A SONG TO SAVE THE SALISH SEA

MUSIC, NATURE, PLACE
Sabine Feisst and Denise Von Glahn

A
SONG TO SAVE
THE
SALISH SEA

Musical Performance as
Environmental Activism

MARK PEDELTY

Indiana University Press
Bloomington & Indianapolis

This book is a publication of

Indiana University Press
Office of Scholarly Publishing
Herman B Wells Library 350
1320 East 10th Street
Bloomington, Indiana 47405 USA

iupress.indiana.edu

∞ The paper used in this publication
meets the minimum requirements of
the American National Standard for
Information Sciences—Permanence
of Paper for Printed Library Materials,
ANSI Z39.48-1992.

Manufactured in the United States of
America

Library of Congress Cataloging-in-
Publication Data

Names: Pedelty, Mark, author.
Title: A song to save the Salish Sea : musical
    performance as environmental activism /
    Mark Pedelty.
Other titles: Music, nature, place.
Description: Bloomington ; Indianapolis :
    Indiana University Press, 2016. | Series:
    Music, nature, place
Identifiers: LCCN 2016021950 (print) |
    LCCN 2016035381 (ebook) |
    ISBN 9780253022684 (cloth : alk. paper) |
    ISBN 9780253023001 (pbk. : alk. paper) |
    ISBN 9780253023162 (ebook)
Subjects: LCSH: Ecomusicology—Salish
    Sea (B.C. and Wash.) | Music—Political
    aspects—Salish Sea (B.C. and Wash.) |
    Environmentalism—Salish Sea (B.C.
    and Wash.)
Classification: LCC ML3799.3 .P44 2016
    (print) | LCC ML3799.3 (ebook) |
    DDC 780/.0304—dc23
LC record available at https://lccn.loc
    .gov/2016021950

1 2 3 4 5 21 20 19 18 17 16

Back Cover Image: Towers and Trees
performs at Butchart Gardens. Photo by
Tyson Elder; used by permission.

This one's for the band—Tim Gustafson, Leon Hsu,
Robert Poch, and Bryan Mosher—the Hypoxic Punks

FERDINAND: Where should this music be? i' the air or the earth?
—William Shakespeare,
The Tempest, act 1, scene 2

CONTENTS

ACKNOWLEDGMENTS

THE OLDER I get, the greater my debt. I will start by thanking thousands of students who have taught me so much. It would be impossible to mention them all, so I will note two with whom I coauthored related publications: Joy Hamilton and Morgan Keucker. I have been working with Joy nearly as long as I have been doing this research, and our weekly discussions concerning environmental communication have had a profound influence on this project. Also, Christian Angelich's bomb train research stands out among many student projects that have informed my thinking over the past several years. Without students, this would be a meaningless pursuit.

I would like to thank all of my colleagues in the burgeoning field of ecomusicology, especially members of the American Musicological Society's Ecocriticism Study Group (ESG) whose work has informed various aspects of this research. I should specifically mention Aaron Allen, founding chair and leader of the ESG and a central leader in the development of ecomusicology. This book literally would not have been possible without Aaron's kind assistance and mentorship.

I would also like to thank Aaron's coeditor and fellow organologist Kevin Dawe, whose scholarship and ideas have positively influenced this work.

And then there is Tyler Kinnear. Tyler's work as editor, author, organizer, and soundwalk composer has greatly influenced this work, and I owe him a deep debt of gratitude. Which brings me to William Bares, who along with Tyler organized the Ecomusicologies III conference at the

University of North Carolina in Asheville, a watershed event. Thanks, guys. The academy needs a lot more like you.

Thanks as well to ESG leaders and members Rachel Mundy, Kate Galloway, Michael Baumgartner, Robert Fallon, Michael Silvers, Sonja Downing, Andrew Mark, and Maja Trochimczyk and the entire group. As an interdisciplinary scholar with obligations to several disciplines and departments, I have been somewhat mercenary, taking more from groups like the ESG than I am able to give back. Please know how much I appreciate all that you have so generously offered. As an anthropologist who studies music in environmental contexts, I am continually surprised by the kind and giving reception offered by musicologists, ethnomusicologists, and popular music researchers to my work.

And that's just the musicologists. Ethnomusicologists and popular-music researchers have been highly influential in this research as well, and I owe them all my heartfelt thanks. First and foremost is Jeff Todd Titon, whose research and mentorship have been absolutely essential to the development and execution of this project. Jeff's combination of listening skills and insight greatly advanced my understanding of these issues, and he is among the first colleagues to whom I should apologize for any areas of the book that fall short. My armchair theorizing involving Thoreau will, I hope, lead readers to Jeff's extensive research on the topic. Getting to know Jeff, one of the University of Minnesota's most outstanding alums and a foundational figure in ethnomusicology, has been one of the highlights of my career.

Thanks also to Tony Seeger, for his kind thoughts and comments at the Wesleyan Shasha conference, as well as hip-hop artist Manifest, for providing inspiring ideas at that same event and letting me tag along to see him in action at the community center.

I have been fortunate to get to know Jennifer Post at the Ecomusicologies conferences. I read Jennifer's work on applied ethnomusicology at a crucial point in this research, and her thoughts on applied ethnomusicology exerted a profound influence. Seeger, Titon, and Post provide models and language for applied work like this, and I hope that this project lives up to their calls for cultural relevance.

Likewise, many thanks to colleagues in Environmental Communication, also too numerous to fully acknowledge here, but I would like to single out Jennifer Peeples, Richard Besel, and Tema Milstein for their very direct help and great ideas.

Also, many thanks to environmental artists who shared their work and ideas with me during this research, especially poets Laurie Allmann and Sandra Alcosser, Likewise, thanks to all of the artists who contributed to the Ecomusicology Listening Room (ELR) projects in New Orleans and Pittsburgh. Directing that living exhibit radically enhanced my understanding of sound and music as they connect to place.

Here, at the University of Minnesota, I wish to thank my colleagues in environmental studies, communication studies, anthropology, and music studies, friends who have thoroughly informed this project. In particular, I would like to thank the resident fellows in the Institute on the Environment (IonE) for challenging and expanding my understanding of the relationship between culture and environment. There is not space to list all of my IonE colleagues who have influenced this research, but I would be remiss if I did not cite Lewis Gilbert for his leadership and Todd Reubold for his valuable insights into environmental communication. Directors Jonathan Foley, and now Jessica Hellmann, have created an interdisciplinary space where scholars from different fields can come together to inform each other's research.

Beyond the IonE, Dan Phillipon (English), Sumanth Gopinath (Music), Matt Rahim (Music), Bill Beaman (Anthropology) are among several University of Minnesota colleagues who have offered their ideas and support during the course of my work on this project.

Thanks also to Ron Greene, Chair, and my colleagues in the Department of Communication Studies, including Catherine Squires for her insight into intersectionality. Much remains to be done in regard to connecting identity, place, and environmental justice issues, and I have just scratched the surface in this work, but Catherine's research and collegial feedback have inspired me to take the research further.

Which brings me to the editors of Indiana University Press's Music, Nature, Place series: Denise Von Glahn and Sabine Feisst. They were incredible colleagues before they became my editors, welcoming me into the musicological fold and offering up their ideas on music and environment. Their work in regard to composition, performance, and place was incredibly influential in my past publications, and, as cited in the following pages, their published work has had a significant impact in this research as well. Denise's work on the role of listening has not only helped me understand issues of voice and listening but also helped me become a more skillful listener (a useful skill for an ethnographer). In addition to her other work, Sabine's interpretations of Luther Adams's compositions have caused me to think about environmental musicianship in new ways and provided a key comparative reference for the musicians I studied in the Pacific Northwest. I am extremely fortunate to have had editors who know this subject so well. Denise and Sabine provided extensive feedback after each iteration of the manuscript, radically improving the text. Thanks, Denise and Sabine.

I would like to thank Raina Polivka, sponsoring editor at Indiana University Press. From her detailed feedback to her patience, Raina has helped elevate this book project beyond anything I could have imagined when starting out. Thanks also to Janice Frisch for her hard work on the visual design and layout, and to Indiana University Press for encouraging me to produce Ecosong.net and advancing the exciting Hydra/Fedora project. Thanks to Deborah Grahame-Smith and her team for their excellent editorial work. Also, thanks to a series of anonymous reviewers who made this book better at each stage. I hope that my revisions are worthy of your quality feedback.

A big shout-out to the Hypoxic Punks, with special mention of three talented musicians who have formed the core of the band for the past decade—Leon Hsu (violin), Bryan Mosher (bass), and Robert Poch (drums)—and to our newest member, Tim Gustafson (guitar, voice), for bringing a fresh voice to the band. Performing music with you talented artists has taught me a great deal.

Thanks to the entire Salish Sea community and our friends on Orcas Island, in particular, who have contributed to this research. Which brings me to the most important contributors to this research, the informants. My deep appreciation for your work is played out in detail in each of the following chapters. However, I would like to take this opportunity to offer my genuine gratitude for your having invited me into your musical lives. I hope that this book does justice to your innovative examples and apologize in advance for all shortcomings.

Going beyond music, thanks to my in-laws throughout the Pacific Northwest. If I forget anyone, I will never hear the end of it, so I will not list your names. Nevertheless, please know that you have helped me understand this special part of the world in ways that reach far beyond scholarly research. From kayaking the islands and cooking s'mores, to hiking the mountain passes and watching the Huskies, you have given me an in-depth introduction to the Salish Sea region over the past thirty years. To my entire family, both in the Midwest and the Pacific Northwest, thank you for everything.

Finally, and most importantly, I would like to thank Karen Miksch for introducing me to the Salish Sea three decades ago and giving me a lifetime of happiness since. Karen made this book possible.

A grant from the Andrew W. Mellon Foundation supported the creation of an online resource companion to this book, which includes additional archival and multimedia materials. The companion can be accessed at http://indiana.fulcrumscholar.org.

A
SONG TO SAVE
THE
SALISH SEA

FIGURE 0.1

The Salish Sea and surrounding basin. Stefan Freelan,
Western Washington University, 2009, used by permission.

Introduction: Why Environmentalist Music?

A band in a small boat bobbed up and down on Puget Sound. Behind them, a giant oil rig moved slowly along, dwarfing their trombones, drums, saxophones, and tuba. Movitas's goal on May 16, 2015, was to stop the behemoth machine from coming in for repairs and going back out to drill in sensitive Alaskan waters. The band's music did little to stop the oil rig's slow advance, but their celebratory sounds lifted the spirits of protesting kayakers while bringing national public attention to the dangers of offshore oil drilling. The protest was nicknamed the "Paddle in Seattle."

As we sat and talked a month later, members of Movitas made it clear that they never expected their music to work Joshua's magic. Instead, they make music hoping that their rousing marches will add to fellow protesters' esprit de corps, bring public attention to important matters, serve as an alternative headline service, help organize a movement, bring protest events alive with sound, and provide band members themselves with a little pleasure and camaraderie. There is great magic in that.[1]

Months earlier, and many miles east of Seattle, singer-songwriter Dana Lyons performed his witty repertoire for conservative ranchers throughout Montana. It was a different audience with similar goals. The ranchers wanted to quash an energy company's plans to ship coal through eastern Montana and on toward the coast. They did not want their ranchlands invaded by twenty mile-long coal trains a day, dirtying local streams and pastures on the way. So the Bard from Bellingham was there to help them sing, shout, and laugh their way to victory against seemingly unstoppable economic forces.

A similar impulse moved the singing Raging Grannies of Victoria, Canada, to commandeer a rubber raft and steer it into the path of the world's largest nuclear navy. It resembles the unshakable faith that compels Sharon Abreu to perform her musical *Climate Monologues* in places like Anacortes, Washington, in the shadow of massive oil refineries. It is what drives Idle No More activists in British Columbia to sing sacred songs in protest against Kinder Morgan's pipeline plans. It is the musical impulse that sent Adrian Chalifour up a tree to sing "This Land Is Your Land" on Galiano Island and sent Bobs & Lolo to teach kids environmental ideas through song. This book is about environmentalist musicians' musical magic, how they compose and perform, and what we can learn from their innovative examples.

Why write about these exceptional cases? Because the environmental movement needs more music. Movements have always been propelled by song. In the 1950s and 1960s, civil rights demonstrators sang "We Shall Overcome" while marching down contested streets. They sang songs like "We Shall Not Be Moved" at lunch counter sit-ins. In the 1970s and 1980s, peace activists rallied around popular songs including "I Ain't Marching Anymore" and "Give Peace a Chance." Throughout the 1980s, millions of rock fans participated in the global human rights movement at "mega-benefit" concerts.[2]

Thus far, there is no musical equivalent for the environmental movement. Musicians have produced songs about nature and environmental degradation, but unlike peace, civil rights, and labor anthems, few environmentalist tunes have worked their way as deeply into activist practice or the popular imagination.

There are several reasons for this. First, the environmental movement is comparatively young compared to civil rights, peace, and labor movements. The repertoire has had less time to grow. Second, environmental themes are harder to fit into popular music genres or narrative conventions. It is difficult to point fingers at problems that are invisible (e.g., toxins) and everywhere (e.g., climate change). And who is there to point at? Blame and promise are more widely shared compared to dialectic labor struggles or human rights abuses. It is more difficult to define good and bad guys than in most other movements.

The relative lack of universally recognized songs might also have to do with the decentralized nature of the environmental movement. The environmental movement is, in reality, hundreds of organizations, issues, and events taking place around the world, often without much coverage in national and international news media. Therefore, the place to look for environmentalist musicianship is on the regional and local level, not in the headlines or among headliners. The global climate change movement might not yet have found a musical headliner, but in places like Anacortes, Vancouver, and Victoria, activist musicians have been playing their part apace. Their voices may not be heard on the radio, featured on the evening news, or written about in the way that other movement music has been in the past, but these musicians are part and parcel of the environmental movement nevertheless.

The goal of this book is to document, dissect, and understand their music. Why? What can a book say about music that music cannot communicate on its own? As the saying goes, "Writing about music is like dancing about architecture."[3] Music works just fine on its own, and textual retellings almost always fall short of the goals of explaining, evoking, or enhancing the musical soundscape. However, this is not a work of musical appreciation per se. I am not here to verbally articulate the ineffable power of sound. For that, I recommend visiting Ecosong.net to listen to these performers' music and watch them in action.

Nor is this a work of musical critique in the traditional sense. Dissatisfaction with traditional musical criticism is one of the things that drove me to this project. My earlier book on the topic, *Ecomusicology: Rock, Folk, and the Environment*, is more of a typical work in that regard. I identified and researched problems but then produced little in terms of finding ways to move forward. Presumably, practical application was someone else's job. Now it is my job. This book is about figuring out how musicians, citizens, consumers, activists, organizers, and communities might make music work more effectively from an ecological standpoint. The best way to do applied work is to learn from those who do musical activism well.

In another sense, writing about music is quite literally like dancing about architecture. Movement brings architecture alive, and physical space is integral to dance. Architecture and dance are mutually referenced in every human ritual. So, too, writing has a lot to do with music. The backstage contexts for making music are rarely self-evident in the music itself. Therefore, we research and write about those aspects of making music that the music itself does not always reveal. In this case, that includes information about how musicians go about making a living doing something so important, yet so rare, as performing environmentally relevant music. Professional musicians do not always share that information, even though it is vitally important to young musicians, environmental activists, community organizers, music scholars, and educators, among others. That is the main role I envision for this book. Fortunately, musicians often love to talk about their experiences beyond the stage, and these musicians have incredible stories to tell.

THE PLACE: THE SALISH SEA

Why the Salish Sea? The easy answer is that I live along the Salish Sea for about three months every year. I have grown to care about it a great deal. It is a "convenience sample," to use the statisticians' terminology, but just happens to be where some of the most interesting environmentalist art is taking place.

Given that most environmentalist music is place-based, it seems fitting that this research is regionally focused as well. Befitting the series title—Music, Nature, Place—this book is about music in a specific place. The focus on a specific region allows each of these cases to be appropriately contextualized in terms of geography, culture, and history. However particularistic, place-based analyses often travel well. Vancouver Island singer-songwriter Adrian Chalifour made that argument in our conversations. He explained that he prefers specific, place-based imagery to more generic, placeless references. In chapter 7, Chalifour argues that music placed in a richly drawn, recognizable locale resonates better with listeners far away, not because those listeners can relate to the exact locale described in his songs about the Salish Sea, but because those distant listeners also live in places that they love, places with definite contours, identities, and meanings. Generic "environmental" references do not always draw that deeper articulation between people and place. Therefore, the listener in Suffolk might relate better to "California Dreaming" than a song about loss placed in a nonspecific setting. A kid from Kansas might find greater resonance in "London's Burning" (... with boredom now) than a song about existential angst in general. A song's capacity for cross-cultural translation is enhanced, not diminished, through rich references to place. Effective narrative, including musical narrative, requires meaningful settings. So, too, these case studies benefit from their connection to a specific place, the Salish Sea. They are as much about music in the Salish Sea region as they are about environmental musicianship in general.

This undoubtedly raises a question for many readers: "What is the Salish Sea?" The SeaDoc Society provides the most precise definition: the Salish Sea is a "unified bi-national ecosystem that includes Washington State's Puget Sound, the Strait of Juan de Fuca and the San Juan Islands as well as British Columbia's Gulf Islands and the Strait of Georgia."[4] However, referring to this great inland waterway as the Salish Sea is as much about historical tradition and cultural recognition as about ecological accuracy. Conceiving of the Pacific Northwest's connected waterways as the Salish Sea "recognizes and pays tribute to the first inhabitants of the region, the Coast Salish."[5]

The US Board on Geographic Names has made the Salish Sea an official designation, which means it "can now be added to maps and other materials."[6] However, only fairly recently have nonnatives begun referring to these contiguous bodies of water as a single geographic entity. From Dana Lyons and his songs about salmon (chap. 1) to Bobs & Lolo with their playful odes to octopi (chap. 4), all the musicians featured in this book are deeply connected to the Salish Sea. They are profoundly concerned with threats to the marine biome around which they live as well as the densely populated littoral and mountain ecosystems surrounding the Salish Sea. For them, it is a sacred place that has suffered a great deal and is under even greater threat now. The latest symptoms of systemwide decline include a mysterious "wasting disease" that has wiped out 80 percent of the Salish Sea's sea stars and toxin levels in local harbor seals and orcas that put them among the most chemically impaired mammals on earth, to name just two current symptoms of the wider disease.

As if that were not enough to worry about, Enbridge, Kinder Morgan, and Peabody Coal want to turn the Salish Sea into a busy thruway for Montana coal and Alberta shale oil, either of which could have catastrophic effects locally and implications for climate change globally. Those are just a few of the reasons these musicians compose, perform, and organize. From Lyons's Great Coal Train Tour (chap. 1) to Idle No More activists, literally drumming up resistance to the Kinder Morgan pipeline (chap. 3), musicians are turning their love for the Salish Sea into creative resistance.

I chose the Salish Sea region for additional reasons. It represents a rich environmentalist tradition. Greenpeace is just one of several groups that got its start in the heart of Cascadia. With an active environmentalist subculture, Cascadia is a good place to look for innovative environmentalist musicians. Artists need audiences, and the Salish Sea provides a critical mass of people ready to hear about environmental problems and possibilities. While not just "preaching to the choir," these musicians do have a solid community base to draw on and sustain their musicianship.

Unfortunately, there are few examples of truly successful environmentalist musicianship to be found anywhere, and that includes the Pacific Northwest, where I conducted this work. Granted, there are thousands of amateurs cranking out songs about sustainability, environmental injustice, and the sublime beauty of nature, but not all are truly worth emulating.[7] By no means am I dismissing such efforts. They are essential to community organizations and local movements. However, this book is not so much about people dipping their toes into environmental musicianship as it is written *for* such musicians. As a part-time, community musician myself, I have learned a great deal from these accomplished experts, and I believe that other musicians, scholars, activists, and fans will as well.[8]

THE PEOPLE: MUSICIANS OF THE SALISH SEA

In this research, I sought to find what largely eluded me in a previous project: positive cases. After completing *Ecomusicology: Rock, Folk, and the Environment,* I had a better sense of popular music's problematic environmental ethics and aesthetics but few ideas for moving forward. The artists selected for this project present promising new ideas for environmentalist musicianship. I observed and talked to successful environmentalist musicians to find out how they compose music, prepare, perform, earn their living, and work with local movements. I sought out musicians who work with local organizations, communities, and movements as a matter of course, rather than those for whom environmentally inflected performance is a side project. For these musicians, environmentalism is part and parcel of their musicianship.

Given that purpose, I used a slightly different yardstick in this research than in most studies of music. I am less interested in making aesthetic judgments and more invested in exploring the ecological articulations of artists. By "ecological articulations," I am referring to the ways in which musicians communicate environmental concepts as well as how they connect to communities, movements, and ecosystems. Each of the artists profiled in this book has found ways to do that well.

In other words, this book is more about environmental ethics than musical aesthetics. If the reader is interested in aesthetic assessment, visit Ecosong.net to hear and see these musicians perform. My interpretations of a song's aesthetic qualities are no more meaningful than any other listener's. All listeners use personal, genre-bound, and culturally constructed criteria in assessing sound. I remain a cultural relativist when assessing musical quality. One fan's noise is another's nirvana. Therefore, instead of critical assessment of musical aesthetics, this book will explain each musician's life history, cultural context, creative process, and performance strategies. While not a traditional work of musical appreciation in that sense, this book can help us appreciate musical text and performance in new ways through understanding social, political, and ecological contexts.

Once I established that a musician or ensemble had made a substantial ecomusical mark in their community, region, or movement around the Salish Sea, I began the work of finding out how they go about working their magic and continuing to develop as environmentalist musicians. All observations and interviews were conducted from 2011 to 2015, with most taking place in 2013 and 2014.[9] It is difficult to get such information from just listening to a song or simply attending a concert. Hearing the musicians tell these stories and glimpsing backstage realities added a new dimension to my understanding of their music.

My motivation was and remains similar to that of Phaedra Pezzullo, whose groundbreaking book *Toxic Tourism* presents case studies of "toxic tours." Like Pezzullo, I studied these cases not because they are "necessarily typical" or "completely unique" but rather because each represents "an exemplary story."[10] We are in need of good examples. In an age of compounding environmental crises, they are stories worth telling.

The book starts with Dana Lyons (chap. 1), a globe-trotting singer-songwriter known far beyond the shores of the Salish Sea for his environmental artistry.[11] Say the words "environmentalist musician" to activists around the United States and Dana Lyons is often mentioned in response. There is possibly no living musician more well known in that regard, at least in the Anglophone world. Lyons turns musical tours into environmental campaigns and has been doing so ever since he graduated from college in the early 1980s. He maps each of his tours onto an environmental campaign, assisting the efforts of organizations seeking to oppose, change, or create new environmental policies along the route.

For example, in the 1980s, when radioactive materials were being shipped to the Hanford Reach in Washington State along Interstate 90, Lyons executed his "I-90 tour." Much more recently, when massive coal trains and ocean terminals were proposed for the Pacific Northwest, Lyons performed the Great Coal Train Tour. In the decades between, he completed a number of similar tour-campaigns, making a difference through his music. I am not sure why more musicians have not followed Lyons's example. Musicians are consummate thieves, and Lyons's tour-campaign strategy is an idea well worth stealing. After two long interviews, multiple concerts, and dedicated study of Lyons's songs and songwriting, I remain more fascinated than ever by the witty musician's ability to mobilize movements through music. Lyons somehow manages to turn policy issues into interesting art.

Chapter 2 is about the Raging Grannies of Victoria, Canada. Perhaps no group of musical activists has exerted a greater influence on the Salish Sea region than the Grannies. Grannies "gaggles" have popped up all over North America and beyond, a movement that started astride the Salish

Sea in 1987 when twelve women from Victoria got together to sing, scream, and make a nuisance of themselves in public. These brilliant women were tired of being marginalized by opposition leaders and environmentalists alike. It was a privilege to sit, listen, and learn from the original gaggle in Victoria.

The Raging Grannies got their start performing along and atop the Salish Sea. They nearly met an early end when confronting the US Navy with their rickety Anti-Nuclear Armada. They use musical performance to level the playing field. The Navy could easily have overpowered the Grannies' rubber raft, but it and other institutions have yet to figure out what to do with the bad press that comes from swamping a choir of older women who carry ragged parasols and sing deadly-serious-yet-silly songs: "Beneath the nuclear umbrella, we're as safe as we can be!"

The Raging Grannies rewrite popular tunes to express critical sentiments, belting them out with concern for neither decorum nor pitch. They strike fear into the hearts of nuclear navies, corporate polluters, logging companies, and politicians. They rally fellow activists to action, drawing public attention to environmental matters that might otherwise remain out of the headlines. The Grannies use music to comfort the afflicted and afflict the comfortable. Given their musical talents, they typically do more of the latter. The original gaggle bravely showed vocally untrained activists everywhere that music is our birthright as human beings, not to mention one heck of a political weapon.

Chapter 3 is also about movement music and policy-oriented activism. It centers on a specific event, Convergence 2014, a protest organized by the Union of British Columbia Indian Chiefs and peopled by Idle No More activists. Idle No More is a relatively new organization whose method of organizing is based on long-standing, indigenous principles. Musically, as in other ways, Idle No More features indigenous voices leading activists of all backgrounds in opposition to assaults on sacred lands, waters, and cultural traditions while fostering shared commitments to the creation of more just and sustainable institutions. Idle No More got its start in Canada, and is particularly strong in British Columbia, but has now spread into the United States as well. Chapter 3 focuses on the Convergence 2014 protest, including the event's musical soundscape and the voice of its master of ceremonies, Cecilia Point.

Chapter 4 spotlights Bobs & Lolo, an environmentalist duo from Nanaimo, British Columbia, who sing upbeat nature songs to audiences full of dancing kids. When searching for model examples of environmentalist musicianship, I never thought this pursuit would lead me to a pair of children's musicians. Yet after watching Bobs & Lolo in action, I could not imagine leaving them out. Performing joyful music about local animals and ecosystems, the pair is preparing a new generation of environmentalists to think differently about their home place and planet, starting with their backyards and local beaches. They go beyond generic discovery toward drawing deep connections to place. They inspire celebratory reverence and holistic understanding for how living systems work and what it takes to properly steward them. Although Bobs & Lolo's audience, repertoire, and performance goals are different from those of the environmentalist musicians in chapters 1–3, they are nevertheless performing a very essential role within the environmental movement. Their music teaches and mobilizes youth, children who will grow up to either steward or destroy the commons. In movement language, these musicians are creating the base for all future ecological efforts and movements.

Another British Columbia duo performs environmentally themed music for school children. Holly Arntzen and Kevin Wright lead a band they call "The Wilds" (chap. 5). They sing with choirs full of wildly enthusiastic kids, grades 4 and up, filling a slightly different pedagogical niche than Bobs & Lolo. Their musical method is also different from Bobs & Lolo's. Arntzen and Wright develop entire curricula and related songs. Teachers adopt the curriculum and work with students for an entire term. Arntzen and Wright come in at the end of the term for several intense days of rehearsal and a public performance to cap it all off. As is readily obvious in their professional, five-camera videos (viewable at Ecosong.net), the results are truly spectacular. Parents and friends expecting the perfunctory school concert are blown away by the folk-rock intensity of these concerts and the exceptional buy-in of the student choristers. Perhaps the most innovative aspect of all is the way Holly and Kevin pay for it through carefully cultivated sponsorships. Meanwhile, throughout, they have kept alive an allied project, the Artist Response Team (ART), building a new future for eco-music in the region.

There is a community element to all five of the acts outlined above. In each case, however, these artists have developed a reach that far exceeds their local communities, either through touring or, in the case of the Raging Grannies gaggles, by the accidental spread of gaggles worldwide. Chapters 6 and 7 take on a more community-focused set of musicians. Each presents an innovative, yet doable idea for ecomusical performance in one's own local community, whether that community is a small town (chap. 6) or digital network (chap. 7). The musicians are no less talented than those in the previous chapters. However, each provides an eminently doable model for environmentalist performance. We might not all go on regional tours or inspire movements, but we all live in local communities.

Sharon Abreu's *The Climate Monologues* (chap. 6) demonstrates that the resources for social change and environmental stewardship surround us all. Sometimes we just need help putting them all together. Music is an ideal catalyst. Sharon's Anacortes performance of *The Climate Monologues* provides insight and inspiration for community-based activists.

Victoria's Adrian Chalifour offers an online example that shows us how face-to-face place and digital community can work hand in hand. Specifically, chapter 7 revolves around a music video by Chalifour, the driving force behind Towers and Trees. He filmed a creatively reworked rendition of "This Land Is Your Land" performed while sitting in a tree on Galiano Island. His example helped inspire a music video project on Ecosong.net, the digital continuation of this book. His original video and the music of all these artists can be viewed there as well.

Each of these stories will be told with detailed attention to the performers' life histories, musical development, musical compositions, songwriting methods, business models, performance techniques, and ecological connections to the Salish Sea community.

A BRIEF HISTORY OF MOVEMENTS AND MUSIC
IN THE SALISH SEA REGION

The Salish Sea has witnessed a long and strong tradition of movement-oriented musicianship, starting with one of the most well-known movement musicians in North American history: Joe Hill. In 1912, Hill's satirical ballads inspired loggers and miners in British Columbia to organize for better working conditions. Hill used music, such as his song "Where the Fraser River Flows," to mobilize and support workers.[12]

Three decades later, in 1941, Woody Guthrie gave Washington its state song, "Roll On Columbia."[13] As will be discussed later on in the book, Guthrie's relationship to the area was shorter lived than Hill's yet far more complicated from an environmental standpoint.

The labor movement Hill and Guthrie helped create remains alive and well in struggles for living wages and better working conditions. In June 2014, Seattle passed landmark minimum wage legislation requiring employers to pay employees at least $15 an hour. Several of the artists profiled here lent their musical labor to that effort, following in Hill's footsteps. Their environmentalist work is committed to the same tradition of movement-oriented music, connecting social inequities to environmental justice (i.e., healthy ecosystems for all people) and biodiversity (i.e., and for all living creatures). These musicians place environmentalism at the very center of their music, but several have participated in civil rights movements, peace efforts, LGBT rights struggles, and movements for gender equity as well. As part of a political culture that extends beyond ecological concerns, none are single-issue environmentalists.

Moving much further back and deeper than Hill, Guthrie, and the North American labor movement, these musicians are also connected to First Nations histories and traditions.[14] That connection is most evident in the case of Idle No More singers and drummers (chap. 3), but indigenous musicianship is a recurrent theme throughout. Examples include Dana Lyons's collaborations with Lummi musicians and artists (chap. 1) and the Raging Grannies many appearances at demonstrations for First Nations' rights to self-determination (chap. 2). From indigenous instrumentation to the use of native stories, indigenous musical practices have influenced many ecomusical activists around the Salish Sea region.[15]

In addition to a few informants representing direct connections to First Nations traditions (e.g., Cecilia Point is a Musqueam MC), all the artists profiled here share at least one cultural parallel with indigenous musicians: the belief that music is part and parcel of sociopolitical life rather than something to be performed outside of it. As opposed to conceiving of music as abstracted art or entertainment, the musicians featured here view music as integral to a community's political life. Anthropologist Franz Boas's 1888 account "The Indians of British Columbia" is replete with references to music integrated into the social and political life of indigenous communities. He lamented that "the Canadian Government tries to suppress the feasts of the natives" in order to establish hegemony over local nations.[16] Boas was observing that, for First Nations, music is a social and political act as much as a matter of expression and entertainment. Today, music remains a tool of both power and resistance, as evidenced by musical expression in Idle No More protests and Kinder Morgan pipeline ads alike. More to the point, music remains an inextricable part of the Salish Sea ecosystem.

Of course, historical and cultural connections between indigenous and nonnative musicians could be overstated. While cultural connections between indigenous musical traditions and contemporary practices are explicit for Idle No More, involving formal exchanges of song and ceremony (e.g., it is a sacrilege to perform a First Nations song, story, or instrument unless it has been explicitly "gifted"), First Nations and nonnative musicians often operate in separate social spheres. That is not surprising given the region's history of genocide, missionization, and appropriation of indigenous lands and cultural resources.

That fact extends beyond indigeneity to other axes of cultural difference. In addition to all being "environmentalist musicians," each of these musicians represents a separate social circle and subculture. With roughly eight million people crowding the shores of the Salish Sea, there are far more worlds than imagined in a simple cultural binary like "indigenous and nonnative musicians." When I chatted with the members of Movitas in Seattle, for example, the young band members had never heard of Dana Lyons, whereas groups of young environmentalists I encountered in Charleston, South Carolina, and Asheville, North Carolina, idolize him. The country-folk-activist network Dana Lyons belongs to crosscuts region and movement. As another example, the Raging Grannies were similarly unfamiliar with Bobs & Lolo, young women who perform a scant sixty miles across the Salish Sea, although they were very interested in learning more about them. Genre, age, locality, and other social factors separate various subcultures of environmental activists, musicians, and audiences, including those who call the Salish Sea their home.

It is that sense of cultural disconnection that many musicians I spoke with would like to remedy. A universal lament seems to be that despite the growing number of musicians in various parts of the world making environmentally relevant music, there seems to be little coordination between musical subcultures, even in regional contexts. Genre, audience, subculture, and marketing categories determine musical networks more than geography does, for the most part. Other connections, including ecological connections, take a backseat. Yet, given the growing interest in networking among environmentalist musicians, maybe we are observing cultural history in the making. Just as labor, civil rights, and antiwar movements spawned repertoires and musical communities that not only brought together musicians but also influenced the wider popular culture, so, too, environmental musicians might yet make a bolder mark on environmental movements and popular music as a whole. They might even be inventing a style-crossing genre, "environmentalist music," although that is further off and less likely than the development of place-based environmentalist musics of the sort that seem to be in nascent stages of development. Once again, environmentalist musicians do not always know about one another, but they do express interest in seeking the others out.

Nevertheless, for now the point stands: environmentalist music tends to remain a localized, networked, and genre-segregated phenomenon. But does it matter if environmentalist music ever has an impact on global movements and popular culture in a larger sense? Or is regional identification, the making of "local music," what defines environmentalist musicianship and distinguishes it from other styles and genres? These are among the larger questions that this work asks and begins to answer, at least in the case of the Salish Sea.

Granted, making music might not seem like a reasonable thing to do in response to debilitating toxins and extinction-level events, no matter what the location. We should not just fiddle while the world burns. However, these musicians repeatedly make the point that art is more than an entertaining distraction; it is also a mirror. How seriously are we taking environmental crisis if our music barely even acknowledges it? In the future, those looking back to the early twenty-first century might find our music to be surprisingly bereft of references to an environmental crisis that, in Naomi Klein's words, "changes everything."[17]

A BRIEF HISTORY OF SOUND SCHOLARSHIP
IN THE SALISH SEA REGION

In addition to its musical and movement traditions, the Salish Sea region was also home base for the first group of scholars to carefully articulate ecological connections between sound and environment, whose work is highly relevant to this research. The most well known among them are R. Murray Schafer, Hildegard Westerkamp, Barry Truax, and colleagues in the World Soundscape Project at Simon Fraser University in Vancouver. Schafer and his colleagues made the term "soundscape" part of the global vernacular.[18] The work of these Canadian sound scholars reached well beyond the academy. Many architects, engineers, musicians, and urban planners have been adopting soundscape principles in their designs for decades.

More recently, Gordon Hempton made waves with the publication of *One Square Inch of Silence*.[19] The book documents his campaign to change sound policies in wilderness areas throughout the United States, with specific attention to Olympic National Park.[20] He and his colleagues have been seeking to reduce sound pollution through better policies and regulatory practices, thus fostering greater biodiversity in natural areas. Hempton argues that it is essential to maintain areas of relative quietude so that each new generation can learn to appreciate and preserve natural soundscapes and ecosystems.

Which brings us to the rich science of sound in and around the Salish Sea. Bioacoustic research has been particularly important in the region. For example, studies of orcas have demonstrated the negative effects of human noise, leading to regulatory limits on naval sonar while calling the impact of engine noise and propeller vibrations into question.[21] Orcas and other mammals use sound to communicate, educate their young, protect themselves, forage, and mate. The orcas' musical language allows them to form working communities (pods), similar to how humans use sound, spoken word, and music. Bioacoustic researchers working in the Salish Sea have helped scientists, policy makers, military leaders, and ship manufacturers better understand the environmental repercussions of sonar and engine noise. Unfortunately, sound pollution is making it harder for cetaceans, birds,[22] frogs, and other animals to communicate, reducing their chances for survival.[23]

Musicians have been taking part in efforts to make life better for both human and nonhuman residents of the Salish Sea. For example, on San Juan Island, cetacean and human musicians come together each year for the Annual Orca Sing, which raises funds and awareness for whale research and protections.[24] Examples like Bobs & Lolo's "Beluga Song," Dana Lyons's benefits for the San Juan Whale Museum, and David Rothenberg's whale songs demonstrate the power of interspecies performance to help humans learn how to cohabit the Salish Sea and, in general, play nice with others.[25] With eight million humans and several more added each day, matched by only ninety or so resident orcas, such musical lessons are far from trivial.

MEASURING SUCCESS

Admittedly, the title is an alliterative overreach designed to match the hopeful tenor of these artists' music. A song will not "save" the Salish Sea. Perhaps the title should have been something like *Music Plays Several Interesting Roles in Helping Communities and Movements Steward the Salish Sea Ecosystem*. No art could radically change a water body and biome so radically impaired by decades of human abuse. Then again, scientists, politicians, engineers, and educators have had only limited success stemming the tide as well. No single art, practice, or profession can possibly solve the massive problems facing the Salish Sea community. It requires people with various talents and training working together. Historically, collective work has required music. So yes, in that sense music might help save the Salish Sea, by promoting and fostering better stewardship.

However, stewardship also requires effective social movements. People fulfilling professional functions are not sufficient to the task. That is where music comes in. Good music, like clever science, effective governance, and principled commerce, helps us operate ethically and, more specifically, empowers voluntary social movements. To borrow the regulatory language increasingly employed by policy makers, music performs "essential ecological services."

Throughout the Anthropocene, human beings have been crowding out other species at a highly accelerated pace. Clearly, something is not working, and that includes music. Most of our popular music promotes overconsumption, whether through advertising, background music in stores,[26] or more directly in lyrics that tell young listeners that the cool people "really don't care."[27] Conversely, popular music rarely references nature, environmental themes, or environmentalist perspectives. As Shakespeare observed:

Music oft hath such a charm
To make bad good, and good provoke to harm.[28]

Popular musicians have helped transform materialism into a social virtue. Conversely, successful examples of environmentalist music are much harder to find. That is why I set out to find positive examples for this project. I wanted to discover what rare, successful environmentalist musicians do to make their work heard in a culture that eschews environmentalist art, as a general rule. After that initial search, I began to focus solely on the relatively successful cases, positive examples that might supply us with new ideas, a secret or two, and new ways forward.

So what constitutes a "successful" environmentalist musician? For the purposes of this book, successful environmentalist musicians are those who (1) attract audiences, (2) work with environmental movements, (3) have some staying power, and (4) have effectively advocated for biodiversity, healthy ecosystems, and/or environmental justice. Criterion 4 is the most difficult to achieve and the hardest to measure. Arguments for the ability of music and musicians to effect social change rest on evidence that is more probabilistic than empirical. For example, it is reasonable to suggest that Dana Lyons's I-90 tour and his musical organizing in Washington helped defeat the Department of Energy's plans to dump commercial radioactive waste at the Hanford disposal site in the 1980s. His tireless efforts with large audiences probably did every bit as much as scientific data to mobilize activists, sway the public, and change policy. Yet there is no way to measure Lyons's proportional political impact, any more than it is possible to measure the influence of environmental impact reports and white papers. We just have to assume, logically, that such musical efforts matter.

Not only is political impact untestable, it is also unfair to hold musicians to a "social impact standard." Environmental art is probably more catalytic than causal. Music inspires community, creativity, and action, but it is impossible to draw a straight line between musical performance and policy change, let alone ecological outcomes. Yet, once again, the same can be said of scientific data, educational curricula, and other forms of inquiry and communication. Which played a larger role in the American bald eagle's comeback and the banning of DDT, scientific evidence about DDT or Rachel Carson's fictional "Fable for Tomorrow"?[29] Each played an important role. In fact, only the most hopelessly technocratic society would ignore the power of art to interpret, express, inspire, and instruct.

Whether speaking of music or other forms of environmental communication, it is nearly impossible to determine which factors create policy change. To what extent is scientific data persuasive? Do environmental campaigns significantly influence public opinion, regulators, and policy makers, or do economic factors, ideological shifts, and technological developments dominate? Are largely unintentional systemic shifts more or less important than intentional human decision-making processes?

That is all a long way of saying that criterion 4 (success) will be interpreted very broadly here and that criterion 2 (collaboration) is the much more useful proxy for evaluating the ecomusical "success" of a given performer. Collaboration with environmental organizations and movements creates the most tangible link between musical performance and environmental action and, therefore, serves as a useful stand-in for ecological efficacy. Pity the climate scientist, for example, whose work would be judged on whether or not the science leads to effective solutions to anthropogenic climate change. All they can do is speak the truth. All the musician can do is sing the truth.

Whether one can measure musical effects, it is clear that all movements—right, left, or otherwise—need music. For example, when the oil industry wanted to "make pipelines fun," it called on Disney professionals to compose the soundtrack. Its public relations team wisely recognized that a catchy tune would do more than any dry discourse ever could to communicate the "benefits" of fossil fuels.[30] In dialectic fashion, the musicians profiled in this book try to make pipelines sound a whole lot less appealing yet also make their case through song. It is no mystery why corporations and movements alike would turn to music to get their messages across. Music's visceral appeal goes beyond that of verbal rhetoric and works intertextually with all other forms of environmental communication. The emotional power of music makes it useful, even obligatory, for institutional advocacy.

The pipeline example demonstrates that popular music is contested terrain. Unfortunately, far more musicians are currently seeking lucrative licensing deals than working on behalf of sustainability. The current economic model favors consumption-oriented composition and performance methods. Markets favor music that promotes, or at least ignores, environmental degradation.

It is not that everyone should be singing about climate change and toxins. That would be even more annoying than the incessant songs about sex, money, parties, and cars that currently surround us. But maybe every once in a while it would be good for artists to reference the biggest threats to life as we know it. Parties are not much fun without clean food, air, and water, so perhaps there is room for a bit more of the music pioneering artists like Dana Lyons and Adrian Chalifour perform. Perhaps there is a reason to occasionally put down the beer and take a musical walk through downtown Vancouver with Idle No More activists.

The musicians profiled in the following chapters provide clues as to how music might perform more such magic. I hope examples like these will become more common as time passes. If so, we might look back at performers like Dana Lyons and voices like Cecilia Point in the same way we now look back to Joe Hill and Woody Guthrie, as inspiring musicians who helped change the world.

Additional audio-visual material is available at indiana.fulcrumscholar.org.

1. I did not include a chapter on Movitas because the band does not perform in environmentalist contexts very often, as they noted during our interview. However, they provide exceptionally creative support for occasional environmental events like the Shell No protests.

2. Reebee Garofalo, *Rockin' the Boat: Mass Music and Mass Movements* (Brooklyn, NY: South End Press, 1992), 15–36.

3. This quote has been attributed to many famous musicians and comedians, with the most likely source being Martin Mull. See "Writing about Music Is Like Dancing about Architecture," *Quote Investigator*, accessed August 7, 2015, http://quoteinvestigator.com /2010/11/08/writing-about-music/.

4. SeaDoc Society, "Salish Sea Facts," accessed January 4, 2015, http://www .seadocsociety.org/salish-sea-facts/.

5. Ibid.

6. Associated Press, "Washington's Inland Waters Now the Salish Sea," *Oregon Live*, accessed January 6, 2015, http://www.oregonlive.com/news/index.ssf/2009/11 /washingtons_inland_waters_now.html.

7. I will refrain from identifying the less remarkable local acts I encountered while conducting this research. Nor would I want my own name to appear on such a list!

8. For those concerned that a search for best cases might bias the results, please consider the fact that musicologists and popular-music studies scholars have been taking success as their starting point for decades. Scholars join a Bach, Beethoven, Brahms, or Mozart society because they enjoy their beloved composer's music and know that there is musical value and cultural resonance in the life and work of their chosen subject. Following critical acclaim and pecuniary logic, popular music scholars do not have to defend choosing successful musicians like U2 or Kanye West as research subjects. Therefore, there is strong precedent for choosing successful cases as a starting point.

9. For every case covered in the book, several were neglected. For some, that was due to critical evaluation of what constitutes a successful case of environmentalist musicianship, but even some successful musicians were probably missed. For example, readers based in Seattle, Olympia, and the Olympic Peninsula will undoubtedly notice the lack of examples from the Puget Sound area. Every musical act described here hails from the middle to northern part of the region, where I spent most of my time. The Georgia Strait and Strait of Juan de Fuca areas get more coverage than the Puget Sound area.

Most of the observations and interviews took place over a period of four summers, 2011–2014, with activities accelerating in 2013 and 2014. During that period, for example, Chicago's Environmental Encroachment band appeared at Honk Fest West in Seattle. Musician and engineer Graham Smith-White also worked in the South Sound area. In fact, I got a chance to talk with Smith-White about his bike-mounted, solar-powered sound project. It is a creative answer to unsustainable modes of musical production Smith-White is creating a fascinating new model for sustainable recording. See Graham Smith-White, *The Sunrise Review*, accessed January 15, 2015, http://solarpoweredmusic .com/press. Smith-White and the Environmental Encroachment band would have made for excellent case studies. Unfortunately, they are not based in the Salish Sea region. In fact, during my investigations, I was never able to find environmentalist musicians in the lower Puget Sound who fit the basic criteria for "success" laid out in the introduction, but it was not for lack of trying. Nevertheless, my base farther north on Orcas Island might have biased the project toward the Georgia Strait and Vancouver Island areas. When I present the book in Seattle, Olympia, and Port Townsend, I hope to be corrected in person, perhaps by musicians who have been working with environmental movements in the lower Sound. Meanwhile, I hope that they, and you, will add your examples via Ecosong.net.

10. Phaedra C. Pezzullo, *Toxic Tourism: Rhetorics of Pollution, Travel, and Environmental Justice* (Tuscaloosa: University of Alabama Press, 2009), 90.

11. I refer to individuals by their last names in the introduction and conclusion in order to more clearly identify them in context and distinguish them from one another. Conversely, I favor first names in the individual case studies, which lend themselves to more personal treatment, a point explained more completely in chapter 1.

12. Joe Hill, "Where the Fraser River Flows," performed by Utah Phillips, YouTube video, accessed January 2, 2015, https://www.youtube.com/watch?v=7Rww4Fx5NeY.

13. "Roll On Columbia," Woody Guthrie, *Columbia River Collection*, Rounder Records, 1988.

14. These practices have been handed down and kept vibrant (i.e., adapted to changing times and contexts) by local First Nations musicians, storytellers, and elders. However, these are sacred, oral traditions and therefore not "citable" in academic form. Nor would such unauthorized retellings be appropriate. Ethnomusicologists and anthropologists have documented Pacific Northwest musical traditions following appropriate ethical principles. For a useful entry into that literature and archive, including the work of Franz Boas, see Laurel Sercombe, "Researching the Music of the First People of the Pacific Northwest: From the Academy to the Brain Room," *Fontes Artis Musicae* 50, no. 2–4 (2003): 81–88,

15. Some indigenous instruments commonly used in the Salish Sea, including the buffalo drum, were gifted to the coastal peoples from the Interior Plains. Others, like the log drum, are part of local cultural traditions that have been practiced for millennia and, in turn, shared with peoples of the Interior.

16. Franz Boas, "The Indians of British Columbia," *Popular Science Monthly* 32 (March 1988), republished in *Works of Franz Boaz* (Seattle: The Perfect Library, Amazon Digital Services, 2015), page location 1765 of 2087 in ebook, Kindle edition.

17. Naomi Klein, *This Changes Everything* (New York: Simon and Schuster, 2014).

18. R. Murray Schafer, *The Soundscape: Our Sonic Environment and the Tuning of the World* (Rochester, VT: Inner Traditions/Bear & Co., 1993).

19. Gordon Hempton and John Grossmann, *One Square Inch of Silence: One Man's Search for Natural Silence in a Noisy World* (New York: Simon and Schuster, 2009).

20. Krista Tippett, "The Last Quiet Places: Silence and the Presence of Everything," *On Being*, podcast audio, accessed January 4, 2015, http://www.onbeing.org/program/last-quiet-places/4557.

21. Alexandra B. Morton and Helena K. Symonds, "Displacement of Orcinus orca (L.) by High Amplitude Sound in British Columbia, Canada," *ICES Journal of Marine Science: Journal du Conseil* 59, no. 1 (2002): 71–80.

22. Erwin Nemeth et al., "Bird Song and Anthropogenic Noise: Vocal Constraints May Explain Why Birds Sing Higher-Frequency Songs in Cities," *Proceedings of the Royal Society B: Biological Sciences* 280, no. 1754 (2013), accessed January 4, 2015, http://rspb.royalsocietypublishing.org/content/280/1754/20122798.short.

23. Lawrence A. Rabin and Correigh M. Greene, "Changes to Acoustic Communication Systems in Human-Altered Environments," *Journal of Comparative Psychology* 116, no. 2 (2002): 137.

24. Orca Sing 2013 (14th Annual), YouTube video, accessed January 4, 2015, https://www.youtube.com/watch?v=JlEoQcIxdUM.

25. "Beluga Song," Bobs & Lolo, Bobolo Productions, 2004; "Dana Lyons Live in Concert to Benefit the Whale Museum," *Journal of the San Juan Islands*, accessed January 4, 2015, http://www.sanjuanjournal.com/entertainment/91760804.html; David Rothenberg, *Thousand Mile Song: Whale Music in a Sea of Sound* (New York: Basic Books, 2010).

26. Jonathan Sterne, "Sounds Like the Mall of America: Programmed Music and the Architectonics of Commercial Space," *Ethnomusicology* (1997): 22–50.

27. "Really Don't Care," Demi Lovato, *Demi*, Hollywood Records, 2013.

28. William Shakespeare, *Measure for Measure*, act 4, scene 1, *The Complete Works of William Shakespeare*, accessed January 4, 2015, http://shakespeare.mit.edu/measure/full.html.

29. Rachel Carson, *Silent Spring* (Boston: Houghton Mifflin Harcourt, 2002), 1–3.

30. Lindsay Abrams, "Disney Partners with Oil Firms to Make Pipelines Fun," *Salon*, accessed January 4, 2015, http://www.salon.com/2013/12/23/disney_partners_with_oil_industry_to_make_pipelines_fun/.

FIGURE 1.1

The Great Coal Train Tour poster. Photo and design by Bob Paltrow;
used by permission.

Bellingham's Dana Lyons

The Artful Activist

Every movement has its minstrel. The unions had Woody Guthrie. The peace movement had Phil Ochs. The environmental movement has Dana Lyons.

—Captain Paul Watson, Sea Shepherd Conservation Society

For more than thirty years, Dana Lyons has combined a successful professional music career with environmental activism. Thanks to tireless touring and a Top 40 hit, Dana's music has reached well beyond activist audiences. The fifty-five-year-old singer-songwriter remains a popular draw as well as a movement musician.

Each of Dana's tours is designed to bring awareness to a timely environmental issue.[1] He routes his tours through communities affected by a shared policy issue, linking those communities through music. For example, his first tour ran the entire length of Interstate 90, the path proposed for nuclear waste routed to Hanford, Washington. One of his most recent concert series, the Great Coal Train Tour of 2012, followed a route proposed for moving massive amounts of coal from eastern Montana to Bellingham, Washington, and onward to China and other nations. Dana takes advantage of the traditional musical tour structure to increase awareness of pressing environmental issues and to mobilize audiences to do something about them.

Dana's hit song "Cows with Guns" provided much of the notoriety and financing the singer needed to mount subsequent tours.[2] It hit the Top

40 in several parts of the United States and Ireland, reaching number 2 on Australia's national country charts. "Cows with Guns" was number 1 in the Seattle-area radio market and became the top hit on radio's highly rated *Dr. Demento Show* for the year 1997. Proceeds and, more importantly, the notoriety earned from "Cows with Guns" helped Dana maintain an active touring schedule and audience. He has entertained audiences in forty-six American states, throughout Australia and Ireland, and in various parts of England, New Zealand, Mexico, China, Kazakhstan, and Siberia, among other nations. He has shared the stage with Willie Nelson, Lynyrd Skynyrd, Steppenwolf, Nazareth, Blue Oyster Cult, Neil Young, Dave Matthews, John Mellencamp, Lucinda Williams, Stephen Stills, Nickel Creek, Country Joe McDonald, Utah Phillips, Steve Earle, and John Trudell and many other well-known acts.

From Farm Aid concerts to toxic waste dumps, Dana has performed in a variety of locales, including environmentally threatened and marginal sites many other artists avoid. Meanwhile, his sustained local commitments make him an ideal model of environmentalist musicianship and the natural place to start this story about environmentalist musicians in the Salish Sea region. Per the title of his latest album and tour, *The Great Salish Sea*, many of Dana's songs evoke place-related themes, and his tours creatively connect communities to one another and to their local environments. The Bellingham-based performer taps into what Ray Pratt calls "surplus repression,"[3] including audiences' pent-up desires for healthier communities and connection to place.

Occasionally, popular musicians ask for more than applause and money from their audiences, as if that was not demanding enough. Dana asks for action. His music has helped fuel successful campaigns to preserve natural areas and defend communities against potentially toxic development schemes. Conversely, much of popular music encourages us to forget about serious social problems. Music often becomes what anthropologist Jules Henry calls an "anodyne."[4] Our steady diet of pop songs about sex, love, and romance is pleasurable, for certain. However, musicians like Dana demonstrate that music and musicians can entertain us and make us think at the same time.

In a world where much of popular music seeks solely to entertain, Dana's storied career provides clues as to how environmentalist musicians might also inform, inspire, and even mobilize audiences. First and foremost, Dana provides a model method for artistic collaboration with environmental movements. William Roy refers to movements as "collective agents of expression" in his insightful study of how movements "do culture."[5] Roy notes that artists are essential to movements as cultural interlocutors, and here I offer Dana as a prime example and useful model. Dana's methodology of converting musical tours into environmental campaigns is unique and exceedingly effective, as is his comedic songwriting and storytelling. Before delving into Dana's backstory, it is a good time to remind the reader that his music videos, including "Cows with Guns," can be experienced at Ecosong.net.

FROM SEEGER TO SALISH

Dana was surrounded by music from an early age. As a young man, his father was a big band crooner.[6] His mother was musical as well, leading songs at summer camp, and "to this day," he said, she "wanders around making up goofy little songs." Born into a musical family, Dana started piano lessons at age seven and then began playing guitar at twelve. He formed his own rock band the following year. By age fourteen, he was writing his own music.

Dana took an early interest in the environment as well and began combining both passions in high school. After writing a few romantic tunes, he penned his "first environmentally oriented song." I asked Dana if there was anything about growing up in Kingston, New York, that inspired his love for nature. I assumed that he would immediately answer "yes" given Kingston's location in the middle of the Hudson River Valley. After all, that watershed was made famous by the Hudson River School, Woodstock, and Robert Starer's *Hudson Valley Suite*.[7] Until 2009, Pete Seeger's Clearwater project was headquartered in Poughkeepsie, just nineteen miles from Dana's hometown of Kingston. The Hudson River Valley has played a central role in the imagination of American environmentalists, artists, and musicians throughout the nation's history.[8]

Yet, when asked how the Hudson River Valley might have played a role in forming his environmentalist outlook, Dana replied that he had "never thought about that." Once he did think about it, however, he noted a number of ways in which his childhood along the Hudson River afforded special access to environmentalist traditions and values. "Certainly I was influenced at a very young age by Pete Seeger's work on the Hudson River with the Clearwater," he noted rather matter-of-factly, as if such experiences were common for middle-class kids. His parents "talked a lot about the Clearwater and Pete Seeger and the Hudson."

"I got to sail on the Clearwater when I was in my twenties," he added, remembering the moment fondly. Thinking back, Dana noted how the region was tuned to environmental matters: "That's an interesting question because certainly my family influenced it, but now that you mention, I think growing up in that region did influence it. My teachers were way into Earth Day. I had no perspective. I wasn't raised anywhere else, but there was a lot of interest in it there."

A few months later, in an interview with Richard Jenn of the *Whatcom Watch*, Dana reflected on how his childhood experiences might have led him to become to an environmental activist: "We used to play in the apple orchard behind our house. And then when developers bulldozed that apple field when I was ten and wrecked my tree fort, I've been working to stop expanding developers ever since. So it's just kind of a natural for me. I'm not against all development, but I'm against development that's going to wreck beautiful places, important habitats, and important places in certain communities."[9] Early on, Dana recognized the importance of connecting to community, place, and nature. The Hudson River Valley was in the process of rediscovering its natural heritage throughout his childhood. Preservationist values surrounded Dana at home, in school, and even at play.

However, as a child, Dana never dreamed of recording a Top 40 hit or touring. Even as an undergraduate at Swarthmore, he was hedging his bets, preparing for a life of professional musicianship or, if that did not work out, law. He tried "the tougher route first," making music.

In combining music and environmental activism, Dana was by no means riding a popular trend. Activism had ceased to be cool by 1982, when the young political science major graduated from Swarthmore. American youth no longer fetishized the ideals made popular in the late 1960s and 1970s by hippies, the folk revival, and back-to-the-land environ-

mentalists. The Reagan Revolution was in full swing, creating a far different context for young activists. Yuppies were in, and environmentalists
were out.

Dana knew from the start that he was bucking a trend. Perhaps that is
why he makes music somewhat differently compared to previous generations of folk artists. His parodic parables feature lawn-riding cowboys,
militant livestock, and RV-driving dads rather than the more clearly
delineated forces of repression and resistance in the music of folk icons
like Joe Hill, Woody Guthrie, and Pete Seeger. Although his music runs
the emotional gamut, Dana uses humor to scaffold his concert performances, strategically moving back to comedy whenever a rousing anthem
or deeply personal ode to trees, whales, or forests threatens to bring down
the celebratory mood and turn off the audience. Like all successful musicians, Dana is an expert at reading the room. His protagonists are less
polarizing and his tone less accusatory than was typical for folk artists in
the 1960s and 1970s.

By the 1980s, the environmentalist music movement pioneered by
Pete Seeger and Malvina Reynolds in the 1960s had become a recognizable subgenre of folk.[10] Rock musicians took on environmental matters in
the early 1970s, although tending toward slower and simpler rhythms,
acoustic instrumentation, and folk-tinged tonalities when dealing with
ecological themes.[11] By the time Dana came of age, however, it was no longer
hip to write songs with environmental messages. It was viewed, perhaps
even lampooned, as a clichéd musical niche for overly earnest folk artists.
The same could be said of political participation in general. By the mid-
1980s, participatory democracy was no longer cool, even on college cam-
puses. Although almost every university had a group or two participating
in the antiapartheid divestment movement in the 1980s, that movement
was small in comparison to the collegiate peace, civil rights, and free
speech movements of the 1960s and 1970s.

Like Ani DiFranco's disillusioned leftist in "Your Next Bold Move,"
Dana also came of age "during the plague of Reagan and Bush."[12] However, unlike the politically paralyzed activist at the center of DiFranco's
song, he did not simply watch "capitalism gun down democracy." He
became even more involved as neoconservative interests, neoliberal philosophies, and corporate governance grew in social influence. Dana feels

fortunate to have been "surrounded by people" at Swarthmore who "were concerned about the US wars in El Salvador and Guatemala." He "started learning to question the government's version of things" even more than he had as a kid while defending apple orchards along the Hudson.

After graduating, Dana decided to hit the road. That road, and a geographic compromise with his girlfriend, brought him to the Pacific Northwest. Dana's girlfriend wanted to move to California, whereas he would have preferred Alaska. So the young couple settled on Washington, which is "in between." It is surprising that such a long-term commitment to Cascadia could have resulted from a compromise. However, more than three decades later, Dana is still living and working in Bellingham, Washington, having become a model steward in the Salish Sea community.

THE I-90 TOUR

Once situated in Washington, Dana decided against performing heavily traveled tour circuits. Instead, the young musician would trace paths through communities and regions facing imminent environmental threats. The first such tour took place in 1986. Dana toured along I-90 to protest a Department of Energy (DOE) proposal to dump commercial nuclear waste at the Hanford Site. Bordered by the Hanford Reach on the Columbia River, that facility was a dump site for military nuclear waste. US taxpayers have doled out billions of dollars to clean up Hanford thus far, and it will require billions more to complete the job. It is the largest Superfund site in the country.

As if that were not bad enough, in the 1980s the Reagan Administration proposed using Hanford as a dump site for commercial nuclear waste as well. The commercial nuclear materials were to be transported via truck across I-90 in order to join the massive military waste already packed into Hanford. Fittingly, Dana chose to tour along I-90 in order to entertain, educate, and agitate on behalf of a coalition formed to defeat the DOE proposal.

Dana composed "Our State Is a Dumpsite," a "goofy song" recorded as a vinyl record.[13] The songwriter's comedic storytelling strategies are clearly already well developed in the song. A proud protagonist declares the glories of his "ever-glowing state." The song is deadly serious fun. Like Woody Guthrie's word craft (including his unpublished nuclear songs), Dana's lyrical poetry is deceptively deft. He stretches and twists the vernacular to form a surprisingly insightful social analysis. The resulting song is not a simple us-versus-them anthem or cornpone poetry but is instead a fairly complex vision of what might happen should DOE dumping be allowed. In the future outlined by Dana in "Our State Is a Dumpsite," dumping would benefit some Washingtonians, including the protagonist of the song, who loses a "job here fishing" when the nuclear waste does in the salmon runs yet comes out ahead after opening his new nuclear supply store.

Our State Is a Dumpsite
Well I lost my job here fishing and opened up a store
I buy and sell reactors, cooling towers and lead doors
We've got a brand new industry bearing fruit of finer taste
We sell juice to California and get paid to keep the waste

Chorus: Our State is a Dumpsite, Plutonium 239
Our State is a Dumpsite, just set it over there, that's fine
Our State is a Dumpsite, we'll take whatever you send.
Our State is a Dumpsite, where the hot times never end

We don't just make the power, we also build the bombs
The dollars never stop from Washington to Washington
The other states all love us cause we rarely take a stand
They send us little presents and put money in our hands

Chorus

So now I'm fat and wealthy cause my business here has grown
I sell lamps that don't plug in and heaters for your home
Progress and technology, for us they've sure been great
We're singing here in Washington, the ever-glowing state.

Chorus (2x)

The song begins with Dana's matter-of-fact delivery, accompanied by alternating arpeggiated bass lines and strummed chords on acoustic guitar. Dana's voice is more melodic than those of labor musicians like Utah Phillips. Traditionally, labor singers tended to project gruffer voices, shouting as much as singing, performances befitting a loud labor camp. As described in chapter 2, the Raging Grannies have adopted a similar style with great vigor, also performing outdoors and competing with loud soundscapes. Dana, however, is a trained and talented singer whose baritone nicely complements spare guitar accompaniments in stage-based musical performances. In fact, acoustic accompaniment, amplification, and a good mix are needed to fully appreciate Dana's voice in the typical performance context, whereas Utah Phillips's singing-shouting style allows him to belt out the lyrics in practically any performance site, regardless of amplification.

After a relatively subdued introduction and verse, a full band kicks in at the first chorus of "Our State Is a Dumpsite," which reveals itself as a "goofy song." There is a formulaic quality to Dana's first recording, a song that was rushed from composition to distribution as time-dated material. The song's country-blues sound is already clichéd when a tinny honky-tonk piano enters on the second chorus, a track that could have been borrowed from the saloon scene of a Western comedy film. Throughout the song, however, Dana's voice is front and center. In this and in all his songs, words and voice are emphasized over instrumental mix, with acoustic guitar lending harmonic support.

As in Dana's later songs, "Our State Is a Dumpsite" celebrates the protagonist's entrepreneurial American spirit. Nevertheless, listeners get the ironic message: the DOE dumping scheme would lay waste to the Evergreen State's economy and environment. "Our State Is a Dumpsite" is an argument for what risk scholars, scientists, and policy makers call the "precautionary principle."[14] Yet the song also begs us to laugh at, and perhaps even along with, the protagonist's misguided enrichment. Whereas politicized songwriters often ask us to sneer at their opponents, Dana encourages us to laugh with the opposition. From the beginning, he has offered environmentalists a more empathetic orientation toward individuals with opposing views, a way to recognize that they are struggling and to navigate difficult times and problems.

In Dana's music, pleasure is not deferred until some mythical future moment when the movement succeeds. He goes against the tendency among American leftists to equate deadly seriousness with depth of commitment. Those who laugh a little tend to stick around longer, so we might as well enjoy the journey.

That same attitude shows up in Dana's views on conservative fans. Whereas some movement-oriented musicians fear attracting oppositional audiences, Dana cultivates a conservative following and enjoys performing for them. Jerry Rodnitsky notes that many protest singers become concerned when they find their music appealing to the opposition.[15] For example, in 1967, Julius Lester questioned Guthrie's claim, "This Machine Kills Fascists," a saying the folk icon famously carved across his guitar. "Maybe his did," said Lester skeptically. "Mine didn't. The fascists just applauded me." However, Dana does not complain about conservative audiences liking his music or take it as a sign of political impotence. Instead, he takes pride in the fact that his songs entertain people even if the environmentalist message gets lost. After all, that means that people are listening.

Dana describes "Our State Is a Dumpsite" as "the beginning of" his "attempt to make a living as a musician." Dana and his brother, Zach, crafted a tour that followed the proposed waste-transport route, starting in Boston and ending in Olympia, the capital of Washington State. They traveled the entire length of I-90, adding side trips to Minneapolis and cities relatively close to the interstate. In addition to music, the brothers captured people's attention with visual imagery, featuring a fifty-five-gallon drum with a bright yellow radiation warning emblazoned across the side. They stenciled "Not Radioactive" on the drum as well, in case anyone became frightened by their guerrilla artwork.

Many of Dana's later tour strategies were put in place during this first, eventful excursion. For example, the tour was carefully coordinated with partner organizations. Dana and Zach received official sponsorship from the International Firefighters Union. In other words, the brave young duo was practicing a form of political theater far different from Abbie Hoffman's more distracting brand of political humor. According to Todd Gitlin, Hoffman's attention-getting antics distracted from the work and message of peace and justice groups, activists who had been laying the organizational groundwork for years.[16] Conversely, Dana collaborates closely with environmental organizations to see how his music might

further organizational goals. His is not a slapdash, Dadaist effort to dis-
rupt but rather a careful attempt to build movements.

Dana explained the I-90 tour media strategy: "We did press conferences all throughout the United States, stopping at every TV town." He
said the roadside audiences "were very concerned about this toxic waste
being hauled" through their communities. The duo chose to perform
the I-90 tour in the winter of 1986. Winter is generally a slow news period
in the upper Midwest, when unusual outside activities are more likely to
draw the attention of news reporters and their cabin-fevered viewers than
during the busy summer months.

In addition to icy roadsides, Dana and Zach chose a number of school
and hospital settings for their concerts and press conferences. Sometimes
that made for dicey relations with the local constabulary, but not always.
At a stop in Buffalo, New York, state troopers assisted their efforts by
briefly shutting down a road so that Dana and Zach could hold a press
conference without loud traffic noise in the background. It turned out that
a few of the troopers' colleagues had recently died due to improperly labeled toxins, giving the officers a personal stake in the dumping issue.

During our interviews, Dana related a number of stories about police
not only allowing his efforts but also actively assisting. Perhaps the most
poignant was an encounter between Dana and the police in Cleveland
during the Ancient Forest Rescue Expedition of 1989 and 1990. In league
with the organization Conservation Northwest, Dana and about fifty vol-
unteers hauled a 750-year-old Douglas fir around the country. They did so
in order to raise awareness of the ongoing destruction of the nation's remaining old-growth forests. One night in Columbus, Ohio, the group
realized that they had no plans for Cleveland, where they were headed
the next day. They were out of ideas and simply drove the truck into the
heart of Cleveland's downtown district to see what would happen. Police
officers gathered, one after another, curious about the giant tree. Dana told
them each about the tree and explained the logging issue. He then invited
each officer, in turn, to hop up and examine the giant log. Eventually, a
truckload of police officers enjoyed a close-up view of the massive trunk
while hundreds of gawkers filled the street. Dana and company worked
furiously to hand out leaflets.

The anti-logging activists were desperately trying to get all the leaflets distributed before outwearing their welcome on the busy street. Dana thought that time had come when another policeman approached, clearly agitated. As he had done with the officers already astride the truck bed, Dana explained what kind of tree it was and how they were using it to educate people about old-growth forests. In the meantime, local news media had gathered to report on the incident, perhaps hoping for things to escalate. The new cop reacted like the other officers, showing great interest in the tree. However, instead of hopping up to inspect the Douglas fir, he complained, "You guys are pretty inefficient." Then, "Gimme those things," he commanded and grabbed a stack of leaflets. The officer then went around handing out Conservation Northwest materials to the onlookers. Dana characterized it as "a beautiful moment in Cleveland."

Nearly all of Dana's stories are about positive examples like this "beautiful moment in Cleveland." A person who did not know better might mistake him for a New Age minstrel, finding only light and good in an unproblematic world. Instead of apocryphal war stories, Dana's vignettes are about good people acting together toward shared goals. In these stories, people respond favorably to conservation messages, even those connected to the most controversial policy debates. He emphasizes legislative, legal, and electoral victories while largely ignoring bitter defeats. There are at least as many stories to be told of opposition, contention, and failure, but as Dana explained one night over ice cream, there is more to be gained by looking for commonality than by drawing strict lines of opposition. As a movement-oriented musician, he prefers to find emotional inroads that will aid, rather than inhibit, organizational growth and mobilization.

A side trip to Wausau, Wisconsin, was particularly memorable for Dana. It raised interesting questions concerning political culture and the need for more positive approaches. The Department of Energy had proposed the creation of a second nuclear waste dump to supplement Hanford and suggested locating it in Wausau. The townsfolk violently opposed the idea. Thousands of Wisconsinites gathered to protest the DOE plan. They "were going wild yelling at" DOE officials, noted Dana, his concern for the functionaries' safety evident as he told the story. Several guns had to be checked at the door as each citizen was searched. The visitors' cars were tarred and feathered. It was apparent in Dana's voice as he told the story that the singer-organizer did not view this more directly polemical orientation to be as productive as nonviolent coalition-building approaches to the political process.

Unlike Wausau, however, most communities along I-90 had no idea that they were scheduled to become part of a nuclear transport route. Standing in icy roads and even "in the middle of a snowstorm," Dana shouted the same question to each audience: "Are you aware that there's going to be a truckload of nuclear waste coming through your city every ninety minutes for the next twenty years?" He'd wait a beat for that to sink in before adding: "But I know there are never any accidents on your freeways."

The I-90 tour responded to a serious threat, but it was also "really fun." Dana and Zach enjoyed performing their small role in a large movement, an effort that eventually quashed DOE plans to radically expand nuclear dumping at Hanford. It is never possible to say if a campaign succeeds or not, let alone how. There are always a number of reasons for the ultimate success or failure of a given legal initiative, regulatory procedure, or corporate plan. No single individual or even organization ever makes all the difference. It is even more difficult to measure the success of artistic endeavors. However, it seems reasonable to conclude that carefully designed and well-executed performances like the I-90 tour make a positive difference. As has generally been the case, Dana's I-90 tour contributed to a movement that met with remarkable regulatory success. The DOE plan was defeated. In fact, during an era when there were more defeats than victories for environmental movements, an inordinate number of Dana's tours have contributed to successful campaigns.

The I-90 tour left a lasting impression on the young singer-songwriter, so much so that he has used the same basic method several times over, with similar success. His tours form part of an iterative creative process: new environmental issues lead to new songs and tours. Dana's tour experiences then generate new song concepts, and so on. Take "Turn of the Wrench," a song inspired by an experience during the I-90 tour.[17] "Turn of the Wrench" tells the story of farmers and rural residents in southern Minnesota combating large power companies. Utilities were acquiring relatively unfettered rights to run new power lines across rural lands, farms, and local communities. More power was needed to satisfy the growing demands of businesses and residents in the Twin Cities, and rural communities received visual blight and loss of cropland as a result. The itinerant singer-songwriter often learns about problems and opportunities while on the road and then mixes them into his next songwriting cycle, as he did with "Turn of the Wrench."

After the I-90 tour ended, Dana performed the Yes on Referendum 40 tour. The Washington State referendum asked the Department of Energy to nix its dumping plan. To promote the referendum, Dana and a few of his friends built a life-size nuclear-waste cask, painted it fluorescent yellow, and drove it around the state on a flatbed truck. "People would give us the thumbs up or would give us the finger," Dana remembers. The group counted the results of this impromptu "finger poll." The results were "80 percent thumbs versus 20 percent fingers." Perhaps not coincidentally, Referendum 40 passed with an 84 percent majority in 1986. Although the Hanford Site is under federal control, the department had little choice but to simply drop the nuclear dumping initiative once the state demonstrated such strong and overwhelming resistance to the plan.[18]

COWS WITH GUNS

Leader of a moo-vement . . . Catapulted to cult status.
  —*The Portland Oregonian*

Play it once and watch the phones explode.
  —Bob Rivers, *Twisted Tunes*, KZOK, Seattle

Dana followed up the Ancient Forest Rescue Expedition with the Ozone Tour in the early 1990s. Performing at "colleges and little places all up and down the East Coast," Dana promoted a boycott of Tropicana Orange Juice. At the time, Tropicana was owned by Seagram's Whiskey, which in turn owned a large share of DuPont, the world's largest manufacturer of ozone-depleting chlorofluorocarbons (CFCs). Greenpeace called for a boycott of Tropicana. The goal was to use public pressure to publicly embarrass Tropicana and Seagram's. The final objective was to persuade DuPont to reduce or eliminate CFC production. "CFCs were eventually banned," explained Dana, arguing that the Greenpeace boycott was part of a "successful campaign."

Around the same time, Dana performed the Tour of the Dammed. He was working with First Nations and environmental organizations to oppose dam projects in Canada. Hydro Quebec had proposed massive dams that would have flooded Cree lands. Dana and friends dramatized the issue by creating a dam two hundred feet long out of sheets and sticks. They would erect it near each performance venue, including cafés, universities, and community centers. Their immediate goal was to get northeastern states in the United States to stop purchasing electricity from Hydro Quebec.

For Dana, a high point of the tour was when two hundred people dressed up as caribou ran into a reflecting pool outside the New York State Capitol and "drowned," dramatizing what would happen to wildlife and natural habitats if the canyons were dammed. Some of the proposed dams were built later, in the twenty-first century, but on the whole, the Tour of the Dammed succeeded in stopping widespread damming in Cree territories.

It is interesting that Dana equates the success of his tours with the achievement of policy objectives rather than ticket sales, critics' reviews, or aesthetic criteria. In fact, I had to prod the successful singer to talk about his artistic achievements and professional successes. His greatest success, from a sales and popularity point of view, is "Cows with Guns."

Dana composed "Cows with Guns," his best-selling song, after it came to him early one morning in a dream. He jokes that he "may have been visited by the great cosmic cow herself." His cat Oliver "knocked a plant off the shelf or something and woke me out of my dream at five in the morning." With the chorus and several verses still in his head, Dana "scribbled it down" as fast as he could. A few months later, in 1996, the song hit the Top 40 in twenty-five US radio markets. "Cows with Guns" stayed on the Top 40 for six months in Ireland and reached number 2 on the country charts in Australia.

"Cows with Guns" ignited Dana's career and fueled much of his subsequent success on tour. It opened up new audiences for his music as well:

"I think there was one weekend when I played a rodeo one night and the Vegetarian Conference the next night. . . . They both loved it." He particularly loves playing it for "vegetarian groups because it's fun to see the militant side of the vegetarian peaceniks coming out. . . . I think it's healthy," he added with a laugh. When I mentioned hearing a recent story about declining beef consumption in the United States, he whimsically replied, "I can't take credit."

"The most gratifying thing about 'Cows with Guns,'" said Dana, "is that people think it's so funny; I think it just gives them a good laugh." During each interview, we ate dinner, moved on to coffee, and went elsewhere for dessert. At each location, fellow diners came up to Dana to tell him how much they love his music. At a coffeehouse, a local city councilwoman interrupted her business meeting as soon as she caught sight of Dana sitting across the room. "Cows with guns!" she sang, with obvious admiration.

"That was one of our cool city council representatives," explained Dana with a sheepish smile. Dana occupies that rare territory between local musician and pop star, experiencing a bit of both worlds. He is deeply connected to the Bellingham community and Salish Sea region. At the same time, the international reach of "Cows with Guns" allows him to tour beyond the Pacific Northwest and make a living through his music.

"Cows with Guns" has allowed Dana to go to "many interesting places." When I first interviewed him in 2013, the road-weary singer had just finished a three-month tour of Australia. "For most audiences," he explains, "Cows with Guns" is "probably the only song of mine that they had ever heard."

I have listened to Dana perform "Cows with Guns" twice in concert, once in Bellingham and once in Olympia. Older fans seem to recognize the tune as soon as they hear the opening line. However, even younger audience members become fixated on Dana's story about a charismatic cow that leads a bovine uprising.

One thing is apparent when listening to "Cows with Guns" and the earlier tune "Our State Is a Dumpsite" side by side: Dana's songwriting had matured in the intervening decade. The melodic yet no-nonsense baritone is still there, albeit a bit more earnest in "Cows with Guns." He sells the song by taking on the vocal orientation of a war correspondent, juxtaposing the serious tone of his voice with each "bad cow pun" to co-medic effect. Mariachi trumpets add a revolutionary feel to the song about "revolutionary veal." A *ranchera* instrumental accent evokes the cinematic soundtrack of a Western movie, but unlike the honky-tonk piano in "Our State Is a Dumpsite," mariachi harmonies deepen the emotional texture of the song, pulling listeners further into the world of the song rather than jolting them out of it. Mariachis from Dana's favorite Bellingham restau-rant lend a hand to make it all work. In other words, the song is done well. It is a humorous song that required very serious effort. Production values are far better in "Cows with Guns" and all the songs on the album of the same name than in Dana's earlier work.

As opposed to Dana's well-designed tours, it is difficult to know what conclusions to draw from the "Cows with Guns" example. As explained at the outset, the central objective of this book is to garner knowledge and ideas from Salish Sea musicians who have successfully communicated environmental messages through their music and movement work. Dana's case is among the most instructive, a model for informing and inspiring other singer-songwriters or anyone else interested in mounting an envi-ronmental campaign. However, no one can simply choose to write a hit song. No matter how much time and effort most musicians put into their craft, very few receive hits in return.

Perhaps that is what "Cows with Guns" reminds us: all professional musicians need to make money if they are going to continue composing, recording, and performing quality music. Thanks to "Cows with Guns," Dana is now able to pour all his time and talent into advancing a unique synthesis of musical activism and art rather than having to take on studio work, provide music lessons, or front a cover band. At the same time, his success did not happen overnight. Like other professional artists, the middle-aged minstrel works extremely long hours, remains very entrepre-neurial, and has forgone much more lucrative opportunities to take part in environmental campaigns every year.

That same work ethic, creativity, and sense of sacrifice were evident in Dana's professional life long before "Cows with Guns" came along to pro-vide notoriety and a modicum of financial stability. At the same time, his professional life is, like most artistic careers, far more precarious than that of middle-class professionals. As noted on his website, Dana "lives in a nice garage in Bellingham, Washington, with his cat Oliver." And, sadly, Oliver recently passed away. It's a tough gig, but Dana makes it look easy. Projecting a pied piper persona onstage, he communicates a message of hope and possibility, even inevitability, to his audiences. At some point in nearly every concert, Dana nonchalantly reassures audiences, "We are going to win this one."

THE GREAT COAL TRAIN TOUR

The energy consortia's plan was simple: build a new coal-loading facility at Cherry Point, Washington, as well as five other specially designed terminals along the Oregon, Washington, and British Columbia coasts. Once those were built, they would be able to transport coal from mines in eastern Montana and Wyoming to the coast via rail, load it onto giant ships, and send it to power-hungry markets in Asia. Another 2,700 ships, vessels larger than oil tankers, would ply the coast. Many of these would make their way through the Strait of Georgia and out to the Pacific through the Strait of Juan de Fuca on their way to power plants in China, turning the Salish Sea into a thruway for Montana coal. In so doing, they would travel through the home territory of resident orcas, areas where sea stars are already experiencing a crippling "wasting syndrome"[19] and salmon stocks have been on the decline (although 2015 was a surprisingly good rebound year for the salmon runs), threatening an already impaired Salish Sea ecosystem with increased sound pollution, toxins, and direct physical disturbance. What could possibly go wrong?

"They had six coal terminals proposed in Washington and Oregon," explains Dana, "and we've beaten three of them so far."[20] That was how Dana introduced the Great Coal Train Tour during our second interview, not by talking about his music or even the tour concept, but by explaining the issue driving his musical efforts. "Asia can't get enough energy," he explained, so "energy companies in North America want to export as much as they can as fast as they can because all they care about is the money." Regarding the local effects of increased coal transport, Dana complains that these same companies "don't care about how much energy is left for us or the pollution or anything else."

This is a topic that hits very close to home for Dana, even more so than the Hanford Reach issue that inspired his first tour. "If you draw a straight line from the center of North America to Asia," he explains, "it goes right through the Puget Sound." He then launched into his argument against the coal trains and terminals, adding a very personal dimension: "This coal train exporting hundreds of millions of tons to China through my beautiful city of Bellingham and through many beautiful communities all the way from eastern Montana to here is going to really damage our way of life. I have respiratory issues. I'm a light sleeper. The trains wake you up. There's all the pollution from the diesel engines and the coal dust. It just goes on and on: lowering property values, climate change." The residents of Bellingham would have to deal with up to twenty additional mile-and-a-half-long trains per day. Those trains are estimated to lose between 1 to 3 percent of their load on each trip, directly polluting every area they pass through. It would be worse for cities on the main line, like Spokane. Residents there would have to contend with coal trains throughout the entire day, with very few breaks between trains.

"The reason we're going to win comes down to one line," explained Dana, as he has done hundreds of times before. "What do we get out of this deal?" The self-styled "country humorist" revived an old line for the new challenge: "They get the coal mine, and we get the shaft." He repeats, "That's why we're going to beat them."

Dana did not start out with that confidence. Based on people's initial reactions at his concerts and the various small rallies and events he attended, the normally optimistic musician said he got the "impression at the beginning of the tour" that activists in the Pacific Northwest and Mountain West region "culturally didn't believe they were going to win."

The activists' and residents' attitudes gradually changed. Dana was extremely moved when, on several occasions, "people would come up" to him "after the shows and start crying because they thought there was no way we could win." The implication was that after concerts and group discussions, audiences gained greater faith in their abilities to defeat the coal proposals. Before the coal opposition movement started, localized pockets of resistance felt isolated. Music played a role in helping isolated communities feel a sense of regional connection. They became aware of others out there who felt as strongly as they did about stopping the coal trains and ships. "Music is great uniter," concludes Dana.

Several popular-music scholars agree with Dana's assessment of music as a "uniter" and community motivator. In *Acting in Concert*, political scientist Mark Mattern argues that "communities that musicians have helped to form and sustain provide the social basis for political action that would be difficult or impossible among individuals who are not tied together in this way."[21] Marek Payerhin agrees, observing that musicians provide "a sense of political efficacy" to activists facing "the dread of consequences of challenging the status quo."[22] It is a tall order for an organizer, let alone an artist. "People need to believe that they are not alone, that they can trust other potential protestors, and that their collective action will bring about the desired change." In his seminal book on musical politics, *Rhythm and Resistance: The Political Uses of American Popular Music*, Ray Pratt makes a similar argument about musical community. He quotes Pete Seeger, "The real art of politics is to make what appears to be impossible, possible," in making the point that music provides a sense of possibility to weary audiences.[23]

Mattern, Payerhin, and Pratt have identified the sentiment at the center of Dana's songwriting, touring method, and performance technique. One comes away from every conversation with Bellingham's favorite minstrel reassured that the movement will succeed and fairly certain that the corporate coal scheme does not stand a chance. During the Great Coal Train Tour concerts, Dana similarly reassures audiences that they can and will defeat Peabody Energy, Burlington Northern Santa Fe Railroad, and Goldman Sachs. The reader can get a sense of the singer's reassuring rhetoric by watching his testimony at a scoping hearing on the coal terminal.[24] Videos of that and other performances are posted at Ecosong.net.

Dana provides the audience with evidence to back up his positive predictions. During concerts in the summer of 2014, for example, he triumphantly announced that Goldman Sachs, the majority shareholder in the Cherry Point Coal Terminal project, had withdrawn its investment. After peppering his between-song banter with news and information, Dana provides the audience with additional reasons why they should remain hopeful, giving them subtle encouragement to get involved in this winning campaign. His rhetoric makes victory seem inevitable, and his music makes working toward shared goals sound pleasurable.

Noting recent victories against expansive coal and gas development plans in Australia, Canada, and the United States, Dana explained to me during an interview: "We won them all on investor confidence. So on the coal train [tour], I'm just encouraging people to raise hell loud and proud" in order to "scare them [the investors] off."

In a way, Dana's music is a counterpoint to ubiquitous oil, gas, and coal ads, including those prominently featured before and after Public Broadcasting Service programs. "When we watched the TV news every night," remembers Dana, "we'd come away thinking, 'Oh my god! How can we possibly do anything?'" Countering that overwhelming message, environmentalist music like Dana's functions as a headline service for events, issues, and perspectives that rarely find their way into mainstream media. "That was my primary work on the tour," he explained.

In addition to linking communities through music, Dana also appeals to each region's distinct sense of identity. At the end of the Olympia show, for example, he told the audience that people in the Salish Sea region have a unique opportunity to be the first to put a "cork" on fossil fuel exports. Right now, Dana argues, "we get all of the risks, and none of the benefits," which leads him to ask, "Why is North Dakota's economy more important than ours?" He was referring to the parallel issue of oil transport by train but using much of the same rhetoric employed in the coal train controversy. He stokes regional pride by suggesting that if they can stop such fossil fuel shipments, other regions will eventually ask, "How come they [the Pacific Northwest] don't get the dangerous oil trains? Why are they so special?"

Dana's main tool is humor, reaching audiences by making them laugh. However, he seeks to mobilize audiences through inspirational music as well in the tradition of union and civil rights anthems. For example, "Sometimes (The Coal Train Song)" is "a call to action" on the coal-shipping question.[25] Whereas many of Dana's songs contain polysemic possibilities, "Sometimes" allows little such leeway. It is an explicit argument against the coal trains and terminals, employing an explicit thesis, evidence, and logic in evocative personal-story form:

Sometimes
When you feel the ground a'rumbling
When you hear the great horn sound
The big steel wheels a'grinding
The three lights bearing down
When a sound that once seemed friendly
Now is tearing at your heart
There's no backing down

Sometimes the people stand up for a reason

When you see the long train coming
And it's coming to your town
And it's carrying the poison
In a hundred thousand cars
And you hear your daughter coughing
When it wakes her in the night
There's no backing down
When you know it drops the value
Of every home in town
When you know the kids with asthma
Jumping rope on the playground
When you know we're all against it
And our voices do not count
There's no backing down

Sometimes the people stand up for a reason

When they hit you with the sales pitch
While they're buying off the state
While the feds are gonna tell you
That the towns don't have the right
To block interstate commerce
To protect your family's health
There's no backing down
When every mom in Billings
Down through to Bellingham
When every doc and teacher
When every mayor stands
When every child who lives

Within five miles of the track
There's no backing down

Sometimes the people stand up for a reason

In addition to the rousing union- and civil-rights-style tone, there is
also a bit of punk-style agitation evident in the song, especially apparent
in the menacing electric guitar and bass drone driving each verse, tones
evoking trains barreling toward the town. The droning minor exposition
then gives way to a dominant major progression throughout the chorus.
Musically and lyrically, what seemed like an unstoppable external threat
in the verses ends with each rise of the community throughout the chorus.
The chorus wins. Even the melody line is freed from the rail-like melody
line and harmonic dissonance in the song's initial, threatening verses.

After his brief mention of "Sometimes," Dana turned back to the case
against coal ports, focusing on the gulf between corporate institutions and
local interests: "Why would we let Goldman Sachs, Warren Buffet, and
Peabody Energy bring twenty additional trains a mile and a half long through
our community next to our elementary schools and near our hospitals
waking us up at night, polluting the air, lowering the property values, adding to climate change, and all of this to send coal to China so they can
export more jobs? Why would we do that?" He apologizes, "You can hear
my annoyance coming out here," although he sounds less annoyed than
hopeful.

"We have a beautiful community," he notes, adding that the region's
reputation for environmental mobilization is well deserved. "In Washington and Oregon, we pride ourselves on doing the right thing environmentally. I know we screw up plenty, but we really try. This just flies in the face
of who we are. Smaller communities like Bellingham are getting together
to fight. All of the little towns are fighting. We've got our two big siblings—
Portland and Seattle—and they get pleasure out of blocking giant corporations. So I think we're going to be okay.... Our region is surprisingly
well organized.... British Columbia, Washington, and Oregon really care
about the environment."

Motivated by ecological, political, and even personal interest in stopping the coal trains, Dana performed the Great Coal Train Tour. "I went

and met with ranchers who were affected in eastern Montana. I met with five ranching families, and I did concerts the whole way back to Bellingham. What I found particularly fascinating is that all different types of people came to my shows. There were Democrats and Republicans coming to my shows. Not everyone would agree with what I would say, but one thing we all agreed on was that we're going to stop the coal train."

As with past tours, Dana's coal train concerts were linked with organizing efforts and involved a bit of guerrilla theater as well. When I asked about that aspect, Dana handed me a hat. It was a typical camouflage cap, the kind hunters wear throughout the United States. However, as opposed to the usual insignia—the name of a hunting supply chain, gun manufacturer, or popular saying—this camo cap was emblazoned with the words "Coal Train" with a bright red slash running through the middle. Upon seeing the hat, it takes a few seconds to reconcile its seemingly contradictory message. In an era when libertarians tout gun rights and shout slogans like "Drill, baby, drill," camo clothing is typically associated with antienvironmentalist perspectives, not anti-coal movements.[26]

Dana laughed when describing the reaction of politicians trying to figure out how to deal with activists wearing anti-coal camo caps. Like everyone else, government leaders and regulators are used to putting people into ideological camps based on superficial cues, including what they wear. Dana noted that middle-class politicians are often afraid of the working class and tend to pander to what they perceive as bedrock conservatism among working-class white people. The goal with the hats and much of the anti-coal movement was to complicate the politicians, policy makers, and regulators' views of the anti-coal movement as made up of effete, liberal, urban environmentalists. A major goal of the concert tour was to reach the ranchers, farmers, and townspeople most directly affected by the coal trains. Dana found those audiences extremely receptive and upset at having been taken for granted by their political representatives. They were not willing to offer up their land and communities as sacrifice zones. Dana helped give musical voice to their concerns.

However, Dana encourages a sustainable, positive orientation to problems. "To be honest," he admitted, "I always spin positively, because I know that's the strategic way to do it, and you never really know" how things will turn out. "If you do the math on this one," he argued, "it's winnable." He sees the role of musical organizing as helping "people understand how we can win, kind of giving them permission to step it up."

Dana uses humor to create that human connection with his audiences, to communicate (to "make common") ideas that might otherwise seem foreign and perhaps even threatening. He outlined his typical show technique: "I start out all my shows talking a little bit about the coal train proposals. . . . I sing some funny songs, and I describe how we're going to beat it."

The itinerant singer's experience along the route allows him to speak with greater authority. Dana notes that there "have only been a handful of us that have traveled the whole route." He performed the first concert in Friday Harbor, Washington, on San Juan Island, and next attended a Lummi ceremony at Cherry Point, where one of the six coal ports would be located if Peabody Energy's proposal were approved. After a few concerts in his home area, Dana followed the train route from its source in eastern Montana back to Bellingham. Along the way, he served as a musical interlocutor, connecting rail-line communities. "Then (after the Lummi concert), I went straight out to the ranchers. I wanted to get the ranchers' stories to share with all of the city people all the way back because I knew people where I lived in Bellingham, Seattle, and western Washington romanticized the ranchers. It was profound to visit a ranch that they're strip-mining right now and to see the devastation. It was profound and tore at the ranchers who were risking the new train track splitting their ranches."

Once again, Dana's message was that others out there also care, that the communities are not as isolated as they have been made to believe:

> It was really fun to be able to say to the ranchers, 'The eco-freak-os on the coast are going to do their best to not let this happen to you. You've got big allies. You're not alone in this. The ranchers have big allies.' That was my message the whole tour. With little towns just feeling totally overwhelmed. Everyone in Bellingham thought we were going to lose. They feel totally overwhelmed. 'How can we fight these guys?' On the tour, I would just tell the stories of everywhere I had been, and it added up. . . . Then, finally, our big sisters Seattle and Portland came on board.

Dana went on to explain how "the Lummi and the Yakama Indians are talking about lawsuits" to protect their treaty rights against the coal incursion, which includes healthy fisheries. He also mentioned that "endangered species activists" were litigating on "behalf of the orca." Regarding his role as a touring performer, he observed, "It turned out that the region really needed to hear each other's stories." He added that audiences also wanted "to hear my personal take." He was surprised that audiences continue to be interested in his perspective.

In addition to being a "profound" experience for Dana and his audiences, it was also, as he constantly repeats, "a lot of fun."[27] If touring was not rewarding and enjoyable, Dana would not do it. The middle-aged artist beamed like a teenager when describing good times "riding around" with ranchers, visiting Yellowstone, and traveling to some of the most scenic parts of the Mountain West. In other words, there is more than a sense of civic duty behind Dana's touring choices. He explains the complex motivations for the Great Coal Train Tour of 2012, including financial need:

> When I started it, I cared about the issue. I didn't want them to wreck my town. I didn't want them to wreck anybody's town. I needed the tour to make money. I was choosing where to tour. I was listing the choices to my dad. He goes, "You're really into this coal train thing. Besides, you get to go to Montana. Why don't you do a coal train tour?" They hadn't scheduled the hearings yet. I didn't know how much I was going to be able to help. You just don't know. I just needed the tour. I wanted to do it. I booked the tour six months ahead. It turned out that I happened to be doing it right before all of the hearings, which helped promote the hearings.

Soon thereafter, artists, musicians, and activists from the Lummi Nation traveled the route as well with a totem pole crafted by master artist Jewell James, carved especially for the occasion. The Lummi contingent erected the totem pole in front of Enbridge's headquarters in Vancouver, connecting the coal train debate to controversial oil shale and pipeline proposals in Canada (see chap. 3). Just as the Lummi have coordinated with First Nations in Canada, Dana has worked closely with activists throughout Cascadia, including the Lummi, as part of a large and growing coalition.

Environmental threats and opportunities are bringing together diverse allies. Noting that both ranchers and the Lummi have opposed the Cherry Point Coal Terminal, Dana jokes, "Both the cowboys and the Indians are against this." He describes how ranchers, loggers, farmers, business owners, and others have approached him after concerts and identified themselves as "conservative Republicans." "They would joke with me and say, 'I don't agree with everything you're doing, but we're sure going to stop that coal train.'"

"The environmental problems are so big and so many that I might as well put my efforts into organizing issues that everybody already agrees on," explains Dana, noting that the traditional left-right polemic does not always apply to ecopolitics: "This is happening all around the world where the big industries are overreaching. We're talking about destroying ranches. We're talking about destroying farmland. We're talking about destroying local businesses. When the ranchers, the farmers, the Indians, the environmentalists, the teachers, and the doctors all team up and say, 'No,' that's real democracy. That's people power. The Army Corps of Engineers suggests that we don't have jurisdiction (in the Cherry Point Terminal debate). Well, we'll see who has jurisdiction."

Musical campaigns like the Great Coal Train Tour buoy the singer's spirits and supply material for subsequent songwriting, recording, and organizing back home in Bellingham. Increasingly, Dana's music centers on the Salish Sea.

SINGING THE SALISH SEA

More than seventy years of damming rivers throughout the Pacific Northwest brought water to farms and cheap electricity to a rapidly growing population. The dams also led to the extinction of entire salmon subspecies and brought some of the largest seasonal salmon runs to an end.[28] Salmon are the lifeblood of the regional ecosystem, circulating energy and nutrients between ocean, estuary, lakes, and streams as far inland as Idaho. Salmon compose up to 90 percent of the resident orcas' diet in the Salish Sea. Therefore, scientists and environmental activists have been calling for the removal of dams on rivers, where practicable, and the restoration of riparian ecosystems. They achieved a remarkable victory on the Olympic Peninsula, with the removal of the dams on the Elwha River.

The Elwha River is much smaller and far shorter than the Columbia, whose flow is controlled by the Grand Coulee dam as well as forty-five additional dams along its length and its three major tributaries, not counting dams along many smaller rivers and creeks throughout the Columbia watershed. Ironically, the sole remaining wild stretch of the Columbia River is the Hanford Reach, which remains off-limits to farming and other development due to the adjacent nuclear site. Everywhere else along the river, efforts to innovate around the problem of salmon migration have mostly failed, from building expensive and often counterproductive fish hatcheries, to trucking in fingerlings and erecting concrete fish ladders designed to move salmon around dams.

As mentioned in the introduction, two American folk heroes actively worked to change the social landscape of the Pacific Northwest. Joe Hill and his Wobbly allies organized loggers in the early twentieth century. Much later, in 1941, Woody Guthrie threw his artistic weight behind the Bonneville Power Administration's (BPA) dam efforts, composing at least twenty-eight songs in a mere month on the BPA payroll. Guthrie was convinced that the dams would bring power to rural farmers and communities. Like his BPA bosses, Guthrie saw the dam project as a way of curbing the power of large landowners and banks. Large business interests opposed BPA's dam plans and were among those who branded public officials and Guthrie as "communists" for proposing them. Ironically, those same institutions became the main beneficiaries of the cheap power and water those dams provide and are among those most strongly opposed to contemporary activists' efforts at undoing the dams today.

What a difference a half century makes. Today, progressive singer-songwriters like Dana advocate for a very different vision of the region's rivers. Despite sharing Guthrie's egalitarian vision, the ecological outlook of the left has changed fairly radically as environmental health, justice, and biodiversity have become top priorities.

Seventy years after Guthrie penned his celebrated Columbia River Cycle to push dam building, Dana sang "Drop of Water" to mark the first major dam demolition on the Elwha.[29] He did so as part of an emotional ceremony in Olympic National Park marking the removal of the dam. US Secretary of the Interior Ken Salazar, Washington governor Christine Gregoire, and other dignitaries were in attendance for the Saturday afternoon ceremony on September 17, 2011. They gathered to witness the destruction of a dam that had blocked the Elwha's natural flow since 1910.

Leaders and members of the Elwha Klallam Nation were front and center. Dam removal would finally honor their traditions and treaty rights, making it an emotional day for tribal elders like Ben Charles, Sr., who sang to mark the occasion. Ben first gained musical recognition as a member of the Charles Brothers Trio in the 1960s. As Lummi efforts against coal schemes and Idle No More coalitional building in British Columbia demonstrate, the movement to restore and steward the Salish Sea ecosystem has been led by First Nations activists. Alliances with the Lummi, Elwha Klallam, and other First Nations organizations have been central to Dana's efforts as a musical activist as well. At events like the Elwha River ceremony and in the Idle No More rallies described in chapter 3, folk guitar, African *djembe*, and Native frame drums combine to form the environmentalist soundscape of the Salish Sea region.

Before the Elwha ceremony, schoolchildren from nearby Port Angeles painted the dam. To begin the ceremony, everyone in attendance walked over the decorated dam and took a seat across the river. In addition to the brightly painted escarpment, participants noticed a school of king salmon "bumping their noses on the concrete," in Dana's words, looking for a way upriver as they had been doing for the past century. After several speeches and musical performances, Dana took the stage, ending the musical segment of the ceremony with his song "Drop of Water." He considers it one of the most important performances of his career. Secretary of Interior Salazar then gave the order to destroy the dam, and a giant excavator began chipping away at the concrete wall.[30] A video of that performance can be viewed at Ecosong.net.

Despite having moved to the area as a compromise, Dana has committed his entire adult life to the Salish Sea region. Fittingly, his latest album is titled *The Great Salish Sea*.[31] Lyrics to the title song describe how the Salish Sea became a noisier place as wooden boats gave way to ships over the lifetime of a single whale. The ship noise makes it difficult for whales to communicate and, therefore, to hunt, reproduce, and train their young. The song is "written from the point of view of the oldest orca—the matriarch—who is 101 years old now." Cetologists named that elder orca "Granny." As Dana explained during an interview, Granny has witnessed extreme changes, "from the native canoes to the sailboats and the big sailing ships" to "the big freighters and the super tankers." In the song, Granny laments that she "cannot hear your song today."

Another song, "Label GMO Disco," was released to coincide with debate around Proposition 522, a ballot proposal that would have required food producers and distributors to label products containing genetically modified organisms (GMOs).[32] The proposition was defeated but managed to receive 48.91 percent of the vote, leading many to believe that the next attempt stands a good chance of passing.

Much as pop musicians write songs and choose release dates to coincide with certain seasons—an inordinate number of upbeat party songs are released each summer, for example—Dana attempts to anticipate upcoming political issues. He explained above how the timing for the Great Coal Train Tour worked out, coinciding with widespread public hearings. The parallel with other popular musicians is worth considering. Whereas seasonal sales potential drives scheduling for many, for Dana it is a question of maximizing the music's eco-political and artistic impact.

Dana creates performance contexts that help audiences understand issues and ecological connections intellectually as well as emotionally. The Great Salish Sea Tour, to take place in seaside towns and cities around the Salish Sea, promises to do for the local region what the I-90 and the Great Coal Train tours did for towns laid across linear routes. The final stanza of "The Great Salish Sea" best illustrates Dana's intentions:

Oh hush hear the voice from both sides of the border
The rallies, the blockades, the brave sons and daughters
The people speak out for protecting the water
The people are rising to come save the orca

Although Dana has been a major figure in Cascadian folk for decades, the Great Salish Sea Tour is his first to take place solely within his home territory. He hopes the tour will help increase local audiences' cultural and ecological identification with the Salish Sea.

"YOU DON'T WANT TO GIVE IT TO THEM IN AN ENEMA": DANA'S STORYTELLING AND PERFORMANCE TECHNIQUES

Chapter 2 covers the Raging Grannies, a group of women who have been organizing and agitating in Victoria, British Columbia, since 1987. I bring them up here because Anne Moon, one of the Grannies, explained what both Dana and the Grannies are doing with their musical humor. She did so by quoting Canadian musician Buffy Sainte-Marie. "What you're trying to do with a song with social meaning," explained Sainte-Marie, "is to put it in a form that's attractive to people—you don't want to give it to them in an enema."[33]

Musical pain and angst might work for some, and a somber and ominous tone might seem appropriate when writing about the death of entire species, destruction of cherished landscapes, or poisoning of communities. However, live audiences rarely gather to share anger. The popular music concert is generally a celebratory rite. Somber, reverential, or angry styles of music tend to be personal, individualized, and, in a word, private. Conversely, public mobilization seems to work best when made "attractive," as Sainte-Marie pointed out. There is nothing more attractive than humor. No one wants an enema.

Aware of the power of humor and upbeat music, Dana emphasizes his more humorous and uplifting songs at concerts, peppering the performances with more reverential material with great care so as not to give the audience the proverbial "enema." In fact, all the musicians and groups featured in this book use humor as a vehicle for delivering environmental messages. Conversely, the stereotype of the environmentalist folkie is that of the enema specialist, a deadly serious and frighteningly earnest guitarist subjecting others to his or her personal angst over environmental destruction. Successful environmentalist musicians more often use humor to hit the mark.

Dana provided a glimpse into his songwriting process, including how comedy has allowed his music and message to reach unexpected audiences. He uses the example of "Ride the Lawn" (2004), a song that pokes fun at America's obsession with the well-manicured yard:

> One of the things I love about "Ride the Lawn" is that the rider of the lawn is the hero of the song, which is often the way I do my songs. I make who I'm roasting the hero. You can't preach. We all get preached at way too much, so preaching is not a good form of entertainment. However, people appreciate good-humored digs at themselves, especially if they're made heroic while they're being chastised. I have T-shirts of a guy on a bucking lawn mower. The caption is 'I fought the lawn and the lawn won.' People who love lawns and people who hate lawns buy the album and the shirt,

both do. That's actually true with *Our State Is a Dumpsite*. The head of Hanford in the 1980s was given the *Our State Is a Dumpsite* album under his Christmas tree, which I love. That's also true in the ranchers' and vegetarians' love for "Cows with Guns."

Carefully constructed narratives featuring humorous protagonists, settings, and plots keep the audience's attention. "Music combined with stories can just touch your heart," he argues. "It's not about what the rules are and what's supposed to be and all of the technical procedures," notes Dana with a grin, comparing music to other forms of environmental communication. Music works via emotion, which is essential to learning and understanding. He argues that music is not only a more emotional form of communication and expression; it is also a moral force. "Music just cuts it down to the chase: Is this right or is this wrong?"

Dana uses storytelling to deflect attention from himself and onto the issue. "Humor is the best, but also just telling a story from one person's point of view. You can't just disagree with someone's story. You can say that person is wrong—'I don't agree with the sentiment in that story'—but it makes it easier for people to argue about the story rather than reacting to the songwriter." Minstrels have provided critical messages for millennia, sometimes doing so in fairly precarious or even dangerous conditions of sponsorship and employment (e.g., the court troubadour).[34] Not surprisingly, humor and storytelling have been the critical minstrels' rhetorical weapons of choice. Humor and narrative are both self-protective and effective, much more likely to hit home with skeptical audiences than fingerpointing or deadly seriousness prose.

"I've always used humor," explains Dana, estimating that his "concerts are maybe a quarter or a third humor and the rest are ballads and love songs." Based on the concerts I have attended, I would say that the artist underestimates the percentage of humor in his live performances. Dana presents his musical message in "a friendly way, where people can reflect and say to themselves, 'You know, maybe we ought to try to do that better.'" He hopes that audiences "will at least find it funny and begin the discussion" rather than turn off to serious consideration of environmental challenges and the search for more sustainable possibilities. Dana sees his music as a humorous yet thought-provoking conversation starter.

Dana uses punk-tinged playfulness to embrace the conundrums, chaos, and even pleasures of the present crisis. In that way, his artistry differs from other environmental music genres, such as the majority of work developed in the soundscape composition genre, for example. Barry Truax explains that "the real goal of soundscape composition is the re-integration of the listener with the environment in a balanced ecological relationship."[35] While Dana's ultimate goals are similar to those of many soundscape composers, his emotional tone tends toward bemusement rather than balance. Dana's playful recognition and even celebration of disconnection allows audiences to recognize themselves in the music. It is an open-door policy toward performance well suited to how successful movements "do culture."[36]

As Casey Schmitt discovered, people tend to use popular culture to conceptualize and communicate their experiences in nature. "Every single one of my informants," explained Schmitt, "even those individuals who lived, worked, and spent much of their leisure time in the deep woods environment," use intertextual references to popular texts in order to "frame" their experiences in nature.[37] Over the years, Dana has similarly come to believe that music can "help frame the debate" by whittling down complex ecological issues to "a quotable line." That might seem counterproductive at first blush; ecological processes are far too complex for sloganeering. The basic principles of the environmental movement—preserving biodiversity, fostering healthy ecosystems, and promoting environmental justice—mask complex challenges and difficult conundrums that no single line or framing device could fully capture. However, effective communication—clear and meaningful exchange that leads to a relatively agreeable outcome—requires the condensation of complex realities into comprehensible symbols and concepts. Language itself is a system of symbols, a condensation of complexity into relatively simple utterances. The same can be said of music.

Payerhin agrees that musicians play important roles in framing political issues. He points to the case of Polish resistance movements in the 1970s and 1980s as examples: "The songs made a difference by offering a 'natural' way to distribute elements of any tentative agreement among potential adherents of a movement. They aggregated, reinforced, and propagated common symbols and beliefs that allowed movement participants and leaders (to) construct effective action frames. They also helped influence an independent public discourse through framing the issues."[38] Musical communication is not terribly different from other movement messaging in that regard. Where it differs is in its ability to turn framing concepts into artful memes that people remember, repeat, and, at a deeper level, feel.

A CLOSER LOOK AT DANA'S PERFORMANCE TECHNIQUES

As Dana's analysis of musical framing indicates, being a "country humorist" is far more difficult than it appears. It is useful to take a closer look at Dana's performance techniques in order to understand how he employs humor, musical storytelling, and even a bit of logos (rhetorical appeal to reason) to communicate with audiences.

Consider his appearance at the P.S. (Puget Sound) I Love You festival in Olympia, Washington, on Saturday, June 14. About fifty people gathered to sit and listen to Dana while a few others stood around the edges of the open-air tent. During the concert, hundreds more circulated around Percival Landing Park, taking in exhibits by local environmental organizations, buying meals from food trucks, and enjoying the unusually warm and sunny afternoon. "June gloom" had given way to bright blue sky.

After a warm welcome, Dana led off the concert with "The Tree," a deeply personal song written after spending four days camped under a Douglas fir on the Olympic Peninsula.[39] "The Tree" might seem like an unusual leadoff for the "country humorist," but Dana strategically moves back and forth between dramatic and comedic material. The audience finds they are ready for levity after a sober reflection on deforestation ("The Tree"), polluted water bodies ("The Great Salish Sea"), or indigenous knowledge ("Willy Says").[40] The laugh lines would not be as funny, the stories would not be as captivating, the anthems would not be as rousing, and the reverential pieces would be less inspiring if the seasoned singer were to limit his performances to the comedic material alone, although humor is clearly at the heart of his performance.

However, there is no mistaking the comedic core of Dana's concerts for a Seeger-style sing-along, Rage Against the Machine anger fest, or other, more serious contemplation of mass resistance. In case the Olympia crowd feared Dana's P.S. I Love You concert might devolve into a deadly serious event, his performance of "Recycle Wrap" quickly lightened the mood.[41] Once again, ironic juxtaposition makes the song work. When performing the rap, Dana makes no attempt to modify his folksy, older, white voice to the stylistic expectations of hip-hop. Instead of bad satire or cultural appropriation, therefore, the song comes off as a good-natured, self-deprecating attempt to reinforce the importance of recycling. The middle-aged man's creatively bad scat and beat-boxing rhythms reinforce the comedic disjuncture between artist and art. As if that were not brave enough, from a comedic perspective, doing the song a cappella makes it all the more compelling in performance. Conversely, it is one of Dana's songs that did not translate as well to studio recording. Like Guthrie, Dana's use of vernacular rhyme moves his lyrics dangerously close to cornpone poetry, but, also similar to Guthrie, the result is surprisingly complex and genuinely creative.

After "Recycle Wrap," Dana dove back into his more contemplative material, performing "The Great Salish Sea." He occasionally performs an anthem or two. "Sometimes" is one of his best. He summarized the song to me in the following terms: "Are we going to stand up for our communities or not?" Similarly, "The Great Salish Sea" ends with an explicit call for Salish Sea communities to rise up in league with the whales.

Noting that other activist-artists are more likely to write motivational anthems, Dana explains the value of his handful of examples: "Those kinds of songs unify and help inspire people to continue on." Dana would rather make people laugh, however, and does that most effectively. Nevertheless, he is also pretty good at leading union-style rousers when the mood hits.

Next, Dana announced his new Crude Awakening Oil Train Tour to the audience in Olympia. The humor of his explanation matched the gravity of the issue. Dana used a series of puns about the "highly explosive" issue to get people "all fired up." "I make my living off of bad puns," he explained to the giggling audience, his bushy moustache outlining a mischievous grin.

After providing additional updates and information about the train controversies, Dana brought his audience back to the music, announcing,

"OK, more comedy." He sensed, as did I, that the audience gathered at the family-oriented P.S. I Love You concert would tolerate only so much serious material before getting bored.

Ready to go back at it, the audience enthusiastically jumped into Dana's sing-along "Ride the Lawn," one of his most reliable audience-pleasers.[42] (To see Dana leading an audience in a sing-along of "Ride the Lawn" at a similar event, go to Ecosong.net.) It was no accident that at the Olympia concert, "Ride the Lawn" followed his longest spoken-word detour into political issues. The politicking could turn off some audience members, so Dana next brought forth a song with more universal appeal. Whether in love with their lawns or critical of the suburban landscape, everyone can find pleasure in "Ride the Lawn." Unlike "Little Boxes," a song composed by Malvina Reynolds and transformed into a hit by Pete Seeger, Dana's "Ride the Lawn" does not challenge typical American home owner to a contest of wills or present them as the enemy.[43] Instead, the singer invites lawn-loving Americans to laugh and sing along. Sainte-Marie would approve; a Dana concert is anything but an "enema."

SUSTAINABLE PLACE AS A COUNTER
TO CORPORATE CAMPAIGNING

Dana is well aware of the imbalance in resources between environmental movements and industrial opponents like Peabody Energy, DuPont, and the oil industry, as well as their affiliated political consortia, lobbyists, and PR professionals. During our interviews, Dana lamented the fact that chemical and food companies—including DuPont, Coca-Cola, General Foods, Nestle, Monsanto, and PepsiCo—spent at least $21 million to defeat Proposition 522. That sum was far greater than the $8 million spent by proponents of the initiative, money mustered mostly from individual Washingtonians.

Although unrelentingly positive about the possibilities for environmental recovery, Dana remains critical of "industrial capitalism" and "the corporate structure." For example, he had this to say about extractive logging policies:

This is the problem with industrial capitalism. You go into a place. You use it up, and you just leave. Those logging towns really suffered. There was big domestic violence. It's just bad. Losing your job is just horrible. It creates a mess. I understand those feelings in those communities, but if we're going to live sustainably, we're going to have to make some changes. So, the right way to do it, if you're doing something that's going to affect a lot of jobs, is some kind of coordinated effort to help transition people into other jobs, ideally in that area. That's not the way the corporate structure is set up.

In light of such extreme imbalances in financial, political, and PR resources, intangible assets play an important role in environmental movements. Music is one such asset.

The entire news media, our entire society, is telling us from the day we're born that we are powerless—everything, school, you name it. It's all about disempowering. The reason the powers that be have to spend so much time and money convincing us that we don't have any power is because we have a lot of power should we choose to use it. On this coal train thing, the main purpose of my sixty-five-show tour was just to say, 'This is the project, and this is how we're going to beat them,' to lay out a winning strategy. . . . Music can play a big role in that.

Yet environmentalists lose as often as they win. Although he tends not to dwell on failed campaigns, Dana has worked on several losing causes. He laments the fact that 96 percent of Washington's old-growth forests were gone before campaigns to preserve them succeeded in saving the final 4 percent. "We saved some forests," he states. "We lost some." However, nothing has shaken his faith in the power of people and human creativity to solve problems, even in the face of extreme challenges and a well-funded opposition.

Large industries have a national and sometimes global reach, in comparison to the less extensive networking of local communities, not to mention significant corporate advantages in capital and communication resources. To counter that top-down power, Dana's musical campaign-tours add to regional movements' networking efforts. Much like minstrels in Europe's Middle Ages or the traveling *corridistas* of revolutionary Mexico, Dana helps connect communities facing similar needs and challenges. He listens to what an audience has to say in one town and shares the stories, concerns, ideas, and information he hears as he moves down the road to the next community. In that way, concert campaigns like the I-90, Great Coal Train, and Great Salish Sea tours help connect communities. That is one of the ways in which Dana's tours differ from the typical rock or folk tour and why his method is worth emulating by other environmentalist musicians.

It is a different conception of touring than is typical for most American folk and rock musicians. Rock and folk draw on the American love for "the road" imagined as a free space that allows travelers to escape the stultifying confines of community, place, and tradition. The road is where modern individuals go to realize their individual, unfettered potential. Ursula Heise is correct in identifying a degree of "restlessness, rootlessness, and nomadism" in the "American national character."[44] There is certainly an element of the American road motif in Dana's character and motivation, but in many ways his musical campaigns represent the opposite of rootlessness. He seeks to connect communities into collaborative networks, a rhizomatic practice rather than a rootless one.

American environmentalists' more "rooted" sense of place serves as an "ideal counterweight," an equally romanticized conception of a community in relative harmony with its surroundings. Yet, as Heise explains, such conceptions tend to be created by people who lead very mobile lives. For American nomads, place is the sigh of the stressed rather than a real location to which they are deeply connected in a physical sense.

Holly Watkins presents a similar discussion of the conflicted relationship between "place and placelessness." She concludes with a noteworthy caution: "The mobility of music should not discourage place-oriented research, but it does serve as a reminder that, in two perhaps not unrelated senses, music is forever moving in place."[45] Watkins's phrase "moving in place" presents an apt description of Dana's tours as well. His musical campaigns help organize, empower, and connect communities across time and space, a dynamic and continual process that can never be completed. Just as there is no such thing as a natural, unchanging place, mobilized geographies are places in their own right. Dana's tours help make place, whether that place is the I-90 or Salish Sea.

As Watkins reminds us, place is never static. We are creating place all the time, both in conceiving of the world and in acting on those conceptions. Each time and space contains different possibilities, and every static and singular perception of place belies a social contest. Creating a marine sanctuary at Cherry Point, along the Salish Sea, would actualize one vision of place, while erecting a coal terminal would fulfill another. Cherry Point is not a single place, but a material space and time where place is constantly in the making.

At the same time, various conceptions of place are not neutral. Instead, they have radically different ecological consequences. Moving back to the Cherry Point example, competing proposals have radically different consequences for biodiversity, one limiting it and the other fostering it. These competing visions of and for place would have radically different consequences for several companies' bottom lines as well. Artists like Dana— people with creative vision and the ability to express it in ways that engage imaginations—have an integral role to play in that place-making process. Not all artists chose to engage with place and community in that way. Many musicians survive by taking on corporate or business sponsorships whose grants and commissions make critical art unlikely. Some work directly in public relations and advertising contexts. Bourgeois proscriptions against mixing politics with art exert a related ideological influence.

Despite those dominant exigencies and disciplines, artists like Dana manage to weave together a more progressive sense of place and community. For example, Dana's musical performances foster a conception of place that serves as a counter to the coal consortium's dream of converting Cherry Point into an overdeveloped industrial hub.

A LONE VOICE IN THE WOODS

The themes of place and scale introduced above will be developed more completely in section 3, as will considerations of ensemble size. However, it is important to introduce these concepts here in order to illustrate some of the specific ways that Dana advances environmental campaigns and movements with his music.

Regarding ensemble type, when it comes to music and movements, size seems to matter. The environmental soloist, duet, and ensemble represent different aesthetics and goals. The distinction is musical, social, logistical, and even ecological. I first noticed those differences during a previous ethnographic field project, as well as through performing in various solo, duo, and band formats myself.[46] However, the changing meaning of ensemble size became even more apparent during this comparative case study research project.

A topical soloist like Dana represents, among other things, the human struggle against larger, dehumanizing forces. He asks for our collaboration in order to complete the ecology of performance, people, and place. If our collaboration as audience were not necessary to completing the artful project, Dana might as well be out in the woods playing alone. His "solo" performance is, instead, an artful plea for connection, a musical invitation to community.

Conversely, duos represent ideal relationships onstage. Such pairings model ethical comportment and communication between otherwise incomplete and isolated individuals. It might not be wholly circumstantial that the two examples of duos detailed in this book—Bobs & Lolo and Irthlingz—perform mainly children's music. In a way, each pair models an ideal teaching and learning process for young audiences. They model the most elemental form of community, couples, creating a sense of family that children can relate to, one that helps kids make connections between themselves and their own families, as well as with other children. There is much to be learned from watching two people perform music together.

Environmentalist music extends such relationships, feelings, and ethics to a sense of community in the wider, ecological sense. Larger ensembles, groups like the Raging Grannies, model community by performing as one. They model movements by acting as one.

I will deal with duos and groups in later chapters but wanted to lay out the basic argument of scale here to provide comparative context for the following discussion of solo musicianship. The image that leaps to mind for many Americans when they hear the term "movement musician" is that of the soloist, the itinerant singer-songwriter, traveling the road with nothing but a guitar on his back. Musical legends like Joe Hill, Woody Guthrie, and Pete Seeger represent that time-honored folk archetype. Star performers like Bob Dylan, Bruce Springsteen, Ani DiFranco, Billy Bragg, and Tom Morello have extended it into the present. Even as "the road" becomes increasingly metaphoric and decreasingly meaningful as an actual medium for communication (the transportation of things, people, and messages from place to place is no longer essential to communication), the historical road motif lives on in the popular imagination.

At the same time, there is a subtle contradiction, or perhaps irony, within the itinerant tradition. Political movements involve large collections of individuals collaborating to achieve a common purpose. Yet when it comes to music, movements are most often associated with lone artists. For every politically themed ensemble like Sweet Honey in the Rock or Rage Against the Machine, there are hundreds of soloists whose sound and image come to represent entire movements. We could add figures like Joan Baez, Bruce Cockburn, Steve Earle, and many others to the list of politicized soloists, yet I struggle to think of more than a handful of politicized bands that have achieved that same level of reputation.[47]

The soloist appeals to American audiences musically, culturally, politically, and perhaps even ecologically. When it comes to communicating heartfelt music about environmental issues, artists like Dana are more effective than large rock bands as signposts for sustainability. Folk soloists represent voluntary simplicity: music without energy-intensive apparatuses. For example, Dana's simple solo stage presence matches his environmental message, as does his relatively unadorned voice, a voice whose words are made clearer when free of the timbral blending of voices and instruments. The lone singer-songwriter can communicate verbal messages that are more difficult to communicate when words and voice enter into the textual blend of complex ensemble instrumentation.

With those thoughts in mind, I asked Dana to talk about musicians who have inspired him, looking to understand how the singer-songwriter saw himself fitting into various musical traditions. Surprisingly, it took the quick-witted musician a while to answer. It was difficult for Dana to think of examples. Perhaps that is not surprising, given his innovative songwriting and performance methodologies. There are few good parallels.

"Billy Bragg is one of my heroes," Dana volunteered, after a long pause. "If I would try to emulate anyone, it would probably be him," he added. "I just love how he mixes music and songs about issues." He also noted Bragg's "humor and passion."

I then asked Dana, "Why do you solo?"

"I would love to play in a band," he replied, needing no time to think about it. "When I have a chance, I do," he continued. "When I have friends in town, I bring them on." His answer reminded me of Bob Dylan's retort to folk critics who felt he was selling out by taking on a band in 1965. Perhaps those critics did not know that Dylan had performed in a rock band years before he became a solo act or that he had always wanted to go back to performing with others as soon as it became financially feasible.[48] Given enough money and logistical support, many soloists would prefer to play in a band. All things being equal, music is more pleasurable when created with others. However, things are rarely equal. "It's pure economics," explained Dana. "Anyone who has played in the band knows that you get paid the same whether there's one or twenty." Plus, a genre shift tends to accompany increased ensemble size. "I love rock and roll," he continued, "but if I had a band, I don't think I'd be able to pull it off economically."

The itinerant environmentalist might not be able to "pull it off" ideologically either. It is hard to find a like-minded set of talented musicians willing to make coherently themed music together. There are few examples of entire bands maintaining a meaningful social message or movement connections. While there are many solo musicians who are reasonably conceived of as "movement artists," there are few "movement bands" that last. Bands associated with causes tend to have a singularly committed and politically inclined lead singer and songwriter: Michael Franti, Bruce Springsteen, Neil Young, and Eddie Vedder, to name a few. Even these band leaders tend to break away for solo performances when performing highly politicized material. I am not making an essentialist argument concerning links between solo performance and political music, but there are several structural conditions favoring it.

It might be a matter of genre as well. Artists and audiences tend not to view rock as an ideal medium for environmentally inflected music. Rock tends to be impressionistic, whereas folk is associated with story-songs, a narrative tradition. Celebrated Canadian nature artist Robert Bateman made a similar point regarding wildlife art, arguing that representational art is more likely than abstract expressionism to evoke a sense reverence for nature.[49] Similarly, folk music's representational emphasis, its focus on narrative rather than more impressionistic lyricism, might similarly tie in to an audience's expectations of hearing environmental messages delivered in folk styles and genres. Folk musicians use language (lyric), emotional tone, and timbre (e.g., acoustic woods and winds) to deliver environmental messages and meanings that might become lost to the audience when grafted onto rock.

Rock is great for representing electrically charged environments filled with youthful exuberance. Rock revels in the wonders of our built environment, sonically symbolized by instruments that sound like revving engines and screaming sirens.[50] However, it is sometimes difficult to reconcile the rock aesthetic with ecological themes and environmental messages, especially given the more impressionistic aims of rock lyricism. I offer that observation as a passionate fan of rock music rather than a critic seeking to claim superiority for folk environmentalism. The point is simple: environmentalist themes are more often communicated via folk for reasons that go beyond historical happenstance. Contemporary folk music is very well suited to the task. (The same is true for hip-hop; see examples at Ecosong.net.)

Nevertheless, environmental musicianship remains relatively uncommon, even in the folk world. Environment, in the ecological and environmentalist senses of the term, is relatively new to popular music as a whole. Although musicians have been making environmentally relevant, place-based music for millennia, the environmentalist emphasis on sustainability and ecological crises is too new to have produced a large body of musical work to date. We can expect that to change as environmental crises compound, the environmentalist movement grows and ecological concern increases among the wider listening public. Environmental crises are becoming difficult to ignore. However, to date, environmentalist themes remain fairly rare in music.

In that and other regards, Dana has been on the bleeding edge of popular music. Yet he might be on his way to doing for the environmentalist movement what Joe Hill did for labor music, what Paul Robeson did to popularize Negro spirituals, what Woody Guthrie did to popularize American folk music, and what Ani DiFranco did to bring feminist themes to the forefront of popular music. Each of these figures took on some of the most important matters of the day through songwriting and performance. Those issues—labor rights, civil rights, women's rights, and human rights—are as relevant as ever. The work of activists is hardly over when it comes to those areas of concern. However, there are still few professional artists taking on the challenge of environmental degradation, restoration, and justice. Dana is among a small handful of well known examples. Others include Captain Catfeesh in Appalachia and the musicians who belong to Musicians United to Sustain the Environment.[51] However, Dana is distinct in the degree to which he has integrated environmental themes throughout almost all of his songwriting, the way he turns his tours into fully realized environmental campaigns, and the way he wields comedy and storytelling to reach diverse audiences.

A final word is in order concerning how we might understand Dana's music from a comparative perspective. Musicologists, ethnomusicologists, and cultural studies scholars put a fair amount of effort into characterizing the musicians they study, and for good reason. For example, based on his study of Woody Guthrie's Columbia Cycle, John Gold describes Guthrie as a "social documentarist." Previously, Guthrie had been described mainly as a musical activist involved in the struggles of workers and poor farmers, a fiction he actively perpetuated in his art. However, as Gold accurately points out, in truth Guthrie was more observer than instigator. He was certainly not a worker, spent relatively little time among workers, and, given his personality, was the last person one could imagine doing organized political work. Instead of movement-related work, Guthrie's greatest contribution came via acute observation and artistic insight. Gold suggested that we might therefore think of the folk legend as a "social documentarist," a role that had been downplayed for sake of emphasizing Guthrie's fictionalized fame as a movement musician, activist, and organizer.[52] I found Gold's analysis very useful when I began archival research into Guthrie's work with the Bonneville Power Administration.[53]

After completing work in the Guthrie archives, including reading his diaries, I fully agree with Gold's assessment. Guthrie is best understood as a keen observer and clever wordsmith, rather than as the advocate and organizer he has more often been made out to be. The latter reputation resulted from postmortem mythologizing by critics who mistook Guthrie's musical prose and persona for autobiographical fact. Guthrie was a remarkable writer and critical observer. However, he was not a movement musician in the way that Hill was for the Industrial Workers of the World and certainly not to the extent that his protégé, Pete Seeger, organized through song. Guthrie was instead the consummate musician-observer.

So where does Dana fit in relation to those earlier icons? How do we characterize him? Like Guthrie, Dana is an extremely adept lyricist, imbuing his comedic lyrics with point and poignancy. However, unlike Guthrie and very much like Hill, Dana is a movement musician, an artist who turns musical tours into ecopolitical campaigns. Perhaps more importantly, Dana shows us the joy in creating a better world.

NOTES

1. It seems inappropriately cold to use last names for this research, so I refer to informants by their first names. Like Jeff Todd Titon, who refers to research collaborators as "friends," I have chosen to present informants in a more familiar fashion.

2. "Cows with Guns," Dana Lyons, Reigning Records, 1996.

3. See Ray Pratt, *Rhythm and Resistance: The Political Uses of American Popular Music* (New York: Praeger, 1990), 213.

4. See Jules Henry, *Culture against Man.* (New York: Random House, 1963), 43.

5. William G. Roy, "How Social Movements Do Culture," *International Journal of Politics, Culture, and Society* 23, no. 2–3 (2010): 85.

6. Unless otherwise indicated, all quotes attributed to Lyons come from two long interviews conducted by the author. The first took place on August 15, 2013, and the second on December 19, 2013.

7. *Hudson Valley Suite*, composed by Robert Starer, MCA Music, 1983.

8. Denise Von Glahn, *The Sounds of Place: Music and the American Cultural Landscape.* Lebanon, NH: University Press of New England, 2003), 198–225.

9. Richard Jenn, "Profiles of Pacific Northwest Activists: Dana Lyons," *Whatcom Watch Online*, February 2014, accessed January 5, 2015, http://www.whatcomwatch.org/php/WW_open.php?id=1666).

10. David Ingram, " 'My Dirty Stream': Pete Seeger, American Folk Music, and Environmental Protest." *Popular Music and Society* 31, no. 1 (2008): 21–36.

11. Ingram, David. *The Jukebox in the Garden: Ecocriticism and American Popular Music since 1960* (Amsterdam: Rodopi, 2010), 144–152.

12. "Your Next Bold Move," Ani DiFranco, Righteous Babe Music, 2001.

13. "Our State Is a Dumpsite," Dana Lyons, Reigning Records, 1985.

14. Rosie Cooney, The Precautionary Principle in Biodiversity Conservation and Natural Resource Management: An Issues Paper for Policy-Makers, Researchers and Practitioners. *IUCN Policy and Global Change Series* no. 2, (2004).

15. Jerry Rodnitsky, *The Decline and Rebirth of Folk Protest Music* (London: Ashgate, 2006), 24–25.

16. Todd Gitlin, *The Whole World Is Watching: Mass Media in the Making and Unmaking of the New Left* (Berkeley: University of California Press, 1980), 156–174.

17. "Turn of the Wrench," Dana Lyons, Reigning Records, 2004.

18. For additional background, see Washington State Department of Ecology, "Nuclear Waste Program History," accessed January 5, 2015, http://www.ecy.wa.gov/programs/nwp/aboutnwp.htm.

19. Vancouver Aquarium, "Sea Star Wasting Syndrome," accessed January 5, 2015, http://www.vanaqua.org/act/research/sea-stars.

20. As of June 16, 2016, five of the six have been defeated.

21. Mark Mattern, *Acting in Concert: Music, Community, and Political Action* (New Brunswick, NJ: Rutgers University Press, 1998), 5.

22. Marek Payerhin, "Singing Out of Pain: Protest Songs and Social Mobilization," *Polish Review* 57, no. 1 (2012): 6.

23. Ray Pratt, *Rhythm and Resistance: The Political Uses of American Popular Music* (New York: Praeger, 1990), 124.

24. "Public Hearing on the Cherry Point Coal Terminal," YouTube video, accessed January 5, 2015, https://www.youtube.com/watch?v=134C4MNTWLQ.

25. "Sometimes (The Coal Train Song)," Dana Lyons, Lyons Brothers Music, 2012.

26. Of course, conflating gun rights with antienvironmentalism is a mistake. Hunters and hunting organizations have been active conservationists. Alliances between hunters and other environmentalists have been key to several conservationist victories in recent years. Yet Sarah Palin and other conservative leaders have linked working-class interests and imagery with the profit interests of large energy companies, making it difficult for environmentalists to rearticulate environmental health with community interests.

27. Systematic audience ethnography was beyond the scope of this project, and there is no independent website with audience comments. However, the "Concert Reviews" section on Lyons's website provide a fair sense of the reactions I have witnessed at his concerts. Hans Cole of the Jane Goodall Institute summed up the general response of the audience: "Your performances, as always, were incredible: simultaneously entertaining, hilarious, and educational." Cows with Guns, "Press Kit," accessed January 6, 2015, http://www.cowswithguns.com/old-cowswithguns-web/press_kit.html.

28. For a more complete explanation and documentation of the dam issue as it relates to music, see Mark Pedelty, "Woody Guthrie and the Columbia River: Propaganda, Art, and Irony," *Popular Music and Society* 31, no. 3 (2008): 329–355.

29. "Cows with Guns," Dana Lyons, Reigning Records, 1996.

30. "Dana Lyons Performs at Elwha Dam Removal Ceremony," YouTube video, accessed January 6, 2015, https://www.youtube.com/watch?v=bi7Sc4U_YUg.

31. *The Great Salish Sea*, Dana Lyons, Reigning Records, 2014.

32. Kirk Johnson, "Vote on Labeling Modified Foods Spurs Costly Battle in Washington State," last modified October 30, 2013, http://www.nytimes.com/2013/10/31/us/vote-on-labeling-modified-food-spurs-costly-battle-in-washington-state.html?_r=0.

33. Buffy Sainte-Marie, quoted in Courtne Shea, "Habits of Highly Successful People: Buffy Sainte-Marie," *Globe and Mail*, 2014, last modified June 8, 2014, http://www.theglobeandmail.com/arts/music/habits-of-highly-successful-people-buffy-sainte-marie/article19049892/).

34. Simon Gaunt, *Troubadours and Irony* (Cambridge: Cambridge University Press, 1989.

35. Robin Ryan, "Toward a New, Musical Paradigm of Place: The Port River Symphonic of Chester Schultz," *Environmental Humanities* 4 (2014): 50.

36. William G. Roy, "How Social Movements Do Culture," *International Journal of Politics, Culture, and Society* 23, no. 2–3 (2010): 85–98.

37. Casey R. Schmitt, *If a Text Falls in the Woods . . . : Intertextuality, Environmental Perception, and the Non-authored Text* (Oakland, CA: University of California Press, 2012), 17.

38. Marek Payerhin, "Singing Out of Pain: Protest Songs and Social Mobilization," *Polish Review* 57, no. 1 (2012): 5.

39. "The Tree," Dana Lyons, Lyons Brothers Music, 1994.

40. "Willy Says," Dana Lyons, Reigning Records, 1996.

41. "Recycle Wrap," Dana Lyons, Reigning Records, 2006.

42. "Ride the Lawn," Dana Lyons, Lyons Brothers Music, 2004.

43. "Little Boxes," composed by Malvina Reynolds, performed by Pete Seeger, Smithsonian Folkways Recordings, 1999.

44. Ursula K. Heise, *Sense of Place and Sense of Planet: The Environmental Imagination of the Globe* Oxford: Oxford University Press, 2008, 9.

45. Holly Watkins, "Musical Ecologies of Place and Placelessness," *Journal of the American Musicological Society* 64, no. 2 (2011): 408.

46. Mark Pedelty, *Ecomusicology: Rock, Folk, and the Environment* (Philadelphia: Temple University Press, 2012), 174–179.

47. For more information on these famous acts, see Ecosong.net.

48. Ron Rosenbaum, "Playboy Interview: Bob Dylan," *Playboy*, January, 1978, 12–17.

49. Bateman makes that argument in a short, untitled video that introduces his Victoria gallery to visitors.

50. Phillip Tagg, *Subjectivity and Soundscape, Motorbikes and Music* (New York: Routledge, 2006.

51. Travis D. Stimeling, "Music, Place, and Identity in the Central Appalachian Mountaintop Removal Mining Debate," *American Music* 30, no. 1 (2012): 17.

52. Ibid., 84.

53. John Gold, "Roll On Columbia: Woody Guthrie, Migrants' Tales, and Regional Transformation in the Pacific Northwest," *Journal of Cultural Geography* 18, no. 1 (1998): 83–97.

FIGURE 2.1

The Raging Grannies of Victoria, Canada. Back row: Christine Anderson, Sonya Ignatieff, Sheila Rose Richardson, Anne Moon, Alison Acker, Sylvis Krogh, Patty Moss. Front row: Laura Fisher, Ruth Miller, Clara Halber, Fran Thoburn, Freda Knott, Inger Kronseth.

Victoria's Raging Grannies

An Unstoppable Force

For almost three decades, the Raging Grannies have been fighting nuclear navies, corporate polluters, and politicians. Their main weapon is music, although few Grannies admit to musical training or talent. In fact, they wear their lack of talent with great pride. Longtime member Anne Moon once asked a cop, "Am I going to get a record?" "Not with that voice," replied the bemused sergeant.[1]

However, Canadian trade minister Pat Carney had a more positive assessment of the Grannies' musicality: "Your singing is a hell of a lot better than your logic."[2] The Grannies insinuated themselves into an official receiving line for Carney in order to offer up a song. That's what they do, creatively, unashamedly, and with great effect.

The original group of Grannies—teachers, broadcasters, grandmothers, homemakers, retirees, and agitators—banded together in 1987 to sing out against the United States Navy's nuclear incursions into the Canadian shores of the Salish Sea. "Like all older women," wrote Anne Moon, "we were expected to fade into the background along with our looks, our health, our income, and our importance to society." Instead, the Raging Grannies "decided to break the stereotype of nice but negligible grandmothers by becoming outrageous."[3] Indeed, ship captains, CEOs, and political leaders would like these older women to fade with age, but the opposite happens. The Raging Grannies have become more important, visible, and audible as they have aged. Around the Salish Sea, a region known for political ferment, the Raging Grannies are now among the most well-known political organizations. It started in Victoria, a midsize city on Vancouver Island, on the western edge of the Salish Sea. The idea spread. There are now "gaggles" throughout Canada and all over the world.

The Grannies still dedicate much of their efforts to environmentalist causes and take on a range of social justice issues. The Raging Grannies' most prolific academic analyst, Carole Roy, referred to them as "environmental adult educators and cultural activists,"[4] but as her documentary work indicates, the Grannies have been connecting environmental, peace, social justice, and human rights issues throughout their history.[5]

That intersectional sense of politics is represented in the group's official mission statement. In 2000, after thirteen years of existence, the Raging Grannies became an officially recognized "society" under British Columbia's Society Act. The group expressed its mission in the following terms: "To dedicate our efforts to the children of the world so that they may live on a peaceful and harmonious planet, safe from war, injustice and pollution."[6] In other words, the Grannies draw attention to the interconnected nature of social and environmental issues, framing both as a matter of justice.

In the early years, the Grannies protested uranium mining in British Columbia, unsustainable logging practices, Victoria's dumping of raw sewage into the Salish Sea, unsustainable development schemes, and the proliferation of chlorofluorocarbons (CFCs), to name just a few issues that fed their "rage."[7] They have campaigned on behalf of protections for the marbled murrelet, the Vancouver Island marmot, grizzly bears, and monarch butterflies.

As evidenced in these examples, the "environment" for which the Grannies agitate is not some Edenic preserve but rather a world in which humans are deeply involved. They believe that many of the same institutions and ideologies are to blame for both human repression and environmental degradation: corporations, autocratic governance, racism, sexism, and capitalism. In other words, theirs is not a liberal attempt to deal with diffused ideological mind-sets and cultural orientations; they believe in direct action. Whether their target is the local city council or Canada's giant energy company Enbridge, they aim their actions at institutions and policies directly responsible for environmental harm. They rally to support positive alternatives as well.

The Grannies do not pull punches for fear of offending venues (they perform anywhere they like), funders (they have none), or audiences. Their main goal is not to entertain but to draw attention to problems. Unlike most musical professionals or environmental nonprofits, the Raging Grannies do not have to walk a fine line with audiences or negotiate a difficult array of market and cultural forces. That is part of what makes them so dangerous. One hears the raw power of music unchained in their amateur voices and the possibility that more people will recognize their own potential to inspire change. The Raging Grannies boldly model democracy, performing issues in public that those in power would prefer to keep wrapped up in decorous silence. The Grannies cannot keep from singing.

ORIGINS AND HERSTORY

Before telling the story of the Raging Grannies, I have to acknowledge Alison Acker and Betty Brightwell's *Off Our Rockers and into Trouble: The Raging Grannies* (2004). *Off Our Rockers* is a collective memoir, written with the same critical wit the Grannies demonstrate in performances. The book provided invaluable information for this section in particular, as did Roy's extensive research on the Raging Grannies.[8]

I was also extremely fortunate to interview Alison Acker and her fellow Grannies in person: Sonya Ignatieff, Freda Knott, Ruth Miller, Anne Moon, Sheila Rose Richardson, Daphne Taylor, and Fran Thoburn. However, *Off Our Rockers* gave me an excellent head start, allowing us to delve into more detailed questions during the interview. Before starting this project, I had witnessed Grannies at various protests over the years. Their fame among activists preceded them, but I was curious to find out more about their origins, history, personal experiences, songwriting methods, performance techniques, and organizational strategies.

Before the Raging Grannies existed, several of the gaggle's original members belonged to a street-theater troupe called Extenuating Circumstances.

The group's name came about when a Canadian military base canceled an open house, citing "extenuating circumstances." Clearly, those extenuating circumstances were the activists who planned to protest at the open house. Environmentalists and antiwar activists were angered by incursions of nuclear vessels into local waters. Base officials had gotten wind of the group's plans and canceled the event. Extenuating Circumstances performed guerrilla theater opposing the entrance of nuclear-powered craft into Esquimalt Bay, a port on southern Vancouver Island, just five kilometers from downtown Victoria.

In addition to the broader question of nuclear proliferation and the potential for atomic catastrophe, Extenuating Circumstances recognized the probability of damage to local ecosystems: "A coolant leak from the nuclear operating system would pollute local waters, kill salmon, and deter tourists," explained Acker and Brightwell, "whilst the ultimate horror could be a nuclear explosion."[9] Extenuating Circumstances became a training ground for the Raging Grannies. As founding member Fran Thoburn noted in later correspondence, Extenuating Circumstances and the early Grannies were more of an antiwar group than an environmentalist organization per se. As she later wrote, the group "morphed" into an environmentalist and anti-militarist group.

During one early campaign, Extenuating Circumstances members "tested" the water in puddles around Victoria's shopping malls. Group members wore lab coats and draped themselves with various electronic devices. They wandered around busy parking lots using turkey basters to draw water samples from puddles. When approached by curious shoppers, performers would answer onlookers' queries by explaining that US nuclear vessels had started entering local waters. It was a great conversation starter. Those parking lot discussions allowed Extenuating Circumstances to educate the public about potential threats to British Columbia's water, soil, air, animals, and people. The soon-to-be Raging Grannies learned a lot while performing in Extenuating Circumstances.

Feeling marginalized by movement leaders, a small group of Extenuating Circumstances' members broke away to form their own group. The splintering faction, mostly women over forty, included an anthropologist, a businesswoman, an artist, a counselor, and a librarian, as well as a few teachers and homemakers.[10] Despite their eclectic backgrounds and accomplishments, male leaders in Extenuating Circumstances marginalized these activists. Rather than simply rail against patriarchal perceptions or conform to them, the activists did what oppressed peoples have done for millennia: they rendered their stigma absurd and turned a marginalized identity into a rallying asset. From their first shopping spree to buy outrageous granny-wear at secondhand shops, to their unsubtle singing outside the British Columbia Parliament Buildings, the Raging Grannies hit on a recipe for resistance that has been difficult for police, public officials, and corporate public-relations professionals to contain.

The Raging Grannies were determined from the start to bring reason to the public debate by unveiling the absurdity of the status quo, through healthy doses of humor and nonstop public displays of outrage. Those remaining from the early days are uncertain as to which member first uttered the complete phrase "Raging Grannies" but are sure that it happened in 1987 at their formative meeting and that adopting the name was a unanimous decision.

The early days were not always smooth, but they were highly educational. For example, an early coffeehouse performance effectively captivated their tea-sipping audience, but the Grannies realized that it was not a great place for moving audiences toward activism. They decided to find more fitting performance contexts. At one member's insistence, the group performed a Wiccan ceremony, "some spooky circle dancing at Clover Point."[11] The goal was to "put a curse on the USS *Alaska*." When the *Alaska* sailed past with no apparent impact, as most of the group assumed it would, they swore off that sort of ritualistic gesture for good. The Grannies decided to avoid "esoteric experiments" as "wannabe witches." They are political activists, not New Age spiritualists.

The Raging Grannies sang their first original song on Valentine's Day, 1987. "Beneath the nuclear umbrella, we are as safe as we can be," they sang while huddled underneath a tattered "nuclear umbrella." However, neither the government officials they cornered that day nor the press seemed impressed enough to take note of their action, so they decided to become more outrageous for their next protest event.

The group started to take greater advantage of individual members' skills and attributes. For example, Betty Brightwell took the lead "with the press and with officials." Brightwell's "respectability" in dress and comportment made her the natural public relations specialist.[12] Conversely, Doran Doyle was the most experienced when it came to planning acts of civil disobedience, so the group tended to follow her lead in planning protests.[13]

The next act of civil disobedience took place outside the Parliament Buildings in Victoria. Inside, legislators were debating proposals for allowing private companies to mine uranium on publicly held lands. While lawyers, scientists, and activists presented testimony inside, the Grannies presented their own "briefs" outside. They strung underwear on a clothesline hanging across the massive lawn in front of the buildings. Hundreds of fellow environmentalists and unionists cheered the Grannies on as they loaded up their laundry and rushed toward the doors, emboldened by the crowd. Parliamentary police stopped the Grannies from entering. Nevertheless, the Raging Grannies' rock star status was becoming evident as the crowd shouted, "Go, Grannies, go!"[14]

Most of the photos from the period show the Grannies with their mouths wide open, singing at the top of their lungs. Their raucous style of singing effectively grabs public attention. Their inability to lock onto the same pitch or remember melody lines simply adds to the humorous and appealing din. A recurrent cycle of musical preparation and theatrical protest ensued from that point onward and has remained the Grannies' mode of operation to this day. Images and videos of the Grannies in action can be accessed at Ecosong.net.

By the summer of 1987, the Grannies were ready to do battle on the Salish Sea. With their tattered "nuclear umbrellas" unfurled, the group paddled out to engage the Royal Canadian Navy and its allies in the United States Navy, who brought along nuclear-powered ships. It was the Royal Canadian Navy's seventy-fifth anniversary celebration, and the Grannies were bound and determined to spoil the party. Allied with a coalition of First Nations activists and Greenpeace organizers, the Grannies gained a great deal of local and national news coverage by engaging in the unfair fight. The press could not resist the opportunity to display images of women dressed up in long flowing dresses, wide hats, and feather boas bobbing up and down in their tiny boats against the backdrop of massive ships, with their full complement of navy personnel standing at attention on the decks above. Not long after that "battle" on the Salish Sea, the Grannies launched their official Anti-Nuclear Armada in the Peace

Fountain outside Canada's National Parliament Building in Ottawa. The armada consisted of a rubber raft paddled from one side of the fountain to the other. The event received positive coverage across the country while officials tried, unsuccessfully, to dismiss the Raging Grannies' musical theater as misguided and meaningless.

After almost three decades of musical performance, the Raging Grannies continue to garner much more attention than they would if they were to speak out in a less outrageously audible manner. Nor are they content to follow typical protest protocol, which tends to involve marching and chanting in orderly fashion, then gathering to listen to a range of speakers who bore the crowd to tears. Much like Mother Jones, the Raging Grannies lead by example, exhorting activists to invest their passion and creativity in each campaign, to be active participants rather than part of a body count and passive audience. The Grannies' humorous brand of musical "entrainment"— making music together, in rhythm (more or less)—is ideal for representing the collective interests of environmental activists. One of the Grannies' first written goals was "to get the message across with satiric songs," making music the only art specifically cited in their foundational document.[15]

Meanwhile, authorities still have no idea what to do with the Raging Grannies. Roy explains that "the Granny figure allowed older women to claim a public space," and they "often confounded authorities with their unpredictability and imagination."[16]

Political activism involves carefully crafting a message, using subtle rhetoric to persuade policy-making bodies (what advocacy campaign managers refer to as the "primary audience") as well as the public (sometimes referred to as the "secondary audience"). However, the objective of a protest is not the same as that of an organizational campaign like those waged by the Sierra Club, World Wildlife Fund, or Audubon Society. The latter uses a range of tools for reaching policy makers and political leaders more directly, whereas protest tends to be more about public information and mobilization, putting an issue onto the public's radar screen and political agenda. If a topic has not yet entered the public sphere, there is little hope of democratic action taking place. In other words, public protest is an elemental act of democratic communication.

Protest is an alternative headline service. Protesters gather to let the public know when elected leaders are quietly approving uranium mining on public lands, or if a company is clear-cutting the province's few remaining stands of temperate rain forest, or when toxic chemicals are being dumped into rivers leading to the Salish Sea. By acting out in public, groups like the Raging Grannies ritually perform democracy, signaling through their time, effort, and willingness to risk embarrassment that an issue is worthy of public debate.

This is not to say that activists are uninformed. To the contrary, environmental protests are typically the product of serious research by knowledgeable citizens. In fact, the Grannies are some of the most knowledgeable people I have met, deeply versed in every topic they take on. However, as intelligent and savvy activists, they also know that the protest action is not about complex rhetorical messaging. Protest requires bold action, ritual acuity (which involves much more than employment of textual rhetorics and oratory), creativity, and clear messaging. Applying those principles, the Grannies have mastered the art of protest.

Protest expresses collective concerns in public and, when warranted, outrage. Often there is no other forum for expressing such concerns, especially when decisions are being made behind boardroom doors. Making protest work often requires breaking with the rules of decorum, conventional forms of comportment that protect power and the status quo. Powerful individuals and institutions would prefer that protesters adhere to ponderous bureaucratic processes and obey cultural conventions, but such processes are often designed to limit, rather than facilitate, public input and democratic governance. Historically, men with political power have expected decorum and compliance, especially from figures like the Grannies. However, when women representing wives, mothers, and grandmothers suddenly start singing indecorous songs just outside their windows, they are not quite sure what to do with them. In fact, policy makers and CEOs have been uncertain what to do with the Raging Grannies for almost three decades now.

The following list barely scratches the surface of the Raging Grannies' environmental actions, but it does provide the reader with a skeletal outline of their creative responses to significant ecological challenges. The timeline ends in 2002, the year that *Off Our Rockers* was completed. Post-2002 events, covered in the live interview and correspondence, will be discussed later along with the Grannies' performance strategies.

1989: The Grannies marched on the Fletcher Challenge Lumber Company, delivering a clutch of fragile balloon bird "eggs" to company officials, symbolizing what toxic dioxins were doing to birdlife.

1990: At the outset of Operation Desert Storm, the Grannies visited military recruiters. They were protesting the trade of "boys' lives for oil."[17] In accordance with Canadian law, none of the Grannies were asked their age and all were fully interviewed. Two Grannies received callbacks before their requests to enlist were politely rejected.

1992: The Grannies held a "Tea Not Tomahawks" party on the deck of the USS *Texas*, a nuclear-powered, guided-missile cruiser. The ship's captain went ballistic.

1993: The Grannies took part in the Clayoquot Sound forest-protection movement, resulting in several members serving jail time. The larger movement's protests resulted in protections for the Great Bear Rainforest, one of the last remaining sections of old-growth temperate rain forest in the world.

1997: The Grannies helped institute the Golden Piggy Awards, which "recognize and expose" corporate injustice and pollution. Monsanto and Shell have been perennial prizewinners.

1999: In response to the Canadian government expropriating the British Columbian seabed (to stop the provincial government from regulating salmon fisheries), the Grannies mustered an "invasion force" to occupy a rock outcrop "island" near Victoria. Consequently, the Royal Canadian Mounted Police designated the Grannies an official "anti-Canadian force."

2000: The Grannies performed throughout Germany in collaboration with Greenpeace.

2002: The Grannies performed their first "cry-in" to protest welfare cuts.

The year 1993 was particularly pivotal. Acker and Brightwell argue that the anti-logging "battle didn't just save Clayoquot. It lifted the whole environmental movement onto the front pages and brought massive awareness to our planet's fragility."[18] Successful mobilization at Clayoquot helped fuel much larger demonstrations in the following years, including massive protests against the World Trade Organization, the "Battle in Seattle." Of course, Acker and Brightwell are not taking credit for Clayoquot or Seattle, just noting the Grannies' participation in those larger movements. Although it is hard to remember now, mired as we are in the post-9/11 world, there was a period during the late 1990s and into the first twenty months of the new millennium when the post–Cold War peace dividend appeared to be yielding promising gains for environmental, anti-poverty, and human rights movements. Young activists would do well to learn from activists like the Grannies who made that exceptional period possible.

Clayoquot protests led to protections for the Great Bear Rainforest under the aegis of the United Nations Educational, Scientific, and Cultural Organization (UNESCO) Biosphere Reserve program. The agreement curtailed clear-cutting and other unsustainable practices in the area, a success that provided young activists and the Grannies alike with renewed hope. Clayoquot became the symbolic touchstone for a new generation of environmental activists in Canada. The "War in the Woods brought in fresh recruits" for the Raging Grannies as well.[19]

Inspired by the Victoria group's example, gaggles sprang up in sixty towns and cities throughout Canada, as well as in Israel, Australia, and other nations. Their model spread throughout the United States. To this day, San Francisco and Seattle maintain the largest gaggles in the world. A biannual Unconvention of gaggles brings Grannies together from throughout North America. As the original gaggle, Victoria's Raging Grannies are rock stars at the Unconvention. Given their origins and accomplishments, it is not hard to understand why the Victorian troupe remains a model for Raging Grannies the world over. When I interviewed the Victoria gaggle, they were rehearsing their version of *Swan Lake* for an upcoming Unconvention in Montreal.[20] They refer to their new performance as the "Corpse de Ballet."

WHO BECOMES A RAGING GRANNY?

Any story about the Grannies, a fluid organization that values individuality and self-expression, is incomplete without a sense of who joins the group and persists. The eight Grannies I interviewed represent an active cross section of the organization.

Anne Moon was born in Britain but has lived in Canada for her entire adult life. Upon moving to Victoria in 1996, she immediately joined the Raging Grannies. Moon's central role in the Victoria gaggle will become increasingly apparent as the chapter progresses.

Like Moon, Daphne Taylor was born in Britain. She immigrated to Canada with her husband and three children in 1965. She "started being an activist" while she was "living in Halifax, Nova Scotia," where she "joined the Voice of Women."[21] After her family "moved west," Taylor "got involved in more environmental" causes. After taking a break from movement politics, in part to take care of an ailing husband, Taylor thought to herself: "Here I am, and I'm not an activist anymore; I've got to do something about this." She had met Granny Freda Knott through previous protests, so she inquired about joining the Grannies. "So I'm the youngest one here," she jokes, "but I happen to be the oldest one here, too."

Alison Acker moved to Victoria in 1989 after retiring. "I moved here because I wanted to get away from my family, and it was the furthest before I got my feet wet," she joked. "I have a great criminal record," she continued with a smile, summarizing her years with the Raging Grannies. "I love it." A few of the other Grannies feigned consternation when Acker mentioned her arrest record, to which the hardened criminal replied, "Yeah, so I have great street credits." When the discussion turns to songwriting, Acker takes the lead. For most of the group's existence, she has been writing their clever lyrics.

Sonya Ignatieff retired in Ottawa and joined a gaggle of Grannies there. She moved to Victoria in 2001, and "after some deliberation" (which lasted a total of fifteen minutes), the original Grannies gaggle decided to let her into their group. Ignatieff has "always been working in the community," and "towards what might be a better life." She believes that "we should be having a lot more long-term looks at things" and worries about the world her grandchildren will encounter as the century progresses.

Sheila Rose Richardson is from the north of England. Like many activists, Richardson has passed through periods when it simply was not possible to dedicate significant time to a cause: "I was an activist when I could be." She "was a member of the Communist Party in England" but then moved to Canada, where her "downfall was meeting a man." That line received a hearty and empathetic laugh from the rest of the gaggle.

Richardson had a hard time working her way into the Grannies' good graces, largely because her job as a teacher made it difficult for her to set aside sufficient time to rehearsals. "In desperation, I started a drama group called Seniors at Play," she noted, "and then the Grannies took pity on me and took me in . . . I think they are a wonderful group, and I always feel I'm sort of trying to catch up, and I don't think I have. . . . How old am I, seventy-seven? Almost seventy-eight." Richardson ended her introduction on a more serious note: "I'm appalled at the environment, or at least how we're treating the environment and what we're doing to ourselves and everybody else, just absolutely appalled."

Freda Knott also took part in the group interview, an afternoon session involving eight members. Knott was born in Vancouver and then moved to Victoria in 1967. She "was a Red Diaper baby" and "was in the Communist Party until the '90s." Knott has "been very active politically" for her entire life. She "was one of the originators of the peace group here in Victoria" and "until recently was very active on the Council of Canadians."[22] Catching herself, Knott continued, "I still am, but I'm not on the board anymore."

When the Raging Grannies first started, Knott said, "No, I'm not gonna join a group that's gonna make fun of a bunch of old women." "But then I saw how popular they became," she continued, noting that "they all came from the peace movement." Knott had an affinity with the Grannies goals, politics, and members, so she joined up and has been an important force in the group for most of its existence.

Next it was Fran Thoburn's turn to introduce herself. I was fortunate to have some time before the interview to meet and talk to Fran alone in the community center meeting room. In a group made up of movement intellectuals, Thoburn is among the most erudite and politically engaged individuals I have ever met, and she is nothing short of a historic figure. As I was putting finishing touches on this chapter, I was again reminded of the importance of Thoburn's role as a founding Granny as well as her instrumental work in Canadian and global environmental and peace movements. Moon sent along an e-mail from the Canadian Voice of Women, which presented her with the Muriel Duckworth award in recognition of her lifetime achievements as an organizer and activist. The Toronto-based organization acknowledged Thoburn's "environmental sensitivities to travel" but hoped that they might be able to coax her into attending the award ceremony in person. Although these are just the sorts of honors Thoburn dismisses with well-timed jokes, I felt privileged to speak to her in person.

Thoburn related her story in detail:

> Back in '78, my first granddaughter was born. I was living in Ontario, and I thought, "Will there be a world around for her to grow up in?" So I contacted the other grandmother, her other grandmother, and said, "Let's start a Grandmothers for Peace." And she wrote back and said she was really too worried about the Russians coming in and taking over our barbecue backyards. So when I moved out here a few years later, I became active in the peace movement, and we—a group of us took a course—took kind of a weekend thing of learning how to do street theater from David Diamond.

She went on to describe the "nuclear testing" they performed around malls and parking lots:

> We would put on white coats that would have the nuclear symbol on them, and we would have turkey basters, and one woman was wearing a welder's helmet, and we thought we looked official. And people thought we were official because we had this Geiger counter, which really was a metronome, an electric metronome. And we would go out, and we would test the puddles when there was a ship that was run by nuclear power in the navy base. And we would do this downtown, and we would test people and let them know. And we had printed material to give them about the nuclear ships that were going right past our city all the time, up the Strait of Juan de Fuca and so on, just to make people aware of the nuclear [threat].

Although becoming increasingly skeptical of the Grannies' ability to make a major difference, Fran took note of one of their many successes: "So it was the nuclear issue that we mostly worked on, and we did raise a lot of awareness. There were no emergency plans over at the base until the Grannies started telling people that there could be a terrible accident there. So we did make a difference."

Around the same period, the mid-1980s, Thoburn "looked around" at her fellow protesters "and saw that we were all women," adding, "most of us were old." She explained how Doran Doyle suggested that the group "should change our image and become grannies." Thoburn responded negatively to the suggestion: "'Well, I refuse to be an apple-pie, stay-at-home-and-knit granny.' To which Doran replied, 'Let's be Raging Grannies,' so there we were."

Thoburn's account clarifies a previously indeterminate part of the Grannies' backstory, at least as it exists in published form. Rather than not knowing which of the two women first uttered the group name, as told in *Off Our Rockers*, Thoburn later informed me that, according to her journal, it was Doran, "an ardent feminist," who first uttered the name "Raging Grannies."[23] This might seem like a minor point, but it is one worth clarifying for the archive. Several of the current Grannies joined very soon after the group formed, but Thoburn is the last active member from the original gaggle, having played a foundational role in a group that gave birth to a global movement. The 1987 founders' meeting represents a historic dialogue.

Echoing the others' sentiments, Thoburn captured the group ethos well while bringing her biographical sketch up to date:

> And I now have six grandchildren. I'm extremely concerned, and the main thing that worries me most is that not only are our politicians very self-oriented and unwilling to make a real sacrifice but each of us are not quite getting it. We are not making—-we're not cutting back on our personal behaviors. And as far as I'm concerned, I'm the only one I have real control of, and that's true for everybody. But we haven't quite got there yet, and I'm not sure that we will. I think that's just the way human beings are put together. So I have a pretty bleak picture of the future, and I'm now actually a great-grandmother, so it worries me a lot.

As the last active member from that original gaggle, and as one of the most important intellectual and creative forces in the group, Thoburn radically underestimates her importance to the Grannies. Born to a family with a long history of political organizing, she brought decades of political experience and education to the table when the Grannies were formed. She has undoubtedly put her psychology degree to work on more than one occasion in keeping the group together and moving forward. However, like the rest of the Grannies, Thoburn is also well schooled in gender and family relations after "bringing up four children and two husbands." After her children and husbands were grown, she moved to Victoria and began producing a biweekly radio show, among other public efforts.[24] However, decades from now, Fran Thoburn will undoubtedly be best remembered for her foundational role in the Raging Grannies.

Ruth Miller also comes "from a long line of social and political activists." She grew up in Victoria and was connected to the local left from the outset. She also "lived away" from Victoria for "a long time" but eventually came back and joined the Communist Party, where she met Knott, who became her entry point to the group, as was the case for Taylor. At one protest, Miller saw a group of women performing in outrageous granny-wear. "It was the Grannies," Miller remembers. She also remembers thinking, "Gee, that's kind of interesting." She asked Knott, "Who are these women that you're with, and what were they doing?" Miller recalled, "Freda told me" about the Raging Grannies, "and I wondered if I could join." And "here I am thirteen years later," she smiled, pleased with her successful tenure.

The other Grannies volunteered additional information about Miller, including the fact that she belonged to the Black Panthers while at Yale. Miller interrupted, noting that she left the Panthers when the group became violent. At Yale, Miller learned valuable lessons regarding protest and performance. One of her interesting insights involved protesters' relationships with the police. She and her classmates learned that it is a good idea to offer gum to riot police. They have to lift their face shields to chew it. Once protesters and officers make face-to-face contact, she explained, officers are more likely to treat protesters like human beings.

As is evident in Miller's anecdote, the Raging Grannies humanize policy making and protest. They refuse to let governance become reduced to technocratic procedures. Similarly, they eschew dry and lifeless expressions of dissent. Instead, they rage, laugh, and sing, pouring the entire palette of human expression into their public artistry.

SONGS AND SONGWRITING

The Raging Grannies have written and performed more than 150 songs. Most often, they put new words to well-known songs. For example, Fran

Thoburn and her friend Hub Meeker turned "Take Me Out to the Ball-game" into "Take Me Out to the Clear-cut":

> Take me out to the clear-cut.
> We'll picnic on a few stumps.
> I want you to know I'm a tree-farming nut
> Who thinks like a chainsaw that's stuck in a rut.
> MacBloedel* gets a hip-hooray.
> They make black picnic grounds pay.
> So it's one makes it two.
> Dear investors, thank you,
> You have spruced up our day.
>
> Take me out to the clear-cut.
> The timber's been tidied away.
> It's been sold down the stream in a businessman's dream.
> It's swell to stand here on a landscape so clean.
> So it's off to lumbering elsewhere.
> I'll lumber you and you me.
> It's the buzz of the mill that produces the thrill
> Worth a thousand trees.
>
> *Change the name of the timber company to suit.

Jane Mackey composed the Raging Grannies' songs for the first two years. It was Mackey who laid down the foundational dictum for Raging Grannie songwriting: "Don't preach."[25] According to Rachelle Delaney, Mackey "quit because she didn't think the Grannies were musical enough."[26] Delaney published a story about the Raging Grannies based on an encounter with Alison Acker. Acker took over songwriting duties from Mackey but has followed her predecessor's advice well. Her lyrics do anything but preach. Moon regrets that "a lot of the other Granny gaggles have really preachy songs, and we like to think we stand out because we do not preach."

Unlike Mackey, Acker "can't write music." However, unlike many of her fellow Grannies, Acker has sung her entire life, including in orga-nized choral groups. She kindly puts up with the other Grannies' sing-ing, though most have no formal vocal training. Nevertheless, as with a lot of punk, folk, and popular music in general, it is often the uninhib-ited and untrained voice that makes the most pleasing, interesting, and artful vocal sounds. Those who are more classically trained frequently have to unlearn as much as they learn in order to perform popular music well.

Acker explained her songwriting process, emphasizing the speed at which Raging Grannies' songs need to be written and learned: "For instance, today is Thursday. On Tuesday I got an e-mail saying, 'Can the Grannies sing at our antipoverty rally in the city?' Sure. And it was about evictions. So I have about forty minutes, so I did 'All I Want Is a Row Somewhere' and changed a lot of the words around [from *My Fair Lady*'s 'All I Want Is a Room Somewhere']. And then we didn't get together until we rehearsed five minutes before we were there, which is always our problem. As such, it worked very well." The group sticks to well-known show tunes, standards, hymns, and folk songs so that lyrics can be crafted quickly and learned even more quickly. Once Acker knows what the song needs to be about, a recognizable tune usually pops into her head. "I'm not starting from scratch," she reiterates. "Otherwise you would never get anything." However, Acker pointed out that the group has performed one original rap: "We're rebel, rebel Grannies and we're really, really cool. We don't give a damn for any old fool!"

As Acker pointed out, writing songs from scratch is extremely difficult. It is difficult to compose songs with clear messages on predefined topics and also craft original music to accompany the words. It is partly a matter of time but also a function of the complex relationship between lyrical wordplay and musical sound. Composing music with lyrics is typically an iterative process, with sonic considerations that make lyrical composition quite different from writing poetry, for example.

David Boucher provides an insightful comparison of writing songs versus writing poetry.[27] He explains how melodic innovation begets lyrical modification, which in turn influences rhythm, and so on, with all factors becoming mutually interdependent and thus subject to constant change throughout the composition process. A rock, folk, or pop song's ecology is so tightly interconnected that the starting lyrical concept often changes along with musical developments and modifications. One word gets replaced here because it does not fit the developing rhythm. A new word is needed there because it has a prolonged vowel, and a clipped consonant works better from a sonic perspective. New words start leading to new meanings, artful in their multiple evocations but no longer terribly clear in their denotations or original intent. If that very typical form of musical composition sounds like a bad way to go about writing protest music, it is. Typically, the best way to write protest songs is by focusing on crafting clear lyrics with catchy hooks and clever rhyming schemes. That usually means borrowing existing songs and melodies so that one can concentrate on crafting and keeping the right words for the occasion. Acker is highly skilled in that regard. Like movement musicians Joe Hill and Woody Guthrie before her, she borrows her melodies and music from other songwriters.

Acker involves the entire group in the songwriting process whenever possible. Sometimes it is unavoidable. She has to be thick-skinned. "We don't like that line," a fellow Granny will say, or "We need another word here instead." "And they're right," she explains, illustrating the good-natured countenance of a collaborative composer. "I usually e-mail [the new lyrics] out to people," explained Acker, "and generally they don't make too much of a fuss." "Alison is great," said Thoburn, explaining that the entire group appreciates how "she'll accept our fine-tuning."

Moon credits Acker for maintaining a sense of humor. "I think we find that we're very fortunate having Alison because she's got this acerbic sense of humor." Roy is correct to credit the Grannies' "humor and imagination" for their "effective education on public issues."[28] Acker's songwriting has been central to that success. In her hands, "(I've Got You) Under My Skin," became "Under Our Skin," a song about toxic pollution, "Where Have All the Flowers Gone?" was transformed into "Where Have All the Fishes Gone?" and "Climb Every Mountain" evolved into "Behead Every Mountain," a satirical take on mountaintop removal coal mining.[29] "They're tunes that everybody knows," explained Acker.

After updating well-known songs with new lyrics, Acker will often recycle and modify her own words to fit new occasions. "We'll have a word, a song about one president or one prime minister or something, and we just change it," explained Moon. "You know, update it." "For example, when Clinton was in, we had great fun," Acker added. She and other Grannies "admitted" to sleeping with Canadian officials, making hay of the Clinton-Lewinsky scandal.

Unfortunately, not all eras and issues lend themselves to such levity. Acker lamented that "it was hard in the Iraq War finding something you could be funny about." "Some of our songs are serious," Thoburn added. As an example, she noted the following "heartrending" line from the unpublished song "Underneath the Bombers": "The bombs that you're dropping on people to make them free." "I mean, it has funnier parts," she explained, "but that line is just a bombshell in itself." That and other Grannies songs can be accessed at Ecosong.net, which also provides links to several other gaggles' sites in Canada and the United States.

As mentioned, Acker follows a long line of community organizers who used popular tunes to communicate critical messages. Joe Hill is perhaps the most well known, a member of the Industrial Workers of the World (IWW) who converted traditional hymns into satirical union songs.[30] Out-of-work or underpaid loggers and miners often found themselves at the mercy of the Salvation Army or, as Hill referred to them, the "Starvation Army." In exchange for food, they would be subjected to endless proselytizing and dour hymns. Hill's answer to the mine-and-missionary complex was to change a hymn's words, repurposing each song to communicate humorous messages favoring the Industrial Workers of the World. Hill's songs offered earthly change as opposed to "pie in the sky when you die . . . that's a lie."[31]

"The Rapture," the Grannies' response to climate-science denial, is similar to Hill's song about the Salvation Army. "The Rapture" is sung to the tune of "I've Been Working on the Railroad":

Who cares about global warming,
Poverty or war?
Who cares about the future—
We won't be around any more![32]

Every Granny has a favorite song from the group's repertoire. Ruth Miller's is "The Rapture." When a pair of acquaintances asked Miller to "sing something" on a cross-country train trip, she trotted out "The Rapture," surprising everyone in the dining car.

As in "The Rapture," Raging Grannies songs point listeners to specific people and policies, providing an audience with actionable intelligence.

In that sense, their lyrics are what Bob Dylan calls "finger pointing songs."[33] The Grannies want people to clearly hear the name of US president George Bush or Canadian prime minister Stephen Harper in songs like "The Rapture," and they want to explain what such leaders are doing to the environment and not doing in relation to climate change. In other words, clever lyrics are a means to an end, an effective method for delivering environmental messages, rather than art for art's sake. The point is not just to sing about the world but also to change it. It is a burden most songwriters and performers do not face.

Raging Grannies songs connect listeners to specific problems, policies, and people. For example, "Fishies," written by Betty Brightwell, connects federal fisheries policies to local habitat destruction and species endangerment, using Minister of Environment David Anderson as a stand-in symbol for the Canadian government as a whole. The fact that Anderson hails from Victoria makes the song all the more effective.

Fishies
Out in the ocean in a nice polluted sea
Swam a school of fishies, as happy as can be.
We're going back to Canada, where we all began.
But wait a minute, fishes, they've got another plan.

Chorus: Boop, boop. Diddum, daddum, choo (3x)

'cos you'll never make it back up to the river to spawn.

What happened to the turbot, the herring and the cod
Is happening to the salmon, and don't blame it all on God.
Greedy politicians can squabble through the night
But we won't give up our salmon without a good fight.

Chorus: Boop, boop. Diddum, daddum, choo.
Boop, boop, diddum, daddum, choo.
Boop, boop, diddum, we need another plan
And we know we can't rely on David Anderson.

"Fishies" represents the Raging Grannies' relative radicalism. In this song and via protest activities, the Grannies take a stand that is at odds with mainstream conservationists. Anderson has been lauded in the international community as an environmentalist leader. As evidenced in "Fishies," however, the Raging Grannies feel as though Anderson's curbs on overfishing did not go far enough. In this case, they were the loyal opposition rather than party loyalists.

"Fishies" is best read intertextually. The song references science, politics, journalism, and policy. A song like "Fishies" encourages listeners to go out and study issues at greater length and act on that knowledge. Such songs also express the Grannies' collective rage, giving musical form to environmental organizations' public demands. "Fishies" is specifically aimed at returning control of the BC fishery to the provincial government. It is musical advocacy in action, the context in which protest art is best measured.

PERFORMING POLITICS

Once the Grannies agree on the site and purpose of their next public performance, the next steps typically go something like this: the group plans an action, Acker writes a song, and everyone learns the words and rehearses it at the community center. Sometimes they simply update a past performance, especially if time is very limited, but the gaggle's interest is fueled by constant creativity rather than repetition. Therefore, the group prefers to invent new performances whenever possible.

The Grannies' recent Flag Day protests have been particularly creative. Each year, the public gathers to commemorate and honor their national symbol and nation by forming a giant human flag. In 2013, the group donned a giant black sheet and performed an oil slick moving through the human flag, much to the surprise of their fellow citizens gathered on the lawn in front of the BC Parliament Building.

I asked the Grannies to explain their party-crashing performance. "I think it began with Canada Day last year (2013)," explained Moon. She described how "a bunch of people in red and white T-shirts" gather to "form a living flag on the lawn of the legislature every year." The group "decided last year that it would be a really good place to get some profile for the oil problem on the coast."

Enbridge seeks to build a large pipeline to the Pacific Ocean running from the Alberta oil shale region to the British Columbia coast. It is part of a three-ponged approach, piping oil to the Atlantic through southern Canada and the northern United States, sending it to the Gulf of Mexico via the Keystone pipeline, and transporting it to the Pacific through new conduits in British Columbia. Each route has run into environmentalist opposition, although the Koch brothers' Keystone section has received the most news coverage in the United States. As discussed in chapter 3, Enbridge's Alberta-to-British-Columbia proposal has raised the ire of many local organizations, including the Idle No More movement.

"We all got under this black cloth," Moon explained, "and we oozed our way around the flag." The Grannies' human oil slick was visible in aerial photographs of the flag. Yet the Grannies themselves could not see where they were going, so for subsequent protests they cut slits in the cloth so they can pop out their heads. They now wear duck hats, producing the effect of waterfowl popping out of an oil slick.

The week before I interviewed the Victoria gaggle, four of them had taken their oil slick to the annual Oak Bay Tea Party. The slick grew when kids at the event joined in. The group feared that people at the Canada Day and Oak Bay Tea Party events might react angrily to their guerrilla incursions. "I went down there thinking people were going to be telling us, 'Get out of here; we don't want you,'" said Freda Knott, but "it turned out that everybody loved us."

When the Raging Grannies first started, people used to yell things like "'Go back to Russia!' and this sort of thing," added Acker, "but now we get, 'Oh, the Grannies are here! Hooray!'" Thoburn finds that positive reaction "a little bit worrying." Having witnessed the entire life span of the Raging Grannies, Thoburn fears that the increasingly positive reception indicates that they are either "talking to the converted" or that the group's performances are "just laughable." Of course, that concern hovers in the mind of every self-reflective protest performer. Each theatrical activist seeks to find just the right spot on a wide spectrum ranging from avant-garde irrelevance, at one extreme, to pointless "preaching to the choir," at the other.

Of course, all strategies have their benefits. Apathetic and complacent communities often need to be shocked into serious deliberation and action (the term "avant-garde" originally referred to the "vanguard," shock troops at the head of an army). At the other end of the art-as-advocacy spectrum—where artists speak mainly to activist insiders—every choir can use a good pep talk. However, the Raging Grannies hope to communicate their ideas to people who might not otherwise receive dissenting messages. They want neither to be dismissed out of hand as superficially silly nor to be welcomed in as silly entertainment. Thoburn worries that the Raging Grannies might be losing their ability to reach, challenge, and motivate public audiences by becoming simply entertainment.

Thoburn offered the example of the Raging Grannies Anti-Nuclear Armada as a performance that, in the past, more directly challenged the powerful. She noted that the group followed Prime Minister Brian Mulroney "into the Parliament Buildings" before being stopped by police. The Grannies created a wild scene and raucous soundscape with their singing, enough to make the nation's highest officials uncomfortable. Thoburn wonders if they are still having that kind of radical impact.

Thoburn's example brings us back to one of the initial questions in this book: What constitutes "success" for an environmentalist musician? It is a tough question, but one that this self-reflective group is particularly well positioned to answer. In the foreword to *Off Our Rockers*, Anne Moon offers the following thoughts on the ecopolitical impact of the Raging Grannies:

> Strangely enough, we haven't changed the world or accomplished any miracles in the 17 years since we formed the Victoria Raging Grannies. In reality, the world has gotten nastier in spite of us. . . . Sure, we've ruffled a few feathers, gotten a lot of media coverage, annoyed many Canadian citizens and delighted some others, but the differences we have made are largely in raising awareness. You might call us whistle-blowers, catalysts, troublemakers, general nuisances. In our own peculiar fashion, we've worked for peace and nuclear disarmament, safe food and water, saving the forests and an end to poverty, homelessness, injustice and war— sometimes on our own, sometimes with larger groups. It's been a rough ride, with few victories, but we've had a lot of fun on the way.[34]

During our interview, Acker added her thoughts on Thoburn's Anti-Nuclear Armada example. "I'm not sure about whether it worked," but "I liked our cry-in at the Ministry of Health." She continued, "You could just walk in, and it was a three-story sort of amphitheater thing there. All the offices were there. We just sat there, and we cried for nearly an hour. It's hard to cry [for that long, but we did] because our health system was being attacked." After asking, "Was it successful?" Acker answered her own question: "That's so hard to say."

Building on Acker's example, Thoburn described how "people in the building came down and listened to us," again returning the question of who listens to them. "We were being vocal, you know," she added, "saying things as we were crying."

As Acker's and Thoburn's examples demonstrate, soundscape awareness is part of the Grannies' methodology. Officials are not allowed to destroy the environment or health-care system in decorous silence. At the cry-in, police were utterly befuddled by the loud group of women bawling their eyes out. "By the time they came," laughed Thoburn, "we were so hoarse." "Exhausted," added Acker.

"The place was in lockdown because of us," bragged Thoburn. Knott added, "We wouldn't leave, so they picked us up." Miller's sister was observing from the gallery. One of the security people asked her, "Do you think they will leave now?" "No, you had better call the police," she replied, fearing that her sister and the entire gaggle might soon lose their voices. "Because of course we wanted the police to come," added Miller, "and sure enough, they did." Miller noted that the cop escorting her out of the building kindly whispered, "Come again soon" as he released her back into the wild.

Interestingly enough, our discussion about "success" turned the interview conversation toward civil disobedience. Sonya Ignatieff recalled their final act of civil disobedience during the Iraq War anti-recruiting campaign. "We ended up sitting on a couch," she laughed, "and in the end they had to carry it out." She added, "Well, they tried," eliciting laughter from the entire gaggle. "They couldn't lift the couch," explained Thoburn. "There were so many of us on it, and we're not small."

It is possible that the ecopolitical message could get lost in all the entertaining activity. However, the Raging Grannies are not interested in imparting knowledge per se. Neither their songs nor their theatrical performances provide detailed information about issues. They are not performing musical journalism or scholarship. Instead, the Grannies are "aimed at promoting dialogue and raising consciousness by stimulating political debates."[35] In other words, the Raging Grannies are cultural catalysts rather than opinion leaders. They have no desire to lead large coalitions, organize door-to-door, or lobby officials over dinner; instead, they view their role as that of disrupting business as usual, bringing public attention to matters that should be vetted democratically, in public, rather than behind closed doors.

Sitting around a table, talking with the Raging Grannies, including members of the original gaggle, it became apparent that they represent a treasure trove of organizing knowledge. Whereas many imagine protesters as knee-jerk bleeding hearts, these are the types of individuals who study problems in great depth and put in the elbow grease it takes to investigate alternatives. Only when other means of democratic discourse are exhausted, when political, legal, and financial processes have failed to produce a public good, do they take direct action. They are not politicians, lobbyists, lawyers, or accountants; they are activists. Their creativity and humor are products of very sober study, critical thinking, and genuine concern. All those attributes have contributed to the group's success. That success can be measured in their creative contributions to unexpected policy outcomes—such as the movement to protect old-growth forests surrounding Clayoquot Sound and the enactment of radiation monitoring and safety protocols at Canadian naval facilities—as well as their longevity, global spread, and fame in the environmentalist community. Their infamy among industrialists, politicians, and militarists should be added to that list as well. They must be doing something right.

Although music is central to the Raging Grannies' protest performances, the group is reluctant to think of themselves as musicians. "I don't think singing is the best thing we do," observed Acker. "We are lousy at singing." She added, "It's usually our way into things," because "if you're there and singing," it allows both the singers and others to "focus; it's a way to get attention."

"We do not ever want to be entertainers," reiterated Acker, nor does the group want to enter the professional ranks. "We never get paid for anything we do," said Acker. "In fact we're very proud we were once paid $250" as a "non-performance fee" by a group that feared the gaggle would disrupt its New Year's activities. "We went ahead and sang anyway," Miller pointed out.

"The day we sink to being entertainers," concluded Acker, "I think forget it. . . . Songs have to be used as a way in." In other words, for the Raging

Grannies, music is a medium for political communication. Acker provided the example of a public school hearing called over proposals to ban books. A few people were attempting to get books banned on religious grounds. After a woman stood up and argued for the ban, the Grannies performed a sacrilegious song. Negotiation and appeasement are not in their vocabulary. "Everybody screamed with laughter and joy," remembered Acker fondly, "and the poor lady had to be escorted out" because she was so shocked and upset by the Grannies' reaction to her attempt at educational censorship.

Although they play down their musical talent and experience, the Raging Grannies' musical techniques have gained the attention of educators, activists, and fellow musicians. In 1991, just four years after they were formed, the Grannies were invited to lead a workshop at the Kaslo Summer School of the Arts in the Kootenay region of British Columbia. They have been leading workshops ever since.

Freda Knott feels that "singing is a very important part" of the Raging Grannies' performances. "Every time we sing, we have a very good message," she explained. "At the end, there's a message," repeated Knott for emphasis. Knott credited Acker with creating effective "sarcastic" songs that clearly communicate the Grannies' point of view.

In 1987, the Grannies experimented with spoken word but felt it did not really work. Mackey, in particular, argued that music would be more effective and fun. Thoburn remembers a momentous question from Mackey: "Would you guys mind if I made up a song?" "And so the first song was 'Beneath the nuclear umbrella we're as safe as we can be.'" Thoburn sang the first line, fondly recalling the moment when the Raging Grannies became a musical group. She reiterated Knott's point that music has been the group's most effective way to "put out our message."

Music is also an effective medium for creating group cohesion. "I think it brings us together," explained Daphne Taylor. The group uses musical performance to organize internally and externally. "We also do try and get other people to sing with us," added Ignatieff. "We'll often hand out sheets so that people can [sing along] or choose something that is easy where they can sing the chorus or something like that."

Innovation is difficult, however. Ignatieff explained that the group is "always looking to find something new and different . . . some sort of hook that we can really bring out the message that we feel is important at the time." She listed some of her favorite examples and then described the difficulties: "The trouble is that as we're grandmas, we have to cover such a wide swath of things, you know, from the environment to peace to social justice to housing. I mean, the demands on that are incredible, so you can imagine that it's kind of hard to come up with something new." But rather than dwell on the difficulties or downsides to protest performance, Igna-tieff and the rest of the group moved our conversation back to current projects. They were particularly excited about a giant "Granny puppet" they were making for the Victoria Peace Parade, an event that takes place each year on the International Day of Peace, September 21.

Moon compared the puppetry project to a kite festival performance earlier in the year. Their message was "Fly kites, not drones." "Except we didn't have big enough kites," complained Knott, arguing that "if we do it again, we're going to do it with great big kites." That might not jibe well with some members' self-described kite-flying skills, but it is an example of how the Grannies constantly push past their limitations and create exciting performance art. As Lyons illustrated in his performance of "Recycle Wrap," pushing one's boundaries can produce compelling comedy. In the case of the Raging Grannies, it helps them gain public attention.

Thoburn offers an alternative to Knott's big kite proposal: "On the other hand, we could pepper the city with our kites by putting them up on telephone poles." "Or fences," suggests Miller. It was a privilege to watch the group in action as they assessed recent performances in order to plan future actions. Knott noted that they reassess and plan constantly, but most intensively at their annual planning "retreat." "We don't retreat!" shouted Miller, teasing Knott for using the wrong term for their annual planning session.

The group believes their success is due in part to maintaining a constant public presence. Moon explains: "For a while we were every month at the corner of Fort and Douglas, and we go to the Pride Parade, and we go to the Earth Day Walk, and we've got a really high recognition factor because we're almost ubiquitous. So yesterday when we went to the housing pro-test, we were introduced as "my favorite choir," and everybody claps— everybody knows us, and that's because we are out there."

The group discussed their gaggle's distinct identity and how it grew organically from the beginning. A few noted that some members were coming in outlandish dresses, while others arrived at protest sites in slacks, because they bicycled. That led to a consensual use of feather boas and outlandish hats, no matter what else the performer chose to wear that day. There were fond memories of early trips to the Salvation Army store, and each Granny's description of a given member's specific ensemble was accompanied by laughter. However, they resisted the temptation to turn the "Granny look" into a "uniform." Taylor spoke for the group: "I know one time there were gaggles who demanded that everybody wear some sort of a uniform with an apron and that sort of stuff, and we soon nixed that. You know, we said, 'You do it if you like, but piss on that.'" From time to time, other gaggles would suggest matching their costumes for inter-gaggle events. The Victoria Raging Grannies have always politely declined because they prefer to express their individuality and do not want to get too hung up on presenting a singular visual impression. Their approach to costuming is similar to their musical philosophy. It is based on free association, loose coordination, and hard work as opposed to rigid coordination and the hierarchical leadership such coordination inevitably invites and requires. That is part of the recipe for the gaggle's longevity. They recruit creative, hardworking women with good ideas and excellent listening skills but tend to react negatively to control freaks. The Raging Grannies' ethos of antiauthoritarianism is more than external public relations; it is also an internal organizing principle.

TURNING IDENTITY INTO PERFORMANCE

Before moving from the Raging Grannies' performance techniques and on to their organizational strategies, it is useful to think about how the group transforms identity into performance. Earlier in their activist lives, people imposed an ageist and sexist identity on them and role definitions that restricted who they could be and what they could do. In response, the group reappropriated the dismissive "granny" identity and used it for empowering purposes. The "granny" identity became the fuel for their outrageous costuming and musical performances. That was not the only possible choice the Grannies could have made when founding the group. There are other ways to combat stereotyping and silencing.

Take the composers profiled in Denise Von Glahn's *Music and the Skillful Listener: American Women Compose the World*.[36] While each is very distinct in terms of personality, all have expressed their deep reverence for nature through subtle and sophisticated compositions. They serve as expert interlocutors for anyone willing and able to listen. They teach us new ways to listen, to become more skilled at listening to the world around us. As such, the music of composers like Marion Bauer, Louise Talma, and Joan Tower hold the potential to transform hegemonic relations. Such works can reconfigure the way that we all, as listeners and actors, engage with nature and one another, offering us paths through and beyond simple gender polemics. As Von Glahn argues, those who do not yet know how to listen radically underappreciate the musical politics of composers like those she examines in *Music and the Skillful Listener*. Such composers help us appreciate and understand the subtleties of soundscape, including worlds very "close to home."[37] Their compositions have often been overlooked in the same way that quotidian ecosystems are ignored in environmentalist rhetoric.

The composers profiled in *Music and the Skillful Listener* use nuanced composition to invite skillful listening, thus disarticulating women's composition (i.e., the cultural signification of recurrent musical signs as "feminine") from sexist stigmatization and patriarchal articulations (i.e., the interpretation of musical signs crafted by women as "inferior"). Such composers challenge stigmatic tautologies by inviting listeners to better understand their elevated art from the inside, providing entrance into an alternative world of musical listening.

Clearly, the Grannies have chosen a very different strategy from those Von Glahn documents. The complete opposite of subtle, the Grannies craft musical arguments that use the logic of reductio ad absurdum, revealing the ultimate absurdity of hegemonic assumptions by putting ridiculous stereotypes on bold public display where they can be overtly acknowledged, publicly dissected, and changed. They publicly name the game. Perceived as grannies, the Raging Grannies decided to take on that cultural identity with gusto, throwing it back at their oppressors. They brought that sublimated identity to the surface where it could be creatively reexamined and turned into a political asset. They render decorum senseless and rage sensible. From the perspective of hegemonic cultural logic, there is something very "wrong" with a bunch of grandmotherly women singing political songs at the top of their lungs. And, of course, that's what makes it so terribly right.

Anyone watching and listening to the Raging Grannies can hear that there is a method to their madness, a great deal more reason than performed in the sober, decorous presentations of powerful politicians and business leaders. They expose the absurdity of men who brandish weapons of mass destruction while proffering peace. They render the green rhetoric of polluting CEOs ridiculous. Their performances expose the absurd logics underneath the staid sobriety of dominant military, political, and marketing rituals while betraying the solid logic and reasoning hiding just below the insane surface of their songs and bonnets.

Von Glahn's artists teach us much about the power of listening by modeling ethical engagements with nature. Conversely, the Raging Grannies demand that we listen by loudly disrupting silence. Both strategies have their virtues. Both require us to listen.

ORGANIZATIONAL STRATEGIES, MAINTENANCE, AND GROWTH

Dana Sawchuk characterizes the Raging Grannies as a "largely decentralized and non-hierarchical movement."[38] The Raging Grannies base their organization on principles of free association, consensus building, and collaboration. Those principles have led to success, but they also take a lot of work. Achieving relative consensus is not always easy, and there are few mechanisms for resolving conflicts and disagreements, beyond difficult discussions, careful listening, attributions of good faith, and a great deal of elbow grease.

Free association works best in relatively small groups. The Grannies have learned that a dozen is about right. When the group starts to become too small, they lose momentum. Too many, and they begin to lose focus. Plus, twelve is about the number of Grannies that fit comfortably in the "living room" for the group's weekly meetings before they moved operations to a community center.[39]

Collaboration and consensus do not preclude specialization. Acker's songwriting is one example. As another example, Anne Moon takes the lead when it comes to organizational logistics. She is the main group contact and brings the Grannies together for rehearsals. Moon's coordination was also clearly essential to getting *Off Our Rockers* written, edited, and published after earlier attempts failed.[40]

The Raging Grannies are successful despite the difficulties of voluntary organization and lack of clearly defined leadership. Moon points out that they simply have no answer when somebody asks, "Who's your leader?" However, she points out that entrenched leadership does not work in voluntary organizations like the Raging Grannies either. "I know Vancouver has that problem," explained Moon. "They have problems with their groups because one person has taken on the leadership. . . . It doesn't work."

Thoburn agrees with Moon. "Each of us leads," she explained, reiterating the point that leadership is "a shared responsibility." "I keep trying to take on the leadership," joked the founding member, "but I keep getting knocked down." Building on Thoburn's joke, Taylor noted, "Even bossy Anne . . ." pausing in mid-sentence for comedic effect, feigning fear while glancing in Moon's direction. Everyone laughed, indicating that, yes, Moon is the de facto logistical leader but that, by the same token, she wields her power in very limited fashion. They can still laugh at Anne all they want, and Anne welcomes it.

"Yet, I haven't heard you get a word in edgewise," I said to Moon. "Oh, I haven't needed to," she replied to uproarious laughter. "If they get out of line, then . . ." She stopped, miming anger. Humor and what Sartre defined as "good faith"—mutual recognition of collective interest—keep the Raging Grannies together.[41]

As for how that has translated into sister gaggles the world over, that remains a mystery to the Victorian chapter. Much like a video that goes viral, the original Raging Grannies have no idea how their organizational model spread around the world. They were too focused on what they were doing to actively promote themselves as a model for others. It appears that the Raging Grannies brand went viral because observers and allies recognized the merits of their basic performance strategy. Clearly they struck a chord with other women.

Paola Gianturco argues that activist groups composed of older women are on the rise, a phenomenon driven by longer life spans, better healthcare systems, the ravages of patriarchal capitalism, and a feminist revolution that was led by this very same generation of women.[42] Women the world over are taking on increasingly public roles as they age, a life trajectory previously reserved for men.

Given their struggle, the Raging Grannies do not accept male group members. The Grannies' strategy is incompatible with mixed-gender performance. Therefore, they have told more than one male inquirer, "Go start your own group!" "No one has ever done it," noted Knott. The Grannies then began to discuss the matter further, asking one another why men have not started groups similar to the Raging Grannies. Their final consensus was that men tend to react poorly when people make fun of them.

Intrigued by their methods, other communities of women have often invited the Victorian gaggle to perform for them and then instruct them, no matter how briefly, on their methods. Thoburn credits a TV appearance with the Canadian Broadcasting Corporation's Peter Gzowski for initially alerting the nation to their presence. Many women inquired about them after the show aired. In response, Thoburn started sending out tapes with a few songs as well as thoughts on how to start up a gaggle.

Thoburn remembers that women in Thunder Bay, Ontario, formed one of the first gaggles and noted that they even had a man involved in the group. She also expressed regret that the Thunder Bay gaggle fell apart after a few years. However, new gaggles popped up elsewhere, and several have been going strong for many years, especially those in provincial capitals and large cities along the West Coast.

A mere twenty-five miles north of Victoria, one of the most well-known gaggles formed on Salt Spring Island, not long after the original group got under way. "We were peaceniks and that was it," explained Thoburn, playing down the original gaggle's musical prowess, but "we did sing." However, "the next group that started, which was Salt Spring, knew they were going to be singing, so they self-selected singers." The Salt Spring gaggle even published a Raging Grannies songbook in 1993, just six years after the original gaggle formed in Victoria.[43] "They can harmonize," offered Thoburn in praise of the Salt Spring gaggle. "They can start on the same note that they end on." The entire group laughed, content in their lack of formal training. "We've kind of embellished our inability to sing," noted Thoburn, explaining how they have turned their lack of training into an asset. "I mean, we're so unashamed of how we sing that it's quite endearing." It's true that some might prefer their rousing performance of "No Frackin' No Way!" to a traditional chorale.[44]

The original group, made up mostly of self-proclaimed nonmusicians, begat gaggles of musicians the world over. Whereas trained singer-organizers often encourage people to participate—Pete Seeger being the most famous example—the Grannies present a rare case of untrained musicians taking the lead. "Tuneless, perhaps," argues Delaney, a young activist in Victoria, "but the Raging Grannies radiate an enthusiastic spark I've never heard before among activists my own age."[45] The Raging Grannies' performances work in part *because* of their lack of conventional musical skills. As such, they show audiences how to convert anger and hope into musical expression, breaking the artificial boundary between musician and nonmusician. They help people literally give voice to their concerns.

After taking root in Canada, the Raging Grannies quickly spread to Ireland and the United States. Miller remembers that the group was invited to perform for a group of women in Seattle early on. At first, the Seattle group referred to themselves as "Granny Groupies," but they quickly turned into a full-fledged gaggle and have since become one of the most successful chapters in the world.

Miller remembers running into a group of Raging Grannies while vacationing in London. She "met two Raging Grannies" outside the Houses of Parliament. They were "carrying signs protesting the Iraq War." Similarly, Knott met with a gaggle while traveling in Israel. Yet, as Thoburn reminded me, the group never intended to spread. "We just grew," she explained, "and we evolved."

For years, cross-gaggle exchange happened on an ad hoc basic. Now it takes place a bit more formally via a network of gaggles. They keep in contact with a listserv called the "Grapevine." However, it remains an informal network. Some gaggles, even a few in British Columbia, are disconnected from the Grapevine. Gaggles across North America have established a strong web presence, including sites that share songs and lyrics for every protest occasion.[46] Ecosong.net provides a portal to those sites and materials for those wanting to see, hear, and explore more of the Grannies' protest music and performance art.

Regarding the relationship between organization and performance, Thoburn, in particular, wanted me to be clear about the group's primary interest in basic messaging, what I referred to as a headline service at the outset of the chapter. Not only were the original Grannies not looking to expand, explained Thoburn, but they were not even concerned about being creative. "Never mind being creative," she said. "We were more concerned about getting people to listen to us." "The age-old problem is nobody listens to the truth, and of course the Grannies have the truth," she joked dryly. "Nobody was listening to us," she continued when the laughter died down. "We did everything to get people to listen to us and to be aware of the danger of the nuclear stuff right on our doorstep."

To be clear, I asked Thoburn if the overwhelming importance of the nuclear issue drove them toward greater creativity. "That's it," she responded, repeating, "that's it," for emphasis. "The need was there," argued the life-long activist, "and we had to just do whatever we had to do, which of course invites creativity."

Acker added that mutual support keeps the group going. "I think it's also a social event for us all," she explained. "I mean, we're all getting older and our families are God knows where." But she added that they "don't make it into a whining place, you know, sort of, 'Oh, I see you're out of hospital—fine. Next person?'" Others respectfully disagreed with her, arguing that complaining was part of their weekly meetings. Several pointed out the importance of "sharing" as a group ethos, a point that Acker agreed with wholeheartedly before concluding: "Also it is fun coming." She then returned to the point about free association, noting that they keep it all "loosey-goosey."

Ignatieff also argued that free association is key to the group's survival and success as an organization. "We don't always get on," she admitted, "and we have to find consensus sometimes." Ignatieff described life with the group as an invigorating experience. Acker agreed: "I find this gives me energy. I don't know. There's something about being together; if we're not rehearsing or singing, we're bouncing things off each other. I always come out of this enthused, with more energy."

Attempting to piggyback on the initial point, Ignatieff stated, "There was another issue I was going to bring up that seems important, too." She then forgot what she was going to say. Moon jokingly jumped in: "Dementia?" "Yes!" Ignatieff responded, without missing a beat. The Grannies demonstrated throughout the interview that mutual attributions of good faith and humor keep the group functioning. The group gave numerous examples of how members, past and present, take care of one another.

Acker then brought up one of the organization's Achilles heels: recruitment. "We're not very good at getting new people in," she explained. "We want younger people," noted Acker, "but they've got jobs and they're so damn busy." Then she added, "But also I think maybe we are frightening people off."

Of course, openings are few and far between given group size, and although the Raging Grannies operate under an ethos of free association, they remain fairly circumspect early on regarding whether or not they want a new recruit to actually stick around. Acker explained that many people ask to join, "so we say, 'Come to a meeting.'" She went on, "We find out a little bit about them, and very often we never see them again." So the auditioning goes in both directions. Taylor and Knott explained that few people are willing to dedicate a large chunk of their week to a voluntary organization, raising a familiar conundrum for social movements and their reliance on "mechanical solidarity" (Durkheim 2014), voluntarism, to contest powerful and relatively permanent governmental bureaucracies and industries.

All agreed that the group's energizing camaraderie keeps them coming back week after week. Taylor noted that the Grannies each have "tremendous strength." Knott agreed, "We're all very strong women," and wondered if that is "why we're able to get along." However, she fears that their strength might "scare" new recruits. "I mean, I've gone home so mad sometimes," said Knott, a point that led everyone to laugh empathetically, "I say, I'm never gonna come back!" Everyone in the room nodded. "We've been known to cry," added Thoburn.

In other words, the same strength that keeps the group together and propels their success constantly threatens to break them apart as well. It is a creative tension not unlike that which rock bands experience. "There have been lots of groups that have started and then stopped," explained Thoburn, "and it's often over personality problems." She described how the Victoria gaggle once "split and about five people left in extreme, vituperative anger." The group described the moment as a real crisis. "And we just didn't reply in kind and we hung in, and we kept going," noted Thoburn, "and I think every one of them is kind of amazed that we still are going, that we haven't split up." Once again, a combination of humor and commitment seems to keep the Raging Grannies going strong.

While interviewing the gaggle, I was reminded of several famous war correspondents, professional musicians, a NASA scientist, and other highly successful people whom I have interviewed, taught alongside, or spoken to over the years. What these successful individuals all have in common is that they are genuinely curious about the world and what they have to learn from others; they are the sort of people who constantly seek out new information, as if anyone they encounter might aid in their ongoing quest for truly new ideas and useful information. Instead of showing off what they know, such people are constantly learning and focused on creatively solving problems.

That was the sort of genuine curiosity on display during the interview and perhaps an insight into the Grannies' group method. The Raging Grannies focus on social problems and seek ways of creatively solving them, together, doing what they do best. They are able to let group tensions and personal anxieties melt into the background in part because their curiosity, creativity, and interest in issues move them forward, overcoming inhibitions. The Grannies use conflicts and challenges as fuel.

LESSONS

In reviewing the case of the Raging Grannies, I find many of the same lessons emerging as revealed in chapter 1. Like Lyons, the Grannies rejected cultural orthodoxy. Older women are supposed to fade into the background while quietly nurturing the younger generation. They are certainly not supposed to sing out against corporations who clear-cut forests or fight the largest military force in the world. That is behavior most unbecoming of a grandmother.

Lyons made a similar move early in his performing career. A young singer-songwriter is supposed to write about love, pain, and angst, perhaps peppering his or her music with just enough social observation to remain cool and relevant but certainly not turning entire tours into organizing campaigns. As was the case for the Raging Grannies, Lyons bucked convention, including the disciplining demands of musical style and genre.

For the Grannies, going against tradition meant rejecting protest conventions. The Grannies learned that "if we wanted to change society, we'd have to change our methods, because they weren't working."[47] That does not stop most organizations from following time-worn protocols. Convention and groupthink often take precedent over critical reassessment. Instead, the Raging Grannies rejected unwritten rules of culture and comportment, including proscriptions against singing out in public. Imagine how vibrant our democracies would be if more people banded together that way in order to voice their perspectives musically in public.

The Raging Grannies have been bringing relevant issues and information to Victoria's headlines since 1987, putting critical threats to the environment on the public agenda. In each case, conventional methods alone probably would have failed. "Once we were invisible," wrote Anne Moon.[48] Singing loud, humorous songs in public, the Raging Grannies broke with the stultifying decorum surrounding official rites and routines of governance. The Grannies became highly visible and unavoidably audible.

I asked the Grannies what advice they would give new activists and musicians. "Laugh," volunteered Taylor. "Yeah, don't preach," agreed Ignatieff, "laugh." She continued: "I mean, we have a good time together. You know, we enjoy each other's company. We drive each other frantic sometimes, but I do think that humor, you know, is incredibly important. We use irony and humor an awful lot, and I think that it has a strength that you don't have with somebody who's incredibly intense. And, you know, I guess we have fun, even though what we're doing is really serious. Is it a crime to have fun? I don't think so, really." "You have to have fun," Knott agreed. "Otherwise you don't want to do it." "We won't do it unless it's fun," added Acker.

Moon explained the connection between pleasure and protest well in the foreword to *Off Our Rockers*: "We make no apologies for enjoying ourselves while fighting for a cause, because laughter lightens the stress and holds us together."[49]

To answer the same question, Taylor answered "honesty," adding "friendship and love." "You need a thick skin," added Miller, to which Taylor responded, "Oh, yeah, that's good." "No whining," offered Ignatieff, continuing the quick round of concise answers.

Moon finished off the question of success with a climatic argument. She suggested that Victoria's "benign climate" allows them to get "out a lot" to perform in public.

Whatever the reasons for the Raging Grannies' success, a combination of people, personalities, and place gave rise to a phenomenon that remains strong almost three decades later, surely some kind of record for a voluntary organization of its type. Therefore, the end lesson for young musicians or old activists is hardly earth-shattering: once you figure out what works well and what you enjoy doing, keep at it, perfect it, and see how far you can take it. By the end of their first year, the Grannies figured out that musical protest had become their collective reason for being. Once that was clear, they never looked back. They experiment, create, and take risks, but they have never abandoned what they do best: sing in public. The Salish Sea community is better for it, enriched by the beautifully imperfect voices of the Raging Grannies, rare guardians of the public good.

NOTES

1. Alison Acker and Betty Brightwell, *The Raging Grannies: Off Our Rockers and into Trouble* (Victoria, BC: TouchWood Editions, 2004), 179.

2. Carole Roy, "The Original Raging Grannies: Using Creative and Humorous Protests for Political Education," "Herstory," Raging Grannies International, accessed January 6, 2015, http://raginggrannies.org/herstory/.

3. Alison Acker and Betty Brightwell, *The Raging Grannies: Off Our Rockers and into Trouble.* (Victoria, BC: TouchWood Editions, 2004), xi.

4. Carole Roy, "Raging Grannies and Environmental Issues: Humour and Creativity in Educative Protests," *Convergence* 33, no. 4 (2000): 6–18, retrieved October 3, 2015, http://web.b.ebscohost.com.ezp2.lib.umn.edu/ehost/detail/detail?vid=3&sid=32601a8a -5086-4cc3-9ceb-cec065aa1d94%40sessionmgr115&hid=115&bdata =JnNpdGU9ZWhvc3QtbGl2ZQ%3d%3d#db=aph&AN=4931134.

5. Carole Roy, *The Raging Grannies: Wild Hats, Cheeky Songs, and Witty Actions for a Better World* (Montreal: Black Rose Books, 2004).

6. Alison Acker and Betty Brightwell, *The Raging Grannies: Off Our Rockers and into Trouble* (Victoria, BC: TouchWood Editions, 2004), 173.

7. Ibid., 4.

8. All quotations and information that do not specifically cite other authors as sources were derived from a long interview with the Raging Grannies by the author, June 12, 2014.

9. Alison Acker and Betty Brightwell, *The Raging Grannies: Off Our Rockers and into Trouble* (Victoria, BC: TouchWood Editions, 2004), 16.

10. Carole Roy, "The Original Raging Grannies: Using Creative and Humorous Protests for Political Education," "Herstory," Raging Grannies International, accessed January 6, 2015, http://raginggrannies.org/herstory/.

11. Alison Acker and Betty Brightwell, *The Raging Grannies: Off Our Rockers and into Trouble* (Victoria, BC: TouchWood Editions 2004), 19.

12. Ibid., 7.

13. Ibid., 8.

14. Ibid., 25.

15. Ibid., 4.

16. Carole Roy, "The Original Raging Grannies: Using Creative and Humorous Protests for Political Education," "Herstory," Raging Grannies International, accessed January 6, 2015, http://raginggrannies.org/herstory/.

17. Alison Acker and Betty Brightwell, *The Raging Grannies: Off Our Rockers and into Trouble* (Victoria, BC: TouchWood Editions, 2004), 64.

18. Ibid., 102.

19. Ibid., 105.

20. The Montreal Raging Grannies, http://themontrealraginggrannies.com/.

21. Unless otherwise noted, all direct quotes from the individuals introduced in this section are derived from an interview with the author, June 12, 2014.

22. The Council of Canadians/Le Conseil des Canadiens, accessed January 7, 2015, http://www.canadians.org/.

23. Fran Thoburn, e-mail correspondence with author, January 12–15, 2015. See also Alison Acker and Betty Brightwell, *The Raging Grannies: Off Our Rockers and into Trouble* (Victoria, BC: TouchWood Editions, 2004), 3.

24. Ibid., 9.

25. Ibid., 10.

26. R. Delaney, "Musically Challenging," *Horizons* 18, no. 2 (2004): 27.

27. David Boucher, *Dylan & Cohen: Poets of Rock and Roll* (New York: Continuum, 2004), 1–24.

28. Carole Roy, "The Original Raging Grannies: Using Creative and Humorous Protests for Political Education," "Herstory," Raging Grannies International, accessed January 6, 2015, http://raginggrannies.org/herstory/.

29. Raging Grannies. *Raging Grannies Songs*, accessed January 7, 2015, http://raginggrannies.net/.

30. Gibbs M. Smith, *Joe Hill* (Salt Lake City, UT: Peregrine Smith Books, 1984).

31. "The Preacher and the Slave," lyrics by Joe Hill, to the tune of "In the Sweet By-and-By," composed by Joseph P. Webster, first published in the Industrial Workers of the World's *Little Red Songbook*, July 6, 1911.

32. "The Rapture," Seattle Raging Grannies, accessed January 7, 2015, http://raginggrannies.org/seattle/the-rapture/.

33. Nat Hentoff, "Interview with Bob Dylan," conducted in fall of 1965, partially published in *Playboy*, February, 1966, and released as audio file in *Open Culture*, accessed

November 8, 2014, http://www.openculture.com/2014/09/hear-bob-dylans-unedited -bewildering-interview-with-nat-hentoff.html.

34. Alison Acker and Betty Brightwell, *The Raging Grannies: Off Our Rockers and into Trouble* (Victoria, BC: TouchWood Editions, 2004), xii.

35. Carole Roy, "The Original Raging Grannies: Using Creative and Humorous Protests for Political Education," "Herstory," Raging Grannies International, accessed January 6, 2015, http://raginggrannies.org/herstory/.

36. Denise Von Glahn, *Music and the Skillful Listener: American Women Compose the Natural World* (Bloomington and Indianapolis: Indiana University Press, 2013).

37. Ibid., 16.

38. Dana Sawchuk, "Peace Profile: The Raging Grannies," *Peace Review* 25, no. 1 (2013): 130.

39. Alison Acker and Betty Brightwell, *The Raging Grannies: Off Our Rockers and into Trouble* (Victoria, BC: TouchWood Editions, 2004), 165.

40. Anne Moon, foreword to Alison Acker and Betty Brightwell, *The Raging Grannies: Off Our Rockers and into Trouble* (Victoria, BC: TouchWood Editions, 2004), vii.

41. Jean-Paul Sartre, *Existentialism Is a Humanism* (London: Methuen, 1960), 47–48.

42. Paola Gianturco, *Grandmother Power: A Global Phenomenon* (Brooklyn, NY: Powerhouse Books, 2012).

43. Raging Grannies, *Raging Grannies Songbook* (Gabriola Island, BC: New Society Publishers, 1993).

44. "No Frackin' No Way!" lyrics by Vicki Ryder, accessed January 7, 2015, http:// raginggrannies.net/no-frackin-no-way.

45. R. Delaney, "Musically Challenging," *Horizons* 18, no. 2 (2004): 45.

46. Raging Grannies, *Raging Grannies Songs*, accessed January 7, 2015, http:// raginggrannies.net/.

47. Alison Acker and Betty Brightwell, *The Raging Grannies: Off Our Rockers and into Trouble* (Victoria, BC: TouchWood Editions, 2004), 2.

48. Ibid., xi.

49. Ibid., xiv.

FIGURE 3.1

Idle No More "Medicine Wheel" poster. Andy Everson; used by permission.

3

Turtle Island's Idle No More

The Aural Art of Protest

Idle No More began when four women from Saskatchewan decided to take action against Prime Minister Stephen Harper's C-45, a bill that threatened First Nations' sovereignty rights and weakened Canada's environmental protections. Once passed, it became known as the "Jobs and Growth Act," using the sort of language neoliberal regimes the world over have used in order to erode environmental protections.[1] In response, Nina Wilson, Sylvia McAdam, Jessica Gordon, and Sheelah McLean organized a teach-in at Station 20 in Saskatoon on November 10, 2010.[2] They called that event "Idle No More." The origins of Idle No More can be traced much further back over five centuries of indigenous resistance to European colonization.[3]

Although it started in the Interior of Turtle Island (the indigenous designation for North America), Idle No More is very active on the Canadian west coast, in British Columbia. Led by First Nations organizers and joined by nonindigenous allies, the coalition has opposed development plans that would radically affect the Salish Sea. Much of British Columbia is "unceded territory," meaning that indigenous people occupying the land never relinquished their homeland via treaty or other legal mechanism. Idle No More activists are struggling to steward land, water, air, animals, and people within their unceded territories, which requires protecting them from the threat of unhealthy and unsustainable forms of development.

Hundreds of Idle No More activists marched on June 8, 2014, marking United Nations World Oceans Day. They were also rallying against a proposed Kinder Morgan pipeline. The event, Convergence 2014, was organized by the Union of British Columbia Indian Chiefs (UBCIC) and held in Vancouver. However, many of the speakers and most of the activists in attendance belonged to Idle No More, whose communication channels spread word of the event.

This chapter begins with a narrative description of Convergence 2014, emphasizing the protest soundscape. Months after observing the march, I interviewed master of ceremonies Cecilia Point in order to gain her perspective on protest music within the movement. I came to the event seeking to better understand the roles music plays in environmental movements. Although music is discussed below, musical composition and performance are not at the center of this case study. Instead, the chapter focuses on the most elemental human instrument, voice.

"THIS IS NEVER TO BE DONE IN ANGER"

Kinder Morgan, by its own account, is the "largest energy infrastructure company in North America."[4] The company has proposed sending oil from the tar sands of Alberta to the West Coast through British Columbia, via a new pipeline. The UBCIC opposes Kinder Morgan's proposal because of the catastrophic effect oil spills would have on their lands and aquifers. Also, union members know that burning the oil will have a negative impact on global climate. They titled the event "Convergence 2014: Protecting Our Sacred Waters from Tar Sands Oil." Word went out via First Nations media and the Idle No More network, which include websites, Facebook pages, and Twitter accounts.

Heeding that call, protesters began gathering throughout the morning of June 8 at Sunset Beach, a beautiful strip of sand separating Vancouver's dense downtown district from English Bay. UBCIC and Idle No More organizers arrived first, their cars loaded with signs, drums, coolers, lawn chairs, and picnic baskets. Clearly they had done this before. Rather than the excited air of a watershed event, Convergence 2014 had the feel of one Sunday afternoon gathering among many. Constant struggle against energy companies and government officials had turned new rituals into cultural routines.

Idle No More protests have drawn a great deal from American Indian Movement (AIM) organizing strategies and traditions as well as common protest liturgies (gather, march, convene, disperse) yet differ in a few notable ways. First, Idle No More protests are cross-generational celebrations rather than youth-oriented acts of rebellion. Second, instead of making great efforts to demonstrate cultural distinction, Idle No More rhetoric and actions are oriented toward broader community accord. During Convergence 2014, the Royal Canadian Mounted Police had little concern that this diverse group of protesters, including parents pushing strollers and others carrying their kids aloft, were going to do anything more unruly than "take" the Burrard Bridge, and even then only as a means of conveyance between Sunset Beach and Vanier Park, across False Creek and English Bay. The people who participated in Convergence 2014 are very different from the twenty-year-old anarchists who often capture the greatest news attention at Vancouver protests.

Largely without guidance, each new set of arrivals looked about for red T-shirts and other telltale signs of Idle No More gatherings. The group's signs featured Idle No More insignia. One displayed a large circle sectioned into red, white, black, and yellow quadrants on a red background, symbolizing racial unity within the indigenous-led struggle for environmental justice.

The most common graphic at Convergence 2014 was a similar circle graphic with a stylized black pipeline bisecting the foreground and a skull rising out of the flowing stream of oil. Northwest Coast artist Andy Everson created these striking images and gave permission to present them here. The full range of his Idle No More artwork can be accessed through Ecosong.net, as can illustrations and videos of his graphic images as they are employed in protest contexts.

Months later, when interviewing Cecilia Point, master of ceremonies for Convergence 2014, those same images came to mind as she described her collaborative vision: "There is a prophecy that talks about the two-headed serpent making its way across Turtle Island, and to me, that two-headed serpent is the two pipelines, Enbridge and Kinder Morgan. And the prophet, he talks about all people coming together. So black, red,

FIGURE 3.2

No Pipelines. Andy Everson;
used by permission.

white, yellow, all coming together to fight the two-headed serpent and
protect Mother Earth. And to me, that is a nice message." Another common Idle No More image features a fist holding a feather, a reminder that
the movement is led by First Nations and based on cultural traditions that
transcend current policy objectives.

The protesters on Sunset Beach were, in the main, far different from the
stereotypical environmental activists represented in mainstream media.
As per the four founding Mothers of Saskatoon, there are as many or more
middle-aged "hockey moms" as college-age activists in Idle No More. In
fact, that is precisely how Cecilia described herself in the interview.[5]

I sat at a respectful distance as the protesters started to gather. Friends
were getting reacquainted, so I did not feel it would be appropriate to inter-
rupt their reunions. A critical mass of rank-and-file activists had not yet
gathered, although it was apparent that many of the people sitting on scattered benches or lying on the grass nearby were likewise there for the
protest, given away by environmentalist slogans on their T-shirts and the
fact they had shown up on the beach without swimsuits or running shorts.

The first drumbeat could be heard at 11:22, thirty-eight minutes before
the noon protest was scheduled to begin. People were now gathering at an
accelerated pace across from the beach, on a broad stretch of lawn. On my
way across the walking path separating the beach from the lawn, I over-

heard two middle-aged women discussing the protesters as they walked by. They were speed walking, a Sunday morning constitutional. "If I had to choose," said one, "I'd be on the side of the protesters."

The casual passerby seemed to think that she would never have to choose, that someone else would simply decide whether or not a pipeline should bring Alberta's oil—a heavy, black, viscous bitumen squeezed out of subsurface sands and clay, using billions of gallons of fresh water in the process—to the beautiful coast where she walks on Sunday mornings. The molasses-like substance from Alberta tends to sink in water, making it that much more difficult to clean up when spilled and even more destructive than other fossil fuels to the marine ecosystem. However, it was good to hear that if she "had to choose," she would choose clean water over oil. Yet the visual power of protest resonated even there, in the woman's non-committal voice. The mere presence of the protesters moved this casual observer to think about an environmental issue that might not have otherwise entered her consciousness that day.

Sounds and signs of protest slowly began to take over the Sunset Beach soundscape. At 11:31 a.m., a young activist issued a strikingly realistic and surprisingly loud birdcall from the parking lot. It was not a gathering call, so much as a notice to others that he had arrived, marking his sonic territory as young men so often do. It became clear from a growing cacophony of voices, calls, drumbeats, and rattles that protesters were gathering quickly and getting ready to march. Old protesters sat, chatted, and looked around at the gathering mass, pleased to see the healthy turnout. Middle-aged organizers scuttled between groups, carrying signs, delivering messages, welcoming elders, passing out sandwiches, and doing most of the heavy lifting. Most of the young activists were too engaged in socializing to lend a hand with logistics, but their energy and engagement made all the difference.

Many people had come alone to the protest. Like me, they sat sprinkled among larger clumps of families and friends. Everyone seemed to be welcome. There were no clear divisions or sense of who belonged where. The decentralized ethic of Idle No More was evident, as was the emphasis on building community. The day's main task was to oppose Kinder Morgan, but that was more an immediate goal than the ultimate objective. There would be much work to do, so it might as well all be as pleasurable as possible. Convergence 2014 was a community event rather than a deadly serious "struggle." Parents lined up at a nearby pop stand to get their kids ice cream, as if this was just an average day at the beach. A few activists munched on fry bread or sandwiches brought from home. Idle No More protests are an excellent folk remedy for activist burnout. It is the sort of protest movement that can be sustained for the long haul, one that incorporates the full range of human emotion and expression rather than relying solely on momentary outrage.

At noon, Cecilia called everyone to attention. Her call cued gathered drummers and singers to offer an opening prayer. As she explained in our interview, many First Nations songs are prayers, sacred expressions rather than performances in the European tradition. They are to be sung by those to whom they belong, unless explicitly "gifted" for use by another person or group. Most songs sung at Convergence 2014 were offered as prayers and therefore were not participatory music in the Euro-American folk tradition.

One of the drummers led the gathering in a participatory chant, re-peating the refrain "We don't need no dirty pipelines." Everyone enthu-siastically joined in. Musicians played frame drums to keep the cadence, sonically centering indigenous tradition. It is interesting to note that the frame drum has become the central signifier of indigenous music through-out North America, including for Coast Salish peoples. Traditionally, drums in the region were made of cedar logs and other woods, rather than hides. Hides "do not endure or hold their tension well in the constantly humid boreal rain forest."[6] It is a reminder that tradition remains alive through adaptation and exchange. The frame drum was gifted from the Interior and has become a prominent transnational symbol of indigenous identity. The frame drum is as indigenous to the Coast Salish as tomatoes are to Italian culture, that is to say, both not at all and very.

As people gathered into a very large circle, Cecilia shouted: "Everyone get texting and posting on Facebook to get friends and family down here. We need more people to take that bridge." "And Instagram!" added a male drummer, his voice failing to carry beyond the innermost rings of the circle. Unlike Cecilia's, the man's voice was not made for speaking to large crowds. As will be made clear later in the chapter, there are many reasons why Cecilia was selected as the MC and representative voice for the collective body. Excellent vocal projection is one of those qualities.

Cecilia then provided the gathering with a compelling yet pithy explanation of why the group had gathered to "protect our waters" from Kinder Morgan's pipeline. A woman from the drumming group added a few additional points, but her voice was also too quiet to be easily heard. Once again, the comparison showed that Cecilia's vocal presence is perfectly matched to the task. I later learned that she had trained as a jazz singer in high school. This is not at all surprising considering her delivery of these short addresses, unamplified, yet without becoming shrill or sounding as if she is "raising her voice" in anger.

Those qualities of voice made Cecilia's most important message work, both rhetorically and at a deeper level. "This is never to be done in anger," she explained to the gathering, setting the tone for a protest that would, fittingly, be equal parts opposition to Kinder Morgan and celebration of an alternative vision for the future of the Salish Sea.

The event began with drummers and singers standing at the center of a large circle for twenty minutes. The circle continued to expand, starting with a couple hundred and growing to nearly a thousand. Everyone participated, either beating a frame drum, listening intently to songs sung in various local languages, singing along, or, when prompted, chanting refrains against the Kinder Morgan pipeline. The indigenous drummers and singers standing at the center of the circle paused at several points. After thirty seconds or so of such silence, apparently waiting to make sure they would not be encroaching on indigenous drummers, a few nonnative musicians would then play a few lines of rhythm on *djembe* or other hand percussion in order to keep the musical momentum going, adding their sound to the pre-march soundscape.

TAKING THE BRIDGE

Drummers began playing louder and faster as the group got ready to march. Voices became louder, and chants against Kinder Morgan and the pipeline broke out with greater frequency. Then, at 12:18, the eldest drummer offered a song-prayer, signaling that is was time to "take" the bridge, which meant walking across the Burrard Bridge in the driving lanes rather than on the pedestrian causeway.

After decades of attending protests, I found the unscripted sonic cooperation during Convergence 2014 remarkable. In fact, Cecilia's "This is never to be done in anger" would be a very fitting name for the entire soundscape composition. Instead of a chaotic cacophony of shouts, drums, cowbells, and chants, the Convergence 2014 soundscape was focused, organized, and mutually respectful. Musicians used sound to mark their respect for First Nations leadership. Rather than scattered groups of frenetic rhythms competing with one another, there was a coherent soundscape led by indigenous musicians.

As the group entered Pacific Avenue and stretched out across the Burrard Bridge, pockets of sound developed, parade style, but even then there was a remarkable lack of sonic competition or overlap. Instead of a bucket brigade here competing with a group of cowbells over there, warring for primacy where the margins of their respective sound waves overlapped, each section retained a relatively coherent sound focus without invading the next group's sonic territory. These were adults who had learned to listen. They were now teaching their children how to listen. Careful listening was empowering a more productive sound performance, much as it does in any successful ensemble. Rather than music as a "thing," a set text and performance, the protesters were "musicking," to use Christopher Small's term, a fluid, participatory, and highly social form of musical expression.[7] To borrow Denise Von Glahn's term, these activists are skillful listeners.[8]

Visual performance added a great deal to the messaging as well. For example, one group of protesters held painted salmon aloft on wooden dowels. The school of fish "swam" along realistically, undulating up and down as protesters marched forward, slowly raising and lowering their giant fish in rhythm.

The fish contingent had clearly put a great deal of effort, creativity, and forethought into the event. That was much less the case for people like me who merely showed up, willing to respond in kind for each call-and-response. I was reminded that morning just how easy it is to join a protest and vocalize one's views in public. As a further reminder, a fit middle-aged woman left the sidelines on Pacific Street and approached me as we marched by, walking very fast with bike in tow. The woman, whom I will call Sara to protect her identity, asked, "What is the march about?" Clearly she could see that there was an environmentalist theme, but her singular vantage point along the route might not have allowed her to immediately grasp the complete protest message. So I explained the event to the best of my ability. I stated that it was a protest march and rally again Kinder Morgan and for clean water. Sara had been out for a morning exercise ride when she came across the march. Looking in no way out of place in her biking gear, she simply joined in and took part for the duration of the event.

Sara demonstrates how this is by far the most doable example of activism described in this book; any of us can join in a protest event. Yet the simple art of protest is surprisingly under-practiced in North American democracies. There is nothing terribly abstract about a pipeline pumping viscous bitumen into a favorite stream, nor anything terribly difficult about protesting it, at least from the vantage point of joining in a march like Convergence 2014. Protest is a historically proven and highly effective form of public participation, yet most people avoid such activities.[9]

Furthermore, if a person can march, rally, and chant, he or she can also attend scoping hearings, enter legal processes, and campaign for better policies, to name just a few additional avenues for public participation.[10] Not everyone will do all those things, but each act is an effective means of public communication and participation. Yet the term "public participation"—employed by environmental communication scholars and policy researchers—rarely stretches to cover public protest and advocacy campaigns.[11] Nor does protest fit into Gregg Walker's more inclusive term "participatory communication."[12] Both terms imply more institutionalized and professionalized ways of mediating debates rather than equally important forms of public participation, such as public protests and other creative acts.

There are certainly differences between protest actions and more-official forms of public participation. The act of organizing and performing a protest is more akin to performing in a musical ensemble. Effective protest requires intimate listening and adaptive response, performed in the

moment rather than preformed according to codified rules and procedures. As Todd Norton has argued, we need to go beyond "established
institutional mechanisms" in order to gain a more meaningful sense of
how various publics engage environmental questions.[13]

We can rarely determine exactly what will work among these various
approaches to public participation. Each route remains equally likely to
fulfill desired objectives, and it usually takes many forms of public participation, including protest, to succeed.[14] For every individual who takes part
in governmental decision-making processes directly, there are thousands
making their voices known in other ways, from protesting on the streets
to visiting park reserves, signaling to officials that nature matters simply
by showing up.

By virtue of turnout, Convergence 2014 was a fairly successful form
of public participation, with a thousand participants, give or take a hundred at any given time during the three-hour event. The march across
Burrard Bridge went smoothly, for the most part. Unbeknownst to most
marchers, a police motorcyclist sustained a leg injury when a driver tried
to avoid the march and attempted a sudden U-turn. The veteran officer,
who went unnamed in news reports, required surgery to repair his broken knee.[15]

Other than that unfortunate incident, little went wrong during the
afternoon protest. Upon reaching Vanier Park, on the other side of the
Burrard Bridge, people fanned out around a small soundstage. Cecilia
shouted "Sacred waters!" and protesters responded with "No pipelines."
Those previously unfamiliar with the call-and-response chant had a mile-
long march to rehearse it, so almost everyone had it down by the time
Cecilia used it to focus the gathered group's attention.

Once again, nonindigenous activists showed exceptional respect for
the principal organizers. Rather than disrupting the leadership's sonic
messaging with discordantly manic *djembe* and hand percussion, seasoned
activist-musicians waited for the right moments to add their musical contributions, providing a few beats for a flagging chant here or filling in a
sonic gap there. Based on my experience in more chaotic protests in the
USA and Mexico, I found the aural order remarkable, although in a later
conversation, Cecilia said she viewed it as a typical characteristic of Idle
No More protests in Canada.

STAGING PROTEST: MUSIC, VOICE, AND LITURGY

First Nations leaders have carefully developed alliances with nonnative members and affiliated organizations to propose environmental legislation and oppose damaging developments. That is reflected at ceremonial and protest events like Convergence 2014. Nonindigenous activists are formally welcomed as honored guests along with indigenous visitors. A host officially representing the nation or band to which the unceded territory belongs offers the welcome. Cecilia, as a member of the Musqueam Band, welcomed all those who crossed the bridge to Vanier Park. The welcoming ritual and the ethic of respectful collaboration it represents have allowed Idle No More to mobilize a broad and diverse movement without diluting its core values. Idle No More steadfastly articulates environmental justice though a First Nations framework, welcoming all who share that vision to join the effort. Those who do join sign an implicit social contract to abide by the terms of mutual respect, including respect for the elders.

That is a lot to pull off without centralized leadership. However, decentralized is not the same thing as disorganized. Idle No More has been inaccurately compared to the Occupy Wall Street movement in that regard. Part of the difference is that Idle No More draws on five hundred years of tradition as well as a very strong, transnational social infrastructure connecting nations, bands, clans, and tribes throughout North America with allies in environmental justice organizations. Occupy Wall Street took advantage of a momentary flashpoint to experiment with decentralized coalition building around a shared ethic of equity, very broadly interpreted. Both movements have made an impact, but Idle No More is more deeply rooted, focused, and sustainable.

That stability, in turn, allows for collaboration with existing institutions like the UBCIC. UBCIC leaders arranged for a series of representatives and artists to present their ideas to the crowd in Vanier Park. Cecilia was the MC. Speakers led various participatory song-chants throughout to keep the event from becoming overly boring and didactic. A young Coast Salish participant made a particularly strong visual impact by covering himself in oil and walking silently through the crowd, his silence communicating a dystopic sense of dread at what the pipeline could eventually do to the coast.

Councilor K'ána Deborah Baker of the Squamish Nation spoke first. She was followed by Liana Martin and Carleen Thomas of the Tsleil-Waututh Nation Sacred Trust, a group founded and sanctioned by the Tsleil-Waututh Chief and Council to oppose the Kinder Morgan pipeline project.

Next, Chief Stewart Phillip of the Penticton Indian Band and president of the UBCIC outlined the group's reasons for opposing Kinder Morgan. Before starting, he thanked the Coast Salish peoples for inviting him to speak on their lands. Similarly, all the presenters visiting Coast Salish territories thanked their local hosts for allowing them to speak and sing. After providing a general explanation of the pipeline issue, Phillip explained another reason he continues to be involved in environmental justice work: "My wife keeps kicking my butt telling me to do the right thing."

Next, Chief Martin Louie (Nadle Whut'en) and Jasmine Thomas (Saik'uz Nation) represented the Yinka Dene Alliance, five northern British Columbia nations that came together to ban the Enbridge Northern Gateway Pipeline from their territories. Thomas sang a song from the Saik'uz Frog Clan to which she belongs. She explained that she sings for all living beings, including those "who cannot speak, including those who fly, swim, and walk on four legs."

Thomas then led the gathering in song and the refrain "Good-bye, Enbridge!" Most followed suit, offering a sacred prayer-song and short speech before leading activists in a participatory chant. The medium was the message. Each song was a musical expression of identity and an entreaty for respectful dialogue. In Pacific Northwest cultures, there is a strong ethic of mutual respect, performed in rituals that let others know they matter as much as oneself. The potlatch, albeit misunderstood by Europeans as an offering of gifts for the purpose of gaining status (although it is, but only in part), symbolizes that welcoming ethos, as do other longhouse visiting traditions, such as ritual purification with pine boughs before entering another family's home, which represents the principle that a person should not let his or her negativity and problems become an undue burden for the hosts. Idle No More has merged those traditions with rhetoric from the wider environmental justice movement. Their methods have caught the attention of the Canadian government and oil companies, as well as movement intellectuals like Noam Chomsky. Chomsky has repeatedly lauded Idle No More for "taking the lead" in the struggle for a saner approach to environmental risks and injustices.[16]

Chief Martin Louie of the Nadle Whut'en nation is one such leader. In Vanier Park, Louie stated that Convergence 2014 was "fulfilling the dream of Chief Dan George to bring us together with our nonnative brothers and sisters," adding with dry humor, "That is the one good thing Enbridge has done."[17]

Environmental movements in the United States have much to learn from Idle No More when it comes to coalition building. As articulated by Louie and other speakers in Vanier Park, the movement emphasizes shared respect across cultures as a basis for creating structural change. It takes broad, diverse coalitions to make a difference in majoritarian democracies, and Idle No More activists have demonstrated incredible skill in forming them. In an episode of the television series *Rebel Music* titled "Native America," Lakota hip-hop artist Frank Waln made that point this way: "I have never in my lifetime seen our people come together like this, never seen non-natives pay attention to us like they are now; our issues are finally being talked about outside our communities. There's a spirit of resistance. I can feel it in the air."[18]

As demonstrated by the UBCIC, elders are providing much of the guidance. Meanwhile, the youngest generation of activists is bringing new fire to the movement. In Vanier Park, for example, Crystal Lameman of the Beaver Lake Cree Nation combined traditional storytelling and scientific evidence to explain what tar sands development is doing to land, water, and life in Alberta. Lameman is an elementary-school teacher and Sierra Club Canada International Climate & Energy campaigner.

Next, Vancouver's Solidarity Notes Labour Choir sang two songs, "Bella Ciao" and "No Oil Tankers."[19] The Labour Choir's version of "Bella Ciao" is a beautifully simple arrangement with a solo falsetto line that allows a male soprano to deliver a crisp, melodic message, while the full chorus provides textural depth in a punctuated response without getting in the way of the soprano's lyrical message.[20] The Solidarity Notes' version of "Bella Ciao" cleverly adapts traditional choral composition and performance to protest contexts in which, once again, it is paramount to deliver a clear lyrical message.[21] A year later, I listened to the Seattle band Movitas

FIGURE 3.3

"Bella Ciao." Based on an anonymous folk song adopted by the anti-Fascist
movement in Italy during World War II. New lyrics by Dan Keeton, arrangement
by Earle Peach; used by permission.

now, now now la la la la la la la la la la an En-bridge pipe-line is our cash
Could this be our fi-nal

now, now now la la la la la la la la la an En-bridge pipe-line is our cash
Could this be our fi-nal

now, now, now and Ste-phen Harper says we must move fast an En-bridge pipe-line is our cash
now, now, now The land is bur-ning; the fish are dy-ing Could this be our fi-nal

now, now, now and Ste-phen Harper says we must move fast an En-bridge pipe-line is our cash
now, now, now The land is bur-ning; the fish are dy-ing Could this be our fi-nal

cow la la la An En-bridge pipe-line right to our
bow? We will fight them We must

cow la la la An En-bridge pipe-line right to our
bow? We will fight them We must

cow
bow? la la la la la

cow
bow? la la la la la

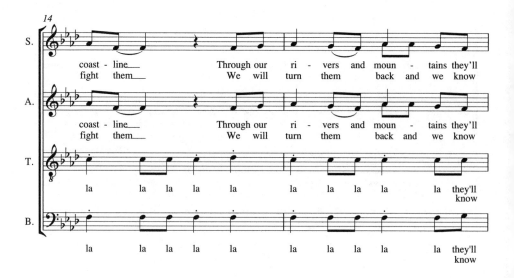
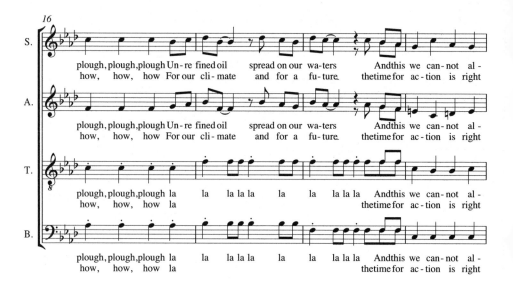

(see introduction) rehearse their lively march version of "Bella Ciao." The rousing, participatory anthem has wide appeal for protest performers, in part because the song's simple verse structure and straight line melody make it easy to adapt to the cause at hand, as witnessed in the Solidarity Notes anti-Enbridge version.

Solidarity Notes Labour Choir's song "Idle No More" demonstrates how nonnative activists have reciprocated interest in Idle No More's efforts and returned the invitation to alliance extended to them by First Nations campaigners:

Idle No More
    Solidarity Notes Labour Choir

Chorus: Idle No More, Idle No More
From this day I'll be Idle No More

We're facing destruction
If we don't understand
The true situation
In this land

Chorus

Our First Nations sisters
Have called us to stand
With them in resistance
To the rape of this land

Chorus

We've waited too long
While injustices stand
Gonna lift every voice
And join every hand

Chorus

Following Solidarity Notes' beautifully rousing performance, Tso'Tine-Gwich'in singer-songwriter Kiera-Dawn Kolson brought many in the crowd to tears with a short prayer-song and well-chosen words. An Arctic campaigner for Greenpeace, Kolson brought the cultures most immediately affected by climate change to the audience's consciousness, no small trick on that warm June day on the southernmost coast of Canada. However, the farther north one lives, the less seemingly abstract and theoretical climate change becomes. Kolson completed her short presentation by begging her listeners to go "beyond tactics of divide and conquer." She became a speaker, or singer, really, for a people, place, and ecosystem few in the audience have experienced directly.

Next, Melina Laboucan Massimo of the Lubicon Cree First Nation spoke about the Tar Sands Healing Walk. Massimo was born in the oil sands region and has witnessed firsthand the devastating impacts of oil sands development. The Canadian government granted leases for development of almost 1,400 square kilometers on Lubicon lands without consent from her people.

Sara Frances Yankoo, an Algonquin "word drummer" and musician, followed Massimo. She has been using music and spoken word to advocate for environmental justice since graduating with honors with a bachelor's degree in environmental studies from York University. Yankoo's performances and musical activism grabbed the attention of Convergence 2014 organizers. Her poetry and mouthbow performance filled the crowd with new energy. Okanagan hip-hop artist Warren Hooley joined Yankoo for a piece she referred to as "impromptu" and "organic." (Yankoo later told me in an e-mail exchange that she had met Hooley just days before the event.) Her mouthbow took on the role of beatbox, which in street rap combines percussive voice and somatic percussion.[22] Yankoo used the mouthbow to add a distinctively indigenous dimension to North American rap, creatively merging indigenous tradition and hip-hop. Storied performer Buffy Sainte-Marie, herself an accomplished mouthbow musician and highly experimental performer, would no doubt applaud Yankoo's creativity.[23]

Chief Judy Wilson of the Neskonlith Band, secretary-treasurer of the UBIC, provided concluding remarks as the sunbaked crowd continued to hang on patiently, possibly a bit stretched by the long program. Perhaps the downside to a broad coalition is the need to have each organization represented onstage. Although ready to retreat from the unusually intense

Vancouver sun, most activists stayed until the end, when a group of drummers from the Interior performed final song-prayers and chants. One of the singers explained that "honor songs are sung seven times" and that he would do so now, to honor the ancestors and the cause to which everyone was committed. People listened, tired yet attentive, until the end of the protest at 3:08 p.m., three hours after we first departed Sunset Beach.

People dispersed, tired but in high spirits, having done their best to bring public attention to the oil pipeline issue. Politicians and news reports often present the oil shale issue as a done deal, as if Alberta's tar sands oil must be brought to a fuel-hungry world and carbon-laden atmosphere as soon as humanly possible. People publicly resisted on June 8.

Will Idle No More win the debate? That remains to be seen. However, Convergence 2014 captured the attention of at least one company. Iven Giesbrecht, the spokesperson for Northern Gateway (Enbridge's name for two proposed BC pipelines), told Marlisse Silver Sweeney of Global News: "Northern Gateway respects the fact that people want to voice their concerns on the issue of responsible resource development. We share those concerns. As an energy transportation company, we look to be part of the dialogue on these important issues. We all need to come together to find workable solutions on a shared responsibility that affects us all."[24] Perhaps the protest made a difference in the public debate and policy-making world. We will probably never know for certain. It is never possible to trace environmental outcomes to specific events or movements, no matter how reasonably inferred. However, the World Oceans Day protest clearly made a difference to those who attended. Their spirits were renewed, sense of purpose redoubled, and minds filled with new information. They would take that energy and information back to their local communities. The beat of the drums, chanting voices, and protest soundscape helped create, communicate, and sustain community. Nothing was more essential to that soundscape than the voice of MC Cecilia Point.

FINDING VOICE, CECILIA POINT

Cecilia became "an activist quite by accident." The self-identified "hockey mom" became active in 2011 when local developers and city planners started digging up the graves of her Musqueam ancestors to build a parking lot and condos. "It's in an area called Marpole," explained Cecilia, a Musqueam village and "a national historic site." Marpole contained one of the largest shell middens in North America due to its advantageous location along the estuary, and, more importantly, it is a sacred site containing the bones of thousands of Musqueam children, women, and men who had lived there. Several buildings had already been built near the site, but they rested on concrete "caps" so that they would not disturb the village and graves below. "Hundreds and hundreds of bodies are buried there," which is why "there was an archaeological covenant on that site."

In 2011, "a developer managed to get a permit to build condos there," Cecilia explained. "They were going to build underground parking, a huge tower, and so on." The government and developers are supposed to consult with the Musqueam Band before excavating heritage sites. They did not.

> Of course, because it was a burial site, they were digging up people. So they would find skulls and hands and bodies. And they dug up two adults and two infants, and so our band was outraged. And what spoke to me throughout that—like the fact that they unearthed two adults and two infants—I immediately said, "You know what? That's my family. I have a husband and two kids." And I looked at my kids, and I just thought, Wow, I can't believe in this day and age I have to explain to them this racism, that First Nations burial sites mean nothing. And we are less than other people. Like I literally up until that moment never had to explain that to my kids before.

As I listened to Cecilia describe the horrors of Marpole, I was reminded of people I interviewed twenty-five years ago in El Salvador, in the late 1980s and early 1990s, survivors of a war in which they had witnessed the loss of family members and neighbors. Many of the people I interviewed in Central America displayed a similar disbelief that anyone could be so cruel along with a calm determination to speak for the dead. Just as Jasmine Thomas did in Vanier Park when she sang for those "who cannot speak, including those who fly, swim, and walk on four legs," Cecilia had earlier become a speaker for the dead at Marpole. She explained that what happened at Marpole is connected to five hundred years of racist colonization, an ongoing process that not even a "hockey mom" who lives "in suburbia" could escape.

What does this have to do with musical activism? Admittedly, this focus on a talented MC is a bit of a detour compared to the explicitly musical acts that performed in Vanier Park and gigging musicians featured in every other chapter of the book. However, I chose to interview Cecilia and feature her story for the same reasons I briefly mentioned Sara, the bicyclist, earlier. Music is more than staged performance. Sara made music by marching and taking part in call-and-response chants. Similarly, Cecilia arranged, orchestrated, and directed the entire event, producing a rich protest soundscape, yet her only claim to musicianship is to have played in the high school band horn section. "I used to be a musician when I was in school," she joked, "and when I say 'musician,' I just mean I played trombone and trumpet and that kind of thing."

As noted earlier, Cecilia also "sang in the jazz choir," something that she laughs off now, as if it were inconsequential. However, hearing her voice at a protest makes the jazz experience seem like a natural part of her preparation for serving as an MC. She has the right voice for jazz and protest, both of which are improvisational genres. An ability to project and maintain pleasant timbre at high volume, as well as an excellent sense of timing, all work in her favor.[25] Those qualities are partly the product of careful listening, which is also required in jazz performance. In other words, the elders were not picking out MCs at random. In Cecilia, they saw a community-leader-in-the-making who had, among her other skills and abilities, a powerful voice, a voice that invites, encourages, and compels rather than shrilly dictates. There is great musicality in that.

Cecilia was in her mid-forties when she became a community activist. So how did a suburban bookkeeper with a deathly fear of public speaking become an MC and spokesperson for one of the most important movements in North America? "I was going to school at the time," began Cecilia, and "I have two kids," she continued, explaining how unlikely and difficult it was for her to take on a leadership role. "People asked every now and again, 'Can you come help with this?' I'm like, 'Hey, leave a message. I'm busy.'" Recalling her resistance makes Cecilia laugh now because now she is the one making calls to recruit reluctant community members. However, her transition from interested observer to committed activist came about fairly suddenly, albeit with a little help from her Musqueam elders:

So I literally do not know why, but the elders asked me to be the spokesperson for that action [against the Marpole development]. I'm a bookkeeper. I don't like to be in front of people. I'd rather be shot in the head than speak publicly. It was a really strange event. Like, I don't know why they asked me. And I remember the next morning going out to the press conference, and all these cameras in my face, and I just started speaking, and I never know how to describe it, except for it was not me speaking. I felt I had this power of all my ancestors behind me. I mean, I said things that I didn't know about. It was very, very strange. And all I can say about that, there are hundreds of our ancestors buried there, and I really felt like they spoke for me. They held me up and let me, you know, speak. And so that action went on for about two hundred days, until it was finally settled. And so I stood on the front lines for two hundred days protecting that property.

As the type of person who really did "not know why" she had been asked to speak for the community, Cecilia can count humility among her positive attributes.

Cecilia laughs now when noting, "I missed my kids' whole summer vacation" and "I lost my job." Her levity thinly veils the continued pain those sacrifices have caused. She describes that transformative period as "bizarre." However, the community was rewarded for Cecilia's sacrifices, starting with a positive outcome to the Marpole desecration. The developer's building permit was rescinded, and, as part of the same injunction, the company will be required to help repair damage to the extent possible. Meanwhile, the Musqueam Band has purchased the Marpole site.

Cecilia's work at Marpole led to connections throughout the local activist community:

Because I was standing there for so long, other groups from around the city came and helped us. People from the environmental movement and a number of mothers who were mothers of murdered and missing children came and brought us food and stood with us. People working against other injustices, like homelessness, and I mean all kinds of people. And so, because all of those people came and stood with us, when our action was finished, we went and stood with them. And so I think that sort of brought me to the forefront. Because I was in the media a lot during that action. So people got to know me. And this is our territory, so it is my territory, and that would be another reason why someone would ask me to speak. They would need someone from Musqueam to open events or say something, for protocol.

Cecilia has been a community leader since those transformative events in 2011. However, rather than feel exceptional, she simply thinks of herself as part of a growing trend: "And I think that you're seeing that a lot more lately, right?" she asked. "People are taking to the streets now because they're concerned about climate change, I think because they're seeing it in their own lives."

When I approached Cecilia, I did not know about her past activities, only that she was an incredibly talented MC based on what I observed at the June 8 event. Listening to her at Convergence 2014 raised several questions: What compels hundreds of people to listen attentively on a loud and crowded beach? What causes a free mass of people to move, chant, sing, and listen together for three hours on a hot afternoon? Several prospective answers leap to mind: A shared sense of purpose? Definitely. Pulsating drums? Probably. The joy of chanting and singing together? Certainly. However, the ritual officiate is essential to such proceedings as well. Without Cecilia's words and voice, no one would listen, because people would have no idea how to coordinate their voices and bodies with those of their fellow protesters. Whether in the hip-hop dance hall or waterside protest, MCs require special talents, including a musical sense of timing and flow.

LISTENING FROM THE CENTER OF THE CIRCLE

Cecilia is a talented listener, a trait common among skilled orators. After I asked her a question, she would pause and think, taking the query seriously, before offering a thoughtful observation in response. For example, I asked her for her thoughts on music in the Idle No More movement. "Well, the song that I always hear at these events is the AIM song, the American Indian Movement song," she observed, adding that there is "some speculation that it was written by a child who was just singing it." The song features a poetic series of nonlexical vocables, sound abstractions rather than words in the semantic sense. This allows it to travel well, to belong to all First Nations and thus serve as a unifying force during intertribal gatherings.

For "First Nations people, our songs are prayers," she explained. "Some belong to people, so not everyone is allowed to sing a song when they hear it," she continued, differentiating indigenous traditions in North American communities from Western traditions, in which folk or community music is defined by the fact that it belongs to no one and thus to everyone who hears a given song. That sometimes makes encounters between indigenous and many other musicians difficult. For example, white activists often appropriate indigenous music and imagery without realizing they are ritually enacting a five-hundred-year-old tradition of theft. What outsiders view as honoring the dignity of First Nations by performing their music is instead a very disrespectful act of sacrilege.

However, that clash of musical values is being worked out surprisingly well within the Idle No More movement. At events like Convergence 2014, for example, the song-as-gift tradition is carefully explained and caringly performed, helping outside activists understand the perspectives of First Nations. These careful lessons treat outsiders with the respect that they are asked to offer in return. It is ongoing, reparative work for five hundred years of settler cultures caring little about the perspectives of First Nations. And so, the broader audience of activists now respectfully listens to sacred song-prayers without appropriating them. They join in on songs that have specifically been gifted to the community at large and very enthusiastically respond to political chants. Meanwhile, the movement also shares publicly available protest songs crafted by world-famous musicians, including songs like "Now That the Buffalo's Gone" by Buffy Sainte-Marie, a Cree singer-songwriter born in Saskatchewan, and "Who's Gonna Stand Up" by her compatriot Neil Young, who grew up one province over, in Manitoba.[26]

These are place-based traditions, musical representations of a broader cultural ethos embedded in daily practice, ritual life, and even architecture. "Like, for us, in Musqueam," explains Cecilia, "we have a longhouse, and those who are very, very cultural spend a long time in the longhouse in the winter." Cecilia took pains to translate the cultural traditions she grew up with into terms that I might understand. "And, um, let's see, I don't really know how to describe it." She gathered the words and offered an effective simile, "I mean, I guess the closest way I can describe it is some nations have like a vision quest, right? Where they go out and fast." Cecilia knew that as someone from the Plains I might be familiar with the vision quest tradition. "In the longhouse, I guess because of the weather, you'd be indoors, up here, and you would, you know, fast and spend a lot of time there," she continued, her careful translation of customs showing why she is the ideal interlocutor for the Musqueam and the larger movement. "So the most spiritual songs come from that place." As if she had not already done a beautiful job translating her traditions through cultural analogy, Cecilia then apologized, "I could think of another comparison to other cultures and religions, but I can't." Knowing that my PhD is in anthropology, she then joked, "That's your job, anyways. It's not mine!"

Fortunately, drawing cultural comparisons is not really my job. Despite my degree, I come to this task as neither anthropologist nor ethnomusicologist but rather with a very practical interest in figuring out how to perform more effectively. Increasingly, I come to this work as a musical activist. Instead of targeting a single cultural site, I sought out the best models throughout the Salish Sea region. That search for ideal types is what brought me to Idle No More. It took me to several protests, but I found few where music, soundscape, and organization harmonized so well. So I wanted to know how Cecilia and her fellow organizers pull it off. She had several insights to share in that regard, once again moving from general principles—"songs in general can rally people and get people motivated"—to more culturally specific First Nations sound principles, including the following:

> We would start every event with a protocol welcome, somebody welcoming them to the territory, and a song. So for us, the song would be like a prayer. Often, people would see Native people on the street singing, and they would say, "Why are they always out there singing?" For us, that's our prayers. Like when we're marching through the streets, and the particular rally that I'm thinking of, [when we] marched from Sunset Beach, I asked the three nations—Musqueam, Squamish, and Tsleil-Waututh—I asked each of the groups, "Sing an old song from your ancestors; don't sing a new one. Reach back and get one of the old ones. And that way, they're coming with us."

In other words, there was nothing accidental about the soundscape composition of Convergence 2014. Cecilia has proved to be a skilled musical arranger, dramaturge, cultural specialist, protest organizer, and MC. This suburban "hockey mom" is exactly what the local movement needed.

Cecilia has observed a couple of changes in the way protest is organized and performed in western Canada, including "a lot more respect for First

Nations communities," although, she admitted, "I'm not really sure why that is." She reminded me that she was fairly new to public activism: "I'm relatively new to the protest movement, like I said, in 2011, but what I am told is that in British Columbia, we see respectful cooperation between activist groups a lot more." She noted that the young people she meets are "not just like university students, the way it was in the '60s," adding that "instead, they're grown people with jobs" who have serious concerns over "what we've left them."

"I'm not really sure why young people are really getting it a lot more than the last generation," she added. "I mean, I'm in my fifties, so when I meet up with friends from high school, they say things like, 'Oh, are you out banging your tom-toms this weekend?'" She laughed, adding "They just don't get it," whereas "the young people really do."

The mention of her high school friends shows how Cecilia continues to spend significant time outside the environmentalist movement. As a result, she, like Dana Lyons and other highly effective organizers, is well aware of what people outside the movement think about problems like climate change. That is what makes Cecilia and other skilled MCs particularly effective as spokespersons, organizers, interlocutors, advocates, and activists. Among her other talents, she can communicate across cultural boundaries.

MUSICAL GIFTS

At the end of our interview, Cecilia provided two additional examples of how songs function. The first shows how indigenous songs retain power when cultural ownership is respected. "The Strong Woman's Song" is "another song that I really gravitate to," explained Cecilia. "It came through these women in prison in eastern Canada." The imprisoned Anishinaabeg women were repeatedly thrown into solitary, "and the song came to them." "I've seen some people put lyrics to it," she lamented, "but I really don't think there's supposed to be lyrics." But "somebody" who was unaware of the tradition "just put lyrics to it one day." The "song came to" the Anishinaabeg women, and "it kept them safe, it kept them protected while they were in the prison."

"That's sort of how songs come about," she explained. Completing the story, Cecilia described how she performed a "welcome" for a "women's treatment center" where abused women receive support. After she performed the welcome, a young woman from the center "came to us, to our action," and "gifted us that song." Once again, activism and tradition intertwined. "So, again, songs have to be gifted to people," she concluded. "You can't just take up and sing them."

Cecilia moved from "The Strong Woman's Song" to a song meant to be shared by everyone in Coast Salish territory. "Something that I'd really like to see happen," she began, "and I don't know how to get the ball rolling on this." She paused, searching for the right words. "There's a men's choir in Vancouver called Chor Leoni," she continued, "and a young man approached me one day, and he said, 'We would really like to sing a First Nations song.'"[27] At the time, "I couldn't think of one," Cecilia lamented, "but now I have one, . . . and it's called the 'Coast Salish Anthem.'" Cecilia later wrote me to say that permission should still be sought from the George family to use their song.

The song has become particularly important across the region, particularly for meetings between multiple bands and nations. On many occasions, it is too time-consuming for each delegation to perform a welcoming song or honor song. So some Coast Salish gatherings will instead begin with the "Coast Salish Anthem," or the "Chief Dan George Prayer Song," as it is also called.[28]

Cecilia feels that the anthem "would just be beautiful if it was sung by a men's a cappella chorus." Ever the organizer, she expressed a "need to find that guy" again and "tell them that idea." She believes it would send "a very powerful message, to see nonnatives coming together and singing the 'Coast Salish Anthem.'" In part through the power of voice, Cecilia Point is the kind of cultural worker and leader who can make such transformative moments happen.

NOTES

1. CBC News, "9 Questions about Idle No More," accessed January 9, 2015, http://www.cbc.ca/news/canada/9-questions-about-idle-no-more-1.1301843.

2. Idle No More, "Living History," accessed January 9, 2015, http://www.idlenomore.ca/living_history.

3. Idle No More, "The Story," accessed January 9, 2015, http://www.idlenomore.ca/story.

4. Kinder Morgan, "About Us," accessed January 9, 2015, http://www.kindermorgan .com/about_us.

5. All quotes not directly attributed to other sources are derived from an interview with the author on December 5, 2014.

6. Native Drums, "Drum Culture," accessed January 9, 2015, http://www.native -drums.ca/index.php/Drumming/Culture?tp=a.

7. Christopher Small, *Musicking: The Meanings of Performing and Listening* (Middletown, CT: Wesleyan University Press, 2011).

8. Denise Von Glahn, *Music and the Skillful Listener: American Women Compose the Natural World* (Bloomington and Indianapolis: Indiana University Press, 2013).

9. Howard Zinn, *A People's History of the United States* (New York: Harper and Row, 2005).

10. Thomas C. Beierle and Jerry Cayford, *Democracy in Practice: Public Participation in Environmental Decisions* (Washington, DC: Resources for the Future, 2002).

11. Jacquelin Burgess, Carolyn M. Harrison, and Petra Filius, "Environmental Communication and the Cultural Politics of Environmental Citizenship," *Environment and Planning* 30, no. 8 (1998): 1445–1460.

12. See Gregg B. Walker, "Public Participation as Participatory Communication in Environmental Policy Decision-Making: From Concepts to Structured Conversations," *Environmental Communication* 1, no. 1 (2007): 99–110.

13. Todd Norton, "The Structuration of Public Participation: Organizing Environmental Control," *Environmental Communication* 1, no. 2 (2007): 146–170.

14. Caron Chess and Kristen Purcell, "Public Participation and the Environment: Do We Know What Works?" *Environmental Science & Technology* 33, no. 16 (1999): 2685–2692.

15. Vancouver Sun, "VPD Officer Injured at Anti-pipeline Protest after Being Hit by a Car," last modified June 9, 2014, http://www.vancouversun.com/touch/news/officer+anti +pipeline+protest+needs+surgery+after+being/9919925/story.html?rel=831135.

16. Martin Lucaks, "Noam Chomsky Slams Canada's Oil Shale Gas Plans," *Guardian*, last modified November 1, 2013, http://www.theguardian.com/environment/2013/nov/01 /noam-chomsky-canadas-shale-gas-energy-tar-sands).

17. Chief Dan George's descendants have continued to play central roles in Coast Salish leadership. For example, Reuben George honors his grandfather's legacy by serving as Sundance Chief of the Tsleil-Waututh Nation while working toward environmental justice, including opposition to the Kinder Morgan pipeline.

18. Shepard Fairey, "Native America," *Rebel Music*, accessed January 9, 2015, http:// www.rebelmusic.com/#!music/rebel-music/episode/native-america.

19. "No Oil Tankers" is unpublished.

20. "Bella Ciao," Solidarity Notes Labour Choir, accessed January 9, 2015, http://www .solidaritynotes.ca/mp3s/bellaciaosoprano.mp3.

21. I would like to thank Gloria Pavez, a member of the Labour Notes Choir, for sending additional information about the group.

22. As of our last correspondence, Yankoo was working on putting their "poem-song" on her Facebook page. She has much to say musically and is a compelling talent, and I hope she will be able to carve out a career as a sound artist.

23. "Buffy Sainte-Marie Demonstrates the Mouth Bow," YouTube video, accessed January 9, 2015, https://www.youtube.com/watch?v=DkWMC2zS1fU).

24. Marlisse Silver-Sweeney, "Anti-pipeline Protest on World Oceans Day," *Global News*, June 8, 2014, http://globalnews.ca/news/1381277/anti-pipeline-protest-on-world-oceans-day/.

25. Vocal timbre varies greatly from person to person. Complex overtones cause voices to take on radically different sonic textures. That is one reason why different voices and even different voicings of the same words by the same person can communicate radically different meanings, even when the speaker strikes the same pitch.

26. "Now That the Buffalo's Gone," Buffy Sainte-Marie, It's My Way! Vanguard, 2006; "Who's Gonna Stand Up?" Neil Young, *Storytone*, Reprise Records, 2014.

27. Chor Leoni, "Chor Leoni," accessed January 9, 2015, https://chorleoni.org/.

28. "Chief Dan George Prayer Song," YouTube video, accessed January 9, 2015, https://www.youtube.com/watch?v=lbXal6XhfAY; "Coast Salish Anthem," YouTube video, accessed January 9, 2015, https://www.youtube.com/watch?v=Nj55oGcNkBs; "Coast Salish Anthem," YouTube video, accessed January 9, 2015, https://www.youtube.com/watch?v=S3KwoaR6VW8.

FIGURE 4.1

Bobs & Lolo. Bobolo Productions; used by permission.

Vancouver's Bobs & Lolo

Raindrop Pop

Bobs & Lolo are based in Vancouver. Robyn Hardy, or "Bobs," and Lorraine Pond, "Lolo," sing tunes like "Ocean Blue," "Sea Turtles Are Special to Me," and "Log Song" (2011) to large crowds of adoring children and their appreciative parents.[1] Their blended voices, tight harmonies, bouncy rhythms, and traveling melodies excite, amuse, and educate thousands of children each year.

I first encountered Bobs & Lolo at their British Columbia Day concert in Victoria, British Columbia. It was August 5, 2013, a warm, dry summer afternoon. Despite the warm sun, many of the kids gathered on the lawn wore full rain regalia. They were dressing up for their favorite song, "Raindrop Pop."[2] When Bobs & Lolo finally rolled out that fan favorite, kids popped their umbrellas and danced around in brightly colored slickers and "wellies" (Wellington rubber boots). The Vancouver-based duo drew at least two hundred young fans to Victoria's St. Anne's Academy National Historic Site park grounds, a typically large turnout for this very successful duo.

Some mothers and fathers get caught up in Bobs & Lolo's music as well. Therefore, I was not surprised during our later interview at the Vancouver Aquarium when star struck parents interrupted our conversation asking for autographs. Several more pointed and smiled as Bobs & Lolo wandered by. The two are popular with family audiences throughout British Columbia, and they reach all of Canada through a syndicated television show.

Every day, environmental educators teach children basic ecological principles, facilitate better stewardship, and inspire them to care about life

on a larger scale. Music and the arts have become an essential part of effective curricula and public programs. Entertainer-educators like Bobs &
Lolo have taken environmental music and education to an entirely different level, with kids clamoring to take part.[3] As with the other cases in this
book, my main objective is to understand how Bobs & Lolo achieved their
success and to mine the case for ideas, strategies, and techniques that
might assist and inspire other environmentalist musicians and activists.

Bobs & Lolo have succeeded by using humor and joy to connect with
audiences, through developing sound business practices, and by practicing
a strong work ethic. They model environmental creativity and perform
ideal identities on stage. The roles they model include good partners, caring
parents, happy children, and, above all, knowledgeable and caring stewards of the natural environment. It is the latter identity that sets the duo
apart from other children's musicians. Bobs & Lolo embody the ideal fa-
milial relationship and ritually demonstrate with each performance how
to reinforce those bonds while extending a similar sense of kinship to all
living beings. Just as Dana Lyons's music connects adult audiences to
environmentalist campaigns, Bobs & Lolo's music connects kids to their
local communities and ecosystems. Bobs & Lolo's music is about "Connecting the Dots" (one of their song titles) between people and place, an
ecological approach to educational performance.[4]

TWO GIRLS FROM NANAIMO

The Vancouver Aquarium interview took place on Thursday, June 5,
2014. Each exhibit contained the memory of a past life for Lorraine and
Robyn. Lorraine once worked for the aquarium, and the duo got their start
performing professionally at the facility. We toured the aquarium with
Lorraine's daughter, Anissa, who is "two going on thirteen," by her
mother's assessment. Anissa's facility with language is very advanced for
her age. She pulled us toward new discoveries around each corner. Anissa's
baby brother, Keshan, joined us as well. "Ke$ha?" I asked, surprised. "Yes,
we are big fans of Ke$ha," joked Lorraine. She was teasing. Her husband
and in-laws belong to the Sikh faith, and in Punjabi, *keshan* means "the
hairy one." Lorraine liked the sound of the word, and the name stuck.

As we started into the first set of exhibits, Lorraine asked if I had been to the aquarium before. "Once," I replied. "The Georgia Strait exhibit is my favorite," I volunteered. Because I live along the Georgia Strait for three months of the year, I find it interesting to see what swims below the surface outside our cabin. "Yeah, that's my favorite," responded Robyn, followed by Lorraine's, "Yeah, it's pretty cool." Over the course of the interview, the two would constantly echo each other like that, virtually finishing each other's sentences, just as they do onstage.

"It's changed a lot over the years," added Lorraine, looking around at all the new exhibits. Lorraine worked at the aquarium before Robyn joined up. She started in the general staff and eventually made her way to fund development, a post that taught her the importance of community investment. That is one reason why Lorraine still pays for a full family membership each year despite offers from the aquarium to give the duo free "celebrity memberships." Bobs & Lolo's music is closely connected to community institutions like the Vancouver Aquarium, similar to the way Dana Lyons has forged symbiotic relationships with environmentalist organizations. Every professional artist needs an institutional sponsor and/or paying audience. Bobs & Lolo have developed both.

Lorraine worried that the presence of her inquisitive daughter and infant son might distract from our more "serious" business during the interview. Admittedly, at times I worried that I was not getting all the information I would later need. But as we made our way into the deeper recesses of the aquarium, I started to realize that I was getting much more than mere information. Lorraine and Robyn were offering me a glimpse into what their music is all about, discussing it within the cultural and institutional context from which it arose. For example, in order to bring home the point that she and Robyn "are personally connected" to their music, Lorraine motioned toward Anissa, who was at that moment transfixed by a colorful fish. It is hard to express a sentiment like that in words, much easier to do so with a gesture or song.

On the day I interviewed them, the duo had just returned from two sold-out engagements in their hometown of Nanaimo. Nanaimo lies directly across the Salish Sea, on Vancouver Island. Lorraine and Robyn first met when they were just eight years old, at a camp in Nanaimo. They became fast friends. Lorraine's and Robyn's mothers were camp leaders, a direct parallel to Dana Lyons's upbringing. Similarly, Denise Von Glahn found that many of the environmentalist composers she interviewed had "early and extremely meaningful experiences with nature." These two best friends grew up in a community, a school system, and families that emphasized conservation.[5]

For Lorraine and Robyn, exploring nature was a shared experience. "We started singing together at the campfire," Lorraine explained, "and still are today." They have "known each other for over twenty-five years now," she added. They are lifelong friends and, like sisters, communicate through subtle gestures and tones, finishing each other's thoughts and sentences. When I mentioned how well they communicate with each other, Robyn laughed: "A lot of people think that we are actually lip-synching our shows. Like the parents are trying to figure out if we're really singing."

However, Lorraine and Robyn are also distinct individuals. Both on- and offstage, Lorraine is the more social partner, an energetic and charismatic force, whereas Robyn is quiet, shy, and deep in thought much of the time. Robyn is happy to let Lorraine take the public lead. During our interview, Robyn tended to listen, nod, and laugh while Lorraine told me about their performing lives together. Robyn would fill in whenever Anissa drew Lorraine's attention to a diving otter, crawling crab, or other irresistible attraction. Otherwise, Lorraine did most of the talking.

Their very distinct personalities offstage gave rise to complementary stage personae. Lolo does more of the talking onstage, while Bobs tends to perform as the model listener, reacting thoughtfully to what Lolo says. Bobs uses nonverbal communication onstage to visually reinforce and illustrate Lolo's verbal cues: [6]

> LOLO: These animals love to wiggle and squirm and crawl [*Bobs wiggles and squirms to illustrate*]. Now you can find them inside. You can definitely find them outside, and if you are very lucky, you might even find them crawling around in your hair sometimes! [*Bobs runs her fingers through her hair*] Only if you're really lucky though.
>
> BOBS: Yeah.
>
> LOLO: So does anyone know what this next song might be about? [*Kids' arms go shooting up into the air*] Shout it out if you know the answer.
>
> BOBS & LOLO (in perfect unison): That's right!
>
> LOLO: This song is all about bugs!

Hearing and seeing the duo perform remind one of the mutually constitutive nature of social relationships and musical performance. The two move and speak using cues that are virtually imperceptible to those of us offstage, and the result is magical, especially for their child audience. As with other examples described in the book, Bobs & Lolo's music videos and live concert clips can be accessed via Ecosong.net. They are must-see media for musical performers and environmental educators who work with children, in particular.

Lorraine and Robyn's relationship was musically infused from the outset, moving from campfire to choir. Both took piano lessons from the same instructor: "I think she [the instructor] knew right away that we were not gonna be classical pianists, so she would let us do duets and kind of encouraged us to enjoy it and then collaborate together, which was, I think, perfect for who we were and what we wanted to do. She just kind of kept us motivated to keep up music."

Next they received support from their high school choir director, Bryan Stovell, a man they remember as "a great music teacher." Robyn and Lorraine often sang with two friends outside class as well, so the four girls asked Stovell to help them form an a cappella quartet. "All right," he replied, "I'll support you and help you as much as I can."

"It's so amazing," recalled Lorraine, "that he would invest that much energy and time into a group of girls singing songs on their lunch hour." She reflected on the girls' first project and performance: "We did all of the arrangements and we wanted to get into a festival, but there was no category for what we were doing. So he had the jazz festival create a category for us. So we could at least get adjudicated and be in front of an audience and have a platform to perform on." Robyn explained that "every holiday," they "would carol and get food for the food donation," and each year they would perform for the school on Remembrance Day.

Also while in high school, Lorraine and Robyn acquired the nicknames "Bobs" and "Lolo." Later, when it came time to choose stage names, "it just felt natural," explained Lorraine, and "more fun," to perform as Bobs & Lolo instead of as Robyn and Lorraine. They do not consider their Bobs & Lolo stage personae to be "characters," however, but rather "the happiest versions of ourselves."

Anissa has started to realize that her mother is a well-known public figure. "You're Lolo," she realized one day. "You're on TV." She knows when Lorraine is "having a show day" because her mother will do her hair a certain way and "get ready for an event" at home. On performance days, Anissa now asks, "Are you going to be Lolo today?" She does not find her mother's behavior unusual. She equates it to the way she takes on imaginary characters "like Rapunzel."

However, Lorraine and Robyn were professional educators before they became Bobs & Lolo, the musical duo. Lorraine worked as a mentor at the Vancouver Aquarium, where it was her "job to interpret what the animals were doing." She worked at the aquarium for five years, from 2001 through 2005. Meanwhile, Robyn was teaching at various elementary schools in Vancouver.

Having grown up singing, both recognized the value of developing lesson plans around music. Lorraine's first experiment with musical pedagogy came in the form of a lesson plan for the aquarium's Sea Stars club. After "bringing the guitar in and strumming it for a sea lion song," Lorraine realized that she was on to something. Music immediately captured the kids' attention and interest.

Around the same time, Robyn was finishing the Fine Arts in Media Education program at the University of British Columbia, the purpose of which is "to work with artistic pre-service teachers to develop leadership in arts education."[7] Both Lorraine and Robyn missed making music on a more regular basis and "just were talking one day about how important it is for kids to learn through music in an entertaining way." "In many cases, they don't even know they're learning," explained Lorraine, "they're sponging it up."

With pedagogical music in mind, the friends decided to "write some songs and use them in our programs.'" "We never thought that we would be doing this full-time," Lorraine reflected, "or it kind of snowballing into something bigger than just a teacher and an educator." She assessed their performance career as "very organic from the start," noting that if they did not "love it," they would not have succeeded.

After a few years performing at the Vancouver Aquarium and other sites around the city, including the Children's Hospital, Lorraine and Robyn wanted to make Bobs & Lolo their full-time job, so they "put some planning into it," explained Lorraine. As with their personalities and stage personae, Lorraine and Robyn feel that they also "complement each other's skill sets well on the business side of things." Lorraine continued, contrasting their anger-free existence with other acts and bands: "Like sometimes there is complication within the group, or personalities don't mesh outside of the music world?" Conversely, Lorraine said that the pair and all involved "really feel like we're a family."

Yet their families were not completely sold on the act in the early days. Lorraine's parents "freaked out a little bit when we first called them and we're like, 'We're gonna quit our jobs.'" Both laughed when recalling that milestone moment in their musical careers. It is similar for many musicians when they decide to make a living through music. Many parents see it as an unimaginable risk, yet making such a leap is an absolute necessity for young would-be professional musicians. "They had just lent us money three years before to put a CD together, and we had already paid them back," noted Lorraine proudly, "but I think they thought this was a fun little side project for the girls." "We were fresh out of university and we still had lots of drive," she added wistfully, looking at the aquarium glass as if it were a window into the past. "I couldn't imagine now starting something like this."

The duo had a lot more to say about the importance of striking out to achieve a musical career rather than hedging one's bets. "I think it will just kind of stay as a hobby job if you can't invest yourself 100 percent," noted Lorraine. "It would be a lot harder now to start from scratch," she continued. In your youth, "you don't have the life responsibilities" and pressures of a "bigger life around you." At that crucial point in their lives, both young women sensed that with sound financial management and hard work, they might be able to turn their part-time interest in performing into full-time careers. "Robyn and I kept kind of getting contracts for special events," noted Lorraine.

In fact, their first contracted gig was right there at the Vancouver Aquarium: "I remember we drafted up our little proposal and presented it to the executive office. We charged nothing, so I think they were like, 'Sure.' . . . We convinced them to hire us for spring break. So we did sixteen days straight, three shows a day. We brought in our band. I think we paid the band, but we didn't pay ourselves. So that was kind of our first real contract. . . . They set up a little stage for us in the underwater gallery."

The Vancouver Aquarium continued to be a great match. In addition to getting other gigs Lorraine characterized as "great contracts," the duo was booked back at the aquarium for the next Christmas season. However, the performers' popularity soon became a problem. "The shows were so insane," noted Lorraine, laughing. In addition to hundreds of dancing and screaming children jammed into the aquarium's performance space, the facility "couldn't accommodate all the traffic." While it was thrilling for the newly minted professional singing duo to bring in so many fans, it was "a guest experience nightmare" for the Vancouver Aquarium administration and staff.

Unfortunately, fans do not always translate into financial success. Bobs & Lolo, the stage act, was not yet paying the bills, so both members had to take on part-time work. Robyn turned to part-time substitute teaching. Having quit her full-time job at the aquarium, Lorraine went to work doing fund development for the Stanley Park Ecology Society, where her boss offered flexible hours, amenable to a budding performance career. It was a heady time to start working for the society. The Stanley Park windstorm of December 2006 took place during Lorraine's tenure. The storm destroyed hundreds of ancient trees and a number of interpretive sites throughout the park. Lorraine helped raise money for recovery and restoration. Among her efforts, she instituted a new concert series called "Playing for the Park."

It was Lorraine who first pitched going pro to Robyn. Following successful Christmas performances at the aquarium, Robyn recalls Lorraine boldly suggesting a change in plans: "Let's quit our jobs and go full-time." Robyn responded with reasonable caution, viewing the move as a "huge risk." "Are you kidding me?" she replied, before agreeing to Lorraine's proposal. A decade later, both are very happy that they found the courage to leap from amateur status to professional musicianship.

SINGING AND SAILING THE SALISH SEA

Robyn explains that she is "still teaching" through singing, but "in a different way" than when she taught conventional classes in a formal school setting. "We still get to do the school shows," she noted, adding, "It's really fun," something she does not say about her seven years in front of a class-room of kids.

The BC Ferries system hired the young duo to entertain travelers throughout the summer of 2005. Having heard that the ferry system was looking for performers to entertain toddlers, the duo put a pitch together. The BC Ferries marketing department "loved the idea," according to Lorraine, and assigned Bobs & Lolo the "key route" connecting Vancouver to Victoria through Horseshoe Bay and Sidney. It was a financial turning point in their professional careers. Although BC Ferries could offer only what they "would pay for one person," it was the first time Bobs & Lolo could pocket a complete contract. Without the need for a backup band, they could keep the money for themselves.

As a teacher, Robyn was off for the summer, while Lorraine had only the weekends free. "So they hired us for weekends for the summer of 2005," explained Lorraine. "We'd ride four sailings a day. We'd get on the ferry in Vancouver and go back and forth to Victoria. Four sailings, so we had a little setup in the children's play area. We'd just released our first album, so we were able to sell them on the ferries, and it was another 'paying your dues' kind of gig. But we got so much experience, because that's like eight hours of music. We sang those songs like crazy, so we really learned what worked with kids, and what wasn't working." Lorraine explained that their repertoire has since grown to more than sixty songs. Back during their ferry days, however, their set was limited to the fifteen songs they had recorded on their first album, *Sea Notes*.[8]

I asked what worked well and what fell flat in those early performances. They said that the sing-alongs and story songs worked well, but the rest of the *Sea Notes* repertoire failed to keep toddlers' attention. As noted in chapter 1, it is not all that different for adult audiences. When Dana Lyons performs sing-alongs like "Ride the Lawn" and humorous song-stories like "Cows with Guns," almost everyone gets on board. When he moves to the more contemplative material like "The Tree," part of the audience loses interest. The festival crowd has to be brought back to the act through heavy doses of audience participation, humor, and storytelling. Adults are not all that different from children in that regard.

Parents on the ferries were particularly grateful for the duo's performances. They were "on the boat for two hours with their kids," and there was "not a lot to do other than run around the deck." As evidence of their appreciation, they often bucked in a bit of extra cash. "We got tips!" beamed Lorraine.

Looking back, I am surprised how much of the conversation in that beautiful place (the aquarium) revolved around logistics, finance, and performance strategies. The discussion kept coming back to making a living and sustaining a career. We would get to matters of environmental meaning in due time, but as is true for all professional musicians, the first order of business was, and is, business. Without a way of paying for the act, no teaching, learning, entertaining, organizing, agitating, or advocacy can take place.

Ferry performances led to paying gigs as far away as Toronto. One group of parents was so enthused that they arranged funding and flights so that Bobs & Lolo could perform for a school fund-raiser in Ontario. The young performers were starting to believe that their act had full-time potential. "Every part of this journey has been like that," said Lorraine. "One opportunity leads to another opportunity." "Yeah," smiled Robyn, "it's very organic."

It would be hard to imagine a more "organic" connection between music and place. While sailing across the Salish Sea on the ferries, they sang about how the sea stars' colors help them "blend in," why sharks are endangered but rarely dangerous, how scientists learn about seals "by looking at their poo," why sea turtles lay their eggs in the sand, and why whales sing to one another. In "Octave the Octopus," they use the coincidental symmetry of octopus arms and scalar notation to teach children a bit about both:

1 2 3 4 5 6 7 8
Let's do the Octopus!
What's that you say?
I said let's do the Octopus!
What's that you say?

Octave the Octopus
Living in the sea
Octave the Octopus
Wave your arms at me

Up, down, wave 'em around
Eight arms I can see
Octave the Octopus
Wave around with me!

"Octave the Octopus" illustrates how Bobs & Lolo balance their interest in teaching with their audience's desire to be entertained. Once again, it is not all that different from what Dana Lyons experiences with adult audiences. Overly didactic entertainment, such as songs explicitly about controversial environmental issues, ceases to communicate anything as audiences seek pleasure in less heavy-handed alternatives. As minority partners in musical conversations with audiences, successful musical activists tend to celebrate the carnivalesque nature of public performance rather than struggle against it.[9] Bobs & Lolo joyfully squiggle, squirm, and dance along with their child audiences, facilitating a deep emotional connection to nature while offering them a really good time.

A CONCERT IN THE PARK

Nine years after their ferry concerts, I witnessed Bobs & Lolo perform in Victoria. As in the other case studies, my goal in observing their concert was to gain insight into the duo's performance techniques.

Bobs & Lolo start each set by warming up the audience, asking them to stretch their bodies to get ready for a song called "Muscles."[10] Bobs suggests that kids think about walking in the nearby mountains or "maybe even to a beach, maybe at a park, or maybe even in your own backyards." Lolo echoes Bobs: "I was going to say, in your own backyard." She continues: "Well, when Lolo and I go for our hikes, we do a bit of a march. Now, we are gonna bring our knees up really high and swing those arms. Excellent. And when we see something really cool on our hiking adventures, we like to skip and throw our hands in the air and wiggle our fingers— perfect, just to let everyone know we saw something really cool. Okay. Let's practice this again. Ready? So we're marching along. We see something really cool . . ."

After getting the kids moving to "Muscles," Lolo tells them Bobs & Lolo's backstory, bringing the narrative back around to nature and the local ecosystem: "Well, it's such a treat for Bobs and I to be here. We actually grew up on Vancouver Island, just down the road in Nanaimo, so it's always a treat to come home. Bobs spent a few years here at Victoria University. But the best thing about growing up on the island and one thing we absolutely loved was being surrounded by the ocean. And I'm sure many of you here today have favorite ocean animals."

Lolo asks the audience to share their favorite animal by shouting it out on "1–2–3." The sea of happy children explodes as they shout out the names of ocean creatures:

LOLO: I heard some good ones. I heard "sharks" down here in the front.

BOBS: I heard "sea stars."

LOLO: And "dolphins" . . .

BOBS: And "turtles" . . .

LOLO: I'm not sure I heard our favorite ocean friend though. Now, this next song is about our favorite ocean animal, and I'm gonna give you some clues to see if you can figure out what it is.

BOBS: Listen carefully.

LOLO: Now, this ocean friend has no eyes.

BOBS: No eyes.

LOLO: It has no brain.

BOBS: It doesn't even have a brain.

LOLO: And you might even say it's not much more than [sings] jelly. Any ideas? That's right. This song is all about jellyfish! Now, I know we have some dancers here today. I saw you did a great job on those warm-up songs, but has anyone here ever done any jelly dancing before?

BOBS: No, Lolo is not talking about belly dancing.

LOLO: It's not belly dancing. This is jelly dancing. And to do jelly dancing, we need to pick up your jelly legs.

BOBS: Let's see those jelly legs everyone.

LOLO: And your jelly hips.

BOBS: Bring out those jelly hips.

LOLO: And your jelly arms. Okay, everybody, turn them into jelly. This song is called "I Wish I Was a Jellyfish."

One gets the sense that Bobs & Lolo's audience participation works without fail, every time, just as Lyons gets his audience to chime in on "Ride the Lawn." Part of the trick, in addition to a solid routine, is that the performers listen closely to their audiences, feeling the kids' emotional feedback and reacting in kind. Audience participation almost always work for these performers because they have become experts at reading the room, subtly matching their tone and pace to the audience's mood. This allows them to bring out the active audience's own musicality. Each act breaks down audience inhibitions in different ways, but both Lyons and Bobs & Lolo bring their audiences on board by using narrative, movement, and humor.

One thing Bobs & Lolo do not do, and the parental audience probably appreciates this, is sing in a higher register when performing for children. Instead of taking on kids' voices themselves, they sing and speak in their natural range, using the same fundamental vocal principles they learned as young singers in Nanaimo. The result is an incredibly pleasant sound, lilting and encouraging, rather than frenetic and disturbing, like the voices of so many kids' singers. Bobs & Lolo energize their child audience without sending them into a frenzy of mindless action. Their banter, lyrics, movements, and music pull kids along and stoke their curiosity.[11]

Bobs & Lolo next led their adoring audience through "I Love Bugs," starting the pre-song banter with descriptions of butterflies, dragonflies, and bees, charismatic mini-fauna of the phylum Arthropoda, before moving on to the less immediately appealing examples of beetles and mosquitoes. It is not a lecture, but rather a conversation. They ask children what they like and like to think about. They share what they like in turn. Information, ideas, and feelings get communicated via musical conversation, but at no time is the performance explicitly didactic. Lorraine showed the same inquisitive patience with her daughter, Anissa, at the aquarium, asking her where she thought a red feather on the ground might have come from (a parrot), why there was mist in the tropical exhibit, and so on. Bobs & Lolo's musical pedagogy is imbued with a similar sense of wonder and discovery.

Next, the kids popped open their umbrellas to sing "Raindrop Pop." Although anyone anywhere can relate to a song about rain, it is one of Bobs & Lolo's most interesting place-based tunes. For much of the year, the Salish Sea region experiences day-to-day drizzle with little letup. "Raindrop Pop" gets kids to appreciate the local climate and biome rather than surrendering to what many in the local area refer to as the "low ceiling" (cloud cover) and depressing drizzle. Instead, "Raindrop Pop" celebrates the rain, the soggy local environment, and the evergreen landscape all the moisture produces. "It seems a lot more effective than simply telling them about the water cycle," I said to Lorraine. "Exactly," she replied.

Regarding the kinesthetic dimension of the song, Lorraine explained that getting out in the rain "was important for us" as kids: "You get muddy buddies on and go outside and just splash and have some fun in the puddles. . . . The lyrical content is really built around the water cycle and at a preschooler level, but, like all of our music, we try to have an element of fun and inspire kids to get outside and play. We love that they're connected so well with 'Raindrop Pop.' And now kids come to our shows in rain boots even on sunny days!" Robyn noted how "fun" it is from the stage to watch kids dance around, twirling their umbrellas. The two take great pleasure in their performances, and it shows onstage. Joy is at the heart of their performances, yet, in addition to pathos, there is a healthy dose of logos (logical argumentation) and ethos (ethical orientations) in their music. Adding those dimensions to the musical conversation can make a performance more difficult to pull off, but Bobs & Lolo make it all look natural.

SONGWRITING THE SALISH SEA

During our aquarium conversation, I mentioned to Lorraine and Robyn that my mother-in-law grew up on Bowen Island, just north of Vancouver. "We love it over there," said Lorraine. "We wrote our last album over on Bowen Island." Their friends invited them to use their island home for an extended writing session.

That led me to ask the duo about their songwriting process, and Lorraine explained their composition process in detail: "It's usually the two of us to start, and then Robyn's husband produces all of our music. On our last two albums he cowrote quite a few of the songs with us. We start with the basic melodies and harmonies, and then he kind of gives them life; . . . he has been involved with Bobs and me from the start. We all grew up together on the island." Lorraine went on, "We call him the ampersand." I did not get it at first, so Robyn spelled it out to me, slowly, patiently, and with the same comforting smile she offers her child audience. "He's the ampersand of *us*," pointing at Lorraine and herself. Mario is the "&" in "Bobs & Lolo." Finally getting it, I asked if Mario has taken on his "ampersand identity." "He does," Robyn replied. "He's got a shirt with an ampersand on it."

Our conversation turned when a sturgeon came into view. "We love the sturgeon," said Lorraine. She explained how she and Robyn wrote a song for "a friend who was working for the Fraser River Sturgeon Conservation Society."[12] It started when the friend joked: "It would be so great to have a sturgeon song." "So we surprised her on our next album," said Lorraine, "and we wrote a song called 'Wish for a Fish: The Sturgeon Song' [2008] It was all about the great white sturgeon."[13] "Our song became part of their curriculum," continued Lorraine, proudly. "We actually perform that live a lot; it's a good, clapping, high-energy folkie song."

"Wish for a Fish" illustrates how Bobs & Lolo's music is integrally connected to local flora, fauna, and folk. From benthos to canopy, their music contributes to the Salish Sea's sonic ecology. It has become common to refer to the "ecological services" and "ecosystem services" of organisms. That is also a good way of describing Bobs & Lolo's music.[14] The duo supplies essential ecological services by providing public knowledge and drawing connections that children need in order to become caring and effective stewards. Therefore, much like an endangered keystone species, Bobs & Lolo's rare music deserves further study and propagation. As we move further and further into the Anthropocene, the fate of ecosystems has become dependent on what human populations know about them and do within them. That knowledge is imparted in many ways. For children, in particular, music is one of the most effective means. The hope is that in ten or twenty years, musicians like Bobs & Lolo will become increasingly common. For now, however, they remain remarkably rare.

MAKING A LIVING, MAKING A DIFFERENCE

If it is hard for a talented soloist like Dana Lyons to earn a living making environmentally themed music, it is doubly difficult for a duo like Bobs &

Lolo. If one member decides to give up, the act is over. Only the bonds of friendship and family have allowed Bobs & Lolo to keep going during uncertain times. Lorraine described their music as a result of passion, love, and hard work. "We would talk to each other and say, like, 'Is this working?' Should we keep going?" "We never lost sight of the value of" teaching and entertaining kids, she added. "It was more like, 'Can we do this as a career?'" "And at every point to date so far," she noted, "we've always been able to say, if we stop now, there has gotta be a reason why it doesn't work." Lorraine provided examples of other acts that simply stopped working. Smiling and pointing to her children, she noted that "this is another little speed bump, trying to transition to starting a young family." She continued: "I'm trying to figure out how we carry all of that, because it is different now. There are other things making it hard for me to invest my day into the business side of things, or the administrative side, or even the creative side. So now we're kind of exploring everything—how do we keep it going? Do we need to bring in somebody else?"

I asked if they had been looking into professional management, having kept that side of the business in-house for their entire career. "Yeah, that's what we're looking at now." They are seeking out professional representation that they can "admire" and "trust." "And that's hard too, after we've been doing it for ten years. So it's hard to let go too, right, even though you recognize that you need the support, but at the same time . . . I don't think we'll be able to finish [the next album] unless we get ourselves some help."

"People are very surprised," explained Lorraine, when booking agents, organizations, and venue managers reach out and discover that they are actually "contacting us" rather than a professional manager or publicist. She notes that thus far there has been no "middleman . . . not a third party." They have been "very careful about protecting" their "freedom and protecting the integrity" of the Bobs & Lolo "brand." Fortunately, three months later Lorraine reported to me that they had contracted with a management company and that they feel confident that their values align with those of their new manager.

The need to tour is also weighing on the duo. "We should be doing more flock booking," explained Lorraine, "where [concerts] are all together, whereas now, we do a lot of one-offs; like we do Ontario and go to Whitehorse." They contrasted the difficulty of doing three shows a day at the

Calgary Stampede with the same sort of scheduling as in years past, when they "were younger and had more energy."

As Bobs & Lolo have pulled back from three hundred shows a year to "maybe fifty," their pocketbooks have been strained. That has, in part, led them to television and social media. Yet even that transformation causes stress. Media that once supplemented live, paid gigs now need to become sources of income as well. Turning social media into a revenue stream is no easy task. For many musicians, social media is a great way of getting music out to the audience, but it pays off for only a select few. "We always joke that we never had a problem with pirating," Lorraine explained, "like that's always been good." "It's sharing the music," added Robyn, "go for it." But now they are wishing that there were more ways to earn a living by selling their creative work directly to audiences. However, they are resigned to the possibility that social media will never become a source of income. "Touring is what is going to pay our bills," Lorraine concluded, adding that television and social media have allowed the duo to develop "a great brand awareness campaign."

As for songwriting royalties, children's music is often boom or bust. "Our population is two- to six-year-olds," explained Lorraine, "and every year there are new ones, right?" That can result in entirely new cadres of adoring fans and paying parents every few years. However, each new generation has to be cultivated, which requires constant work and means that taking a break from the stage entails serious professional risk. Unlike other performers, children's entertainers cannot assume that their fans will still be there when they return to the stage.

Distribution routes are also different for children's performers. "Our 'industry' is parents and educators," explained Lorraine, "versus labels and radio stations." Now, as a parent, Lorraine is thankful that the environments she performs in are family-friendly. She likes having her family at the shows, both because Anissa gets to enjoy the event but also because it allows for travel to places that most kids growing up in urban Vancouver never experience, such as "dog sledding" in Whitehorse, "ice sculpture" and other "things that she wouldn't experience on the west coast." The fact that their business is infused with family has allowed Bobs & Lolo to keep going at a stage in their life cycle when many performers move on to more stable professions.

RECONNECTING TO PLACE AND THE BORDER PROBLEM

Being at the Vancouver Aquarium inspired Lorraine and Robyn to reminisce, including revisiting their initial motivations. They observed that many people, including visitors to the aquarium, were disconnected from the natural environment:

> And it's so ironic that people who have never been to the ocean before would make this stop at the aquarium, when the beach is, like, one hundred meters down the path, right? But it was so crazy to me, because growing up on the island and near the ocean, we were both so connected. Both of our parents had boats, and we were out on the water and exploring tide pools as kids. It was just so foreign, that whole concept, to me, that, hey, this is your first chance in this oceanside city, and you came here first?

Lorraine explained how witnessing that disconnect led them to develop their musical mission. That mission includes helping people who spend "their whole lives in an urban" area gain a "connection with nature and the environment." She noted how easily one falls into substituting simulacra for real living systems. "We just returned from a trip to Maui, and the smell [of a tropical exhibit] totally reminds me of Hawaii." Lorraine used that as an example of how simulations can so easily be substituted for the ecosystems they reference. I was reminded of Canadian journalist Naomi Klein's critique of British Columbia's "tree museums," idyllic preserves sponsored by the same companies that clear-cut and harvest forests unsustainably throughout the province.[15] Klein argues that people are encouraged to mistake the preserved groves for a broader ecological reality, when in fact they are some of the few remaining stands of old growth left. Similarly, Lorraine noted the importance of experiencing biodiverse ecosystems directly and described one goal of Bobs & Lolo's music as providing the motivation for kids to go outdoors and make their own connections and discoveries rather than rely on mediated simulations alone.

One of the most important connections for Bobs & Lolo is the one between people and place. Their most cherished place is the Salish Sea, a body of water teeming with life and ringed by temperate rain forests. However, an imaginary line bisects the Cascadian biome separating its northern and southern sections. Although imaginary, that invisible border is enforced by very real policies, border guards, and bureaucracies. Therefore, even for Bobs & Lolo, movement as traveling artists is influenced as much by nationalistic concerns as by audience, culture, and ecosystem. Bobs & Lolo's experience remains partly dictated by the border. Despite doing about three hundred performances per year, they "have done very little in the US," other than "a little bit in the Pacific Northwest," including "a children's performing art series" in Oregon plus a Bainbridge Island gig. Acquiring "work visas was a challenge." "The first time," joked Lorraine, "I'm pretty sure we did everything wrong, and if they had actually pulled us over and questioned us, we would have been, like, 'Well, we shouldn't be here.'"

"We see lots of events (advertised) around the Seattle area," Lorraine noted, "and we are, like, oh, that would be so amazing, that would be great." At the same time, they have plenty of work in Canada, although increased north-south exchange would be highly beneficial for dealing with those shared challenges. Unfortunately, for most professionals, including Bobs & Lolo, the border remains a serious impediment to broader touring.

THE ENVIRONMENTAL EDUCATION MOVEMENT, OR WHY WE NEED MORE BOBS & LOLOS

Environmental education and enculturation take place constantly. Every day we are taught how to relate to the rest of the living world. Parents, teachers, advertisers, peers, institutions, and industries mold our understanding of the world from the time we are very young and discipline us into specific types of environmental agents: teacher, lobbyist, environmentalist, pipeline welder, commuter, oil company engineer, consumer, and so on. Unfortunately, much of what we learn works against stewardship of healthy ecosystems, reduces biodiversity, and teaches us to ignore ecological crises for the sake of performing niche-specific professional roles in systems designed to produce and distribute goods, but at environmental and social costs that simply cannot be sustained. We learn how to desire and obtain new things at a rate that would startle even the most fashion-conscious consumer of the early twentieth century. We start learning these lessons at a very early age, with every advertisement and visit to the mall. Much kids' music—including soundtracks for cartoons, commercials, and video games—teaches deleterious lessons when it comes to sustainability. That makes Bobs & Lolo's brand of environmental education that much more important.

Bobs and Lolo are building on an important counter-cultural tradition. The modern environmental education movement took root in the nature study movement of the early 1900s. The movement adopted conservationist principles in the 1930s, a reaction to the Dust Bowl and other ecopolitical crises. Starting in the late 1960s, a range of national environmental education acts and initiatives, spurred on by the broader environmental movement, led schools, universities, and community organizations to create environmental studies programs at all levels. The goal was to teach students basic ecological principles, promote stewardship, and support sustainable innovation.[16]

Later still, the environmental justice movement inspired environmental educators to adopt multicultural orientations to nature.[17] Roger Coss argues that music is particularly central to multicultural environmental education, serving a role in fostering the "interdisciplinary way of thinking" needed to steward a "habitable planet."[18] Similarly, Michael Cermak explains how a musically infused environmental studies curriculum is practiced in lab-based science courses in Boston, using hip-hop to help teach ecological concepts.[19] According to Cermak, the study of songs like "New World Water" by Mos Def helps students develop critical ecological literacy that goes beyond simple material relationships.[20]

Learning about the mechanics of living systems is important, but it does not constitute a complete understanding of ecosystems. Human beings, institutions, technologies, and cultural systems are integrally related to animal life, plant life, and inorganic systems.[21] In ecological study, we learn that each element influences others, and that includes the symbolic systems humans produce. Some would like to move omnipresent cultural realities like music to the ephemeral fringe of ecological understanding for the sake of purely material study, but what we perform and listen to, as well as when, where, and how we listen, have demonstrable consequences, influencing if not overdetermining material outcomes in ecosystems. For example, it is no accident that advertising almost always features music intended to compel consumers to purchase goods. Such consumption has material, ecological consequences. Conversely, as in the case of Bobs & Lolo, singing about local animal life can lead to more sustainable mindsets and practices. Just as there is a reason that advertisers pays millions in musical licensing fees, there is a reason that organizations like the Fraser River Sturgeon Conservation Society seek and value musical support from musicians like Bobs & Lolo. Music, like all culture, is part of the contest determining the fates of entire ecosystems.

And so environmental educators work to instill a love of nature in children. Today the onus is on getting children outside the home, away from the Xbox, and moving around outdoors. As Erin Kenny, founder of Cedarsong Nature School, explained: "Children cannot bounce off the walls if we take away the walls."[22] That objective is particularly clear in Bobs & Lolo's third album, *On Your Feet* (2007), a compilation that won the Parents' Choice Award. Their performances reinforce the Ten Pillars of a Good Childhood presented by the Association for Childhood Education International (ACEI), with special emphasis on the fourth, "Creative play and physical activity," the fifth, "Appreciation and stewardship of the natural environment," and the sixth, "Creative expression through music, dance, drama, and the other arts."[23] Environmental education researcher Penelope Wong argues that it is important for educators to link each of these foundational disciplines and is concerned that interdisciplinary environmental education is much less "widely practiced" than it should be, especially as children advance into the higher grades.[24] Robyn's perspective jibes with Wong's. To a significant degree, her frustration with traditional education led to Bobs & Lolo. Taking environmental education beyond the classroom, Bobs & Lolo assist other environmental educators by bringing music and art to bear on the matter.

Unfortunately, for every lesson, song, and dance about bugs or octopi, there are thousands of advertisements teaching kids how to be active consumers. Even green ad campaigns use positive environmental messages to deleterious ends. Called "greenwashing," such ads and campaigns make us feel as though the road to ecological recovery runs through the mall. As Plec and Pettenger point out, the oil industry's public campaigns are nothing short of "didactic" in that regard.[25]

Nor does consumer enculturation end in childhood. Adults are also encouraged to adopt high-consumption lifestyles. Market disciplines are part of that persuasion and professional musicians are not immune to their power. Professional musicianship is a risky career regardless, but uncompromising artists like Dana Lyons and Bobs & Lolo make it that much more difficult for themselves by refusing to compromise their core values. Many of the more profitable revenue streams, including ad licensing and many corporate gigs, are off-limits for those with strong environmentalist ethics. Environmental educators like Bobs & Lolo provide an ethical counterweight to those same market disciplines by teaching children values that go beyond personal enrichment. As pointed out in previous chapters, almost all the musicians featured in this book experienced environmental education early in their lives, whether at camp or in school. The world needs many more Bobs & Lolos.

THE LESSONS OF BOBS & LOLO

Bobs & Lolo have provided fundamental lessons to thousands of children and their parents, encouraging a sense of ecological wonder and joy through their music. They take a positive approach.

Nevertheless, it is almost impossible to determine whether environmental entertainment and education lead to greater sustainability, biodiversity, environmental recovery, or justice. Like most things, art and education are acts of faith. However, it is reasonable to hope that kids who grow up dancing and listening to educational entertainers like Bobs & Lolo are more likely to develop values that lead to environmental stewardship.

But what lessons and ideas can readers extract from the story of Bobs & Lolo? For those who plan on teaching and entertaining children, there is very direct use-value in this case study: develop talent, work hard, make sacrifices, design a sound business plan, and stay the course until it pays off. For the rest of us, we can marvel at their example and support artists like them performing in our local communities. After all, as both Robyn and Lorraine pointed out, making music requires more than musicians. Audiences, managers, organizers, activists, and professionals play a number of essential roles. Bobs & Lolo's "ampersand" is evidence of that. Without caring collaborators, sponsors, and parents, Bobs & Lolo would not be working.

In addition to that broader lesson, a few of Bobs & Lolo's idiosyncratic tactics are worth mentioning. First, Lorraine's and Robyn's connections to environmentally minded community organizations have provided a stable base of operations. The Vancouver Aquarium gave them a launching pad when they were just starting out. Community organizations like the Stanley Park Ecology Society offered the duo invaluable support. They have since returned the favor many times over, so it turned out to be a good investment.

The lesson for young activists is to get involved with community organizations early on, whether that means the local aquarium, state parks system, or community theater. Granted, overtly politicized work is unwelcome in most institutions that receive funding from government sources, taxpayers, businesses, and donors. A particularly strict line is often drawn in the United States between education and advocacy. Sadly, some people believe that the teaching of environmental science is a form of advocacy. That makes the environmental arts particularly vulnerable to criticism, raising concerns among some sponsors that environmental artists will bring unwanted scrutiny and negative publicity.

Fortunately, advocacy is less of a problem in Canada, where there is greater consensus around public funding for the arts and recognition that artists take positions. Nevertheless, even in Canada, it is hard to imagine critical artists duplicating Bobs & Lolo's business plan. For example, neither the Vancouver Aquarium nor government-subsidized television-production companies would be keen on having in-house performers sing about Enbridge's pipeline and shipping plans, no matter how aligned such a position might be with the explicit missions of those organizations (e.g., sustaining the Salish Sea). On both sides of the border, that more overtly political work instead falls to performers like Dana Lyons, the Raging Grannies, and the Idle No More movement.

Nevertheless, Bobs & Lolo's educational case offers a great deal to movement-oriented activists. As Martin Branagan demonstrates, environmental education is a form of environmental activism in its own right.[26] The early ecological education provided by musicians like Bobs & Lolo populates environmentalist movements with new activists.

A key step toward fostering a more environmentally engaged citizenry is to help young people care about the animals, plants, and people in their shared communities and ecosystems. Effective stewardship requires education. Therefore, more educator-artists like Bobs & Lolo are needed. It is good work, and, among the many lessons I have learned from studying their case, it is also joyful work. Lorraine and Robyn repeatedly used the verb "love" to describe what they do. Their passion for music, education, the environment, their audience, and each other comes through in every song and performance. And so I find myself circling back to a point I made at the end of chapter 1: the joy that meaningful environmental work provides more than compensates for the sacrifices it requires. At each concert, Bobs & Lolo see that joy reflected in the faces of children dancing about in colorful rain gear, singing for a better future.

NOTES

1. "Log Song," Bobs & Lolo, Bobolo Productions, 2011; "Ocean Blue," Bobs & Lolo, YouTube video, accessed January 6, 2015, https://www.youtube.com/watch?v=ABFdw7D-jxw; "Sea Turtles Are Special to Me," Bobs & Lolo, Bobolo Productions, 2004; several discographic references in this chapter will point readers to the music video versions of Bobs & Lolo's songs in order to provide a more complete sense of the duo's musical performances.

2. "Raindrop Pop," Bobs & Lolo, YouTube video, accessed January 6, 2015, https://www.youtube.com/watch?v=ok2fEPJ4060.

3. Michael J. Cermak, "Hip-Hop, Social Justice, and Environmental Education: Toward a Critical Ecological Literacy," *Journal of Environmental Education* 43, no. 3 (2012): 192–203.

4. "Connecting the Dots," Bobs & Lolo, *Connecting the Dots*, Bobolo Productions, 2011.

5. Denise Von Glahn, *Music and the Skillful Listener: American Women Compose the Natural World* (Bloomington and Indianapolis: Indiana University Press, 2013), 321.

6. Bobs & Lolo, "'I Love Bugs' Live in Ottawa," YouTube video, last modified March 19, 2011, http://www.youtube.com/watch?v=rX8wIunIwaw.

7. See Peter Gouzouasis, Anne Marie Lamonde, and Martin Guhn, "The Fine Arts and Media in Education Project: The Integration of Creative Arts-Based Activities, Wireless Technologies, and Constructivist Teaching Practices in Practicum Classrooms" Chapter 22 [repaginated pp.1–28] in Karl Veblen, Carol Beynon, Stephanie Horsley, Uresha deAlwiss, and Andre Heywood, eds. *From Sea to Sea: Perspectives on Music Education in Canada*. (London, Ontario, Canada: Scholarship at Western, 2007), retrieved from http://ir.lib.uwo.ca/musiceducationebooks/1/.

8. *Sea Notes*, Bobs & Lolo, Bobolo Productions, 2004.

9. For an insightful analysis of the relationship between Baudrillard's concept of the "carnivalesque" and environmental discourse, see Janet M. Cramer and Karen A. Foss, "Baudrillard and Our Destiny with the Natural World: Fatal Strategies for Environmental Communication," *Environmental Communication* 3, no. 3 (2009): 298–316.

10. "Muscles," Bobs & Lolo, *Action Packed*, Bobolo Productions, 2008.

11. The greater efficacy of the calmer approach is supported by experimental research, starting with a now classic study comparing *Mister Rogers' Neighborhood* to *Sesame Street*,

wherein it was discovered that Fred Rogers's calmer approach taught "pro-social" behavior much more effectively and resulted in more pro-social behaviors in school. See Mabel L. Rice et al., "Words from 'Sesame Street': Learning Vocabulary While Viewing," *Developmental Psychology* 26, no. 3 (1990): 421.

12. Fraser River Sturgeon Conservation Society, "Wish for a Fish: The Sturgeon Song by Bobs and Lolo," accessed January 6, 2015, http://www.frasersturgeon.com/multi _media/wish_for_a_fish__the_sturgeon_song_by_bobs_and_lolo.

13. "Wish for a Fish: The Sturgeon Song," Bobs & Lolo, *Musical Adventures*, Nettwerk Music Group, 2006.

14. Robert Costanza, "Ecosystem Services: Multiple Classification Systems Are Needed," *Biological Conservation* 141, no. 2 (2008): 350–352.

15. Naomi Klein, *No Logo: Taking Aim at the Brand Bullies* (New York: Picador, 2002), 156.

16. Edward J. McCrea, "The Roots of Environmental Education: How the Past Supports the Future," *Environmental Education and Training Partnership*, 2005, ERIC, accessed September 24, 2014, http://files.eric.ed.gov/fulltext/ED491084.pdf.

17. Roger Coss, "Multicultural Perspectives through Music & Sustainability Education," *Multicultural Education* (Fall 2013): 20–25.

18. Ibid., 23.

19. Michael J. Cermak, "Hip-Hop, Social Justice, and Environmental Education: Toward a Critical Ecological Literacy," *Journal of Environmental Education* 43, no. 3 (2012): 192–193.

20. "New World Water," lyrics by Mos Def, composed by Dante Smith, performed by Mos Def, Rawkus/Priority, 1999.

21. Michael J. Cermak, "Hip-Hop, Social Justice, and Environmental Education: Toward a Critical Ecological Literacy," *Journal of Environmental Education* 43, no. 3 (2012): 192–193.

22. Cedarsong Nature School, accessed November 23, 2014, http://cedarsongnatureschool.org/.

23. Lea Pulkkinen, "Ten Pillars of a Good Childhood: A Finnish Perspective," *Childhood Education* 88, no. 5 (2012): 326–330.

24. Penelope Wong, "Greening the Elementary Education Curriculum One Course at a Time," *Green Teacher* 85 (2009): 24.

25. Emily Plec and Mary Pettenger, *Greenwashing Consumption: The Didactic Framing of ExxonMobil's Energy Solutions* (New York: Routledge, 2012).

26. Martin Branagan, "Education, Activism, and the Arts," *Convergence* 38, no. 4 (2005): 33–50.

Holly Arntzen and Kevin Wright lead The Wilds in song. Artist Response Team; used by permission.

Surrey's Artist Response Team

ART for Ecology

olly Arntzen and Kevin Wright lead the Artist Response Team (ART), an activist endeavor and production house that specializes in entertainment that educates; they produce the long-running Voices of Nature music program for schools in British Columbia and across Canada. Like their compatriots, Bobs & Lolo, Holly and Kevin use music to teach environmental concepts to children, but they do so in a very different way. Instead of performing for preschoolers, Holly and Kevin work with children in grades four and up. Also, instead of single concerts, Voices of Nature is a complete curriculum bringing together music, environmental science, and related disciplines. At the end of two to three months of study, students mount the stage with Holly and Kevin and their band, The Wilds, and put on concerts for the local community.

In terms of style, Holly and Kevin's music is different from Bobs & Lolo's as well. They call their hybrid sound "folk pop to rock your world." Most of their songs are rock-tinged if not straight-up rock. Whereas Bobs & Lolo compose catchy pop songs appropriate for preschoolers, Holly and Kevin target an older, school-age audience. Kevin's voice, with its ability to harmonize as effectively as lead, could be compared favorably to AC/DC front man Bonn Scot. Holly's folk-jazz vocal style, when combined with her exceptional keyboard and dulcimer skills, makes for an appealing folk/pop/rock sound, edgy enough for kids to bite into but not so sonically challenging as to scare off school administrators.

Holly and Kevin have also hit upon a particularly successful business model. Whereas Bobs & Lolo perform on an opportunity basis, maintaining a busy yet ever-changing gigging schedule, Holly and Kevin have developed a formalized method and schedule dictated by the school term. Schools adopt Holly and Kevin's entire curriculum. Teachers teach the environmental studies curriculum, as well as Holly and Kevin's songs, for an entire term. Near the end of the term, Holly and Kevin show up for several intense days of rehearsal with the students, capped off with a public concert featuring the kids' chorale and Holly and Kevin's full band, The Wilds. It took Holly years to develop that methodology, working with her late husband, Stephen Foster, and then Kevin, who started taking part in 2003, first on the technical side and then, a few years later, musically as well.[1]

I enjoyed a sunny afternoon in Surrey listening to the duo's fascinating story, from childhood training to the present day, peppered with several live performances in their living room. Theirs is a unique story containing valuable lessons for young musicians, environmental educators, music scholars, and activists. Many young musicians dream of making music for a living. Some dream of creating catalytic art, the sort of music that can change people and aid community efforts. Few achieve those dreams in the way that Holly and Kevin have managed to do. There is often a disconnect between how local musicians earn their living and the music they would most dearly love to perform. The gulf between dream and reality drives many artists from the professional music world. Many have the talent to make the music they love, but few find the business model, drive, discipline, and perseverance to make a living doing so. Holly and Kevin's case provides a number of innovative ideas and examples for those seeking to make music that matters to audiences, communities, and ecosystems.

MUSIC AND METHOD

Minutes after arriving at Holly and Kevin's home in Surrey, I found myself sitting on the couch listening to a live rendition of their newest song, "The Watershed Song." Kevin introduced the song by explaining that it resulted from "a recon trip up the Fraser River to Prince George, down through Quesnel, Williams Lake, Lillooet, and then Mission and New Westminster." These are "all different little watersheds in the Fraser Basin" and place-names evoked in their newest album and pedagogical project.

Holly and Kevin's method is not that different from Woody Guthrie's when he traveled the Columbia River basin making observations and taking notes sixty years earlier or Joe Hill's a century ago in some of the very same areas that Holly and Kevin reconnoitered recently. Joe Hill composed "Where the Fraser River Flows" based on his experiences not far from Holly and Kevin's home in Surrey. Obviously, direct experience, travel, and observation play important roles in the production of place-based music.

Less obvious are the myriad ways landscapes inspire artists. Place exerts a certain sense of agency via music; a case for that thesis will be made at the end of the chapter. However, the divergent nature of compositions created in Cascadia and their radically different consequences temper more romanticized notions of the power of place to influence art. Guthrie's pro-dam music is very different from Kevin and Holly's anti-dam music. Joe Hill's turn-of-the-century Fraser River, lined with logging camps, produced a very different musical vision than the community-stewarded watershed imagined in Holly and Kevin's songs. Guthrie's, Hill's, and Holly and Kevin's repertoires are based on equal parts observation and aspiration.

As for professional aspirations, Holly and Stephen started calling their school program "Voices of Nature" in 1999. Environmental education "was starting to be included in BC curricula," explained Holly. Knowing that music is such a great way to enliven learning, the pair began "creating learning resources that provide teachers with activities that are connected to the song lyrics." Holly handed me two large volumes to take home, each an entire school-term's worth of environmental studies curricula filled with scientific information, art, song lyrics, and other ecological learning materials, carefully interconnected. According to Holly, the curriculum works because "kids like the songs" and teachers who are "pressed to fill (the BC) curriculum requirements" are drawn to the complete, ready-made curricula that Voices of Nature provides.

Increasingly, K–12 institutions around the Salish Sea emphasize environmental studies. School programs place a strong emphasis on experiential learning. Students participate in stream recovery work, for example, restoring salmon runs and spawning grounds along the Salish Sea's urbanized edge.[2] The area's universities have taken on a strong leadership role in the environmental education movement. For example, the Evergreen State College in Olympia, Washington, is a flagship institution for training environmental educators. In Canada, national curricular mandates have created a strong demand for environmental studies resources. As a result, nonprofit sponsors like Parks Canada and private businesses have been willing to bankroll programs like Voices of Nature. However, it took a very talented, savvy, and hardworking pair of musicians to identify that niche and turn it into a successful ecomusical program.

Holly handed me CD after CD filled with songs the duo have created for Voices of Nature over the years, recorded with their full band, The Wilds. Their second compilation, fittingly, is *The Salish Sea*, a "CD of songs about marine conservation" through which Holly and ART "pioneered" the successful method they have been practicing ever since.[3] "Every CD you see," notes Holly, "represents quite a massive project." The duo has produced French-language versions of several CDs. Between their studio recording schedule, curricular development, and touring, Holly and Kevin find very little time for rest.

ORIGINS

Holly and Kevin's successful model developed from trial and error, hard work, and creative convergence. If there is some luck involved as well, it is in their good fortune of meeting after they had both already become accomplished in their own skill set. Each started a musical life at an early age. Kevin "started playing violin in grade two," then took up saxophone and eventually singing. He "always wanted to be a singer," so he began writing lyrics to existing tunes. "I used to perform these little songs in the backyard for the neighborhood kids with my little red record player," explained Kevin. "I had this little microphone you could plug into it with a little speaker." By grade eight, Kevin "really wanted to be a rock singer." He "found a bunch of guys" and "eventually put a band together" to perform AC/DC songs. Kevin is still in a professional AC/DC tribute band called

"TNT." Gigging professionally before they could drive, the band wheeled beat-up equipment around the Oak Bay and Fairfield neighborhoods of Victoria in stolen grocery carts.

Next, Kevin "got into a more substantial band," but by that time, the young singer was becoming disenchanted with the direction of heavy metal music. "I just wanted to become more of a singer instead of a yeller because that's what they wanted, and I didn't want to go that route." High-pitched and raspy metal vocals were starting to give way to the loud growling made famous by death metal bands like Brazil's Sepultura. "That's what they wanted," lamented Kevin, "but I was like, 'No way, I don't want any of that; I'm gonna move on now.'" Kevin "ended up in a band called 'Turk and the Rat,'" a Van Halen–style rock band that needed a bass and backup vocals, so Kevin learned bass as well. Turk and the Rat became a hit in Victoria, winning the first-ever Rocktoria competition in 1988, which allowed Turk and the Rat "to go in and record in the real big studio and get lots of airplay."[4]

Turk and the Rat separated before achieving wider success, and Kevin ended up in Toronto, where he put his musical career on hold. A subsequent move to Windsor, Ontario, led to work in a cover band that played "hard rock stuff from Black Sabbath, to Judas Priest, to Faster Pussycat, LA Guns, and a little bit of the newer stuff like Alice in Chains and stuff when that was first coming out" in the 1990s.

Kevin missed Victoria, so he returned, "got married, had a child, and met Holly and Stephen." He was attending Camosun College at the time, taking "applied communications," including "audio and TV production, website design, and graphic design." As part of his two-year program, Kevin took a "job as the afternoon radio show host" for the college station in 2003. Around five in the afternoon one day, there "was a knock on the window." Kevin went to see what the "stranger" wanted. It was Stephen Foster. Foster described the radio show that he and Holly had already proposed to the station manager, Doug Ozeroff, who had left for the day. Kevin forgot about the encounter until Ozeroff later asked him to produce the new show. "So we started the first year of *Voices of Nature* radio shows" in 2004, said Kevin, running sixteen shows per season. The trio produced their own songs, "lots of them performed by kids," explained Holly," including recording and broadcasting "big live concerts with school choirs" and reader's theater script readings live on air, "like old-time radio shows," added Kevin, with characters that included Vito the Codfather and Tony the Shark.

The radio show complemented Holly's developing school program. "In a season, we did eight full school programs with kids learning songs for several months," she remembered, "and then we would go in and rehearse with them, and then we would do the concert and record it, and then produce this radio show." By the time the radio show came into being, the educational component of Voices of Nature had already been developing at local schools, starting in 1999 at the "tiny Durrance School" on the Saanich Peninsula, just north of Victoria. Holly asked a friend who had children at the school, "Do you think the school might like to have their kids learn environmental songs?" She visited the Durrance School "once a week for five weeks and taught the songs to the kids."

The unit ended with a concert, "and the gym was just packed to the gills," because "the kids had been singing these songs, and they'd been talking about them a whole bunch at home." The audience "jumped to their feet at the end of the concert." For Holly and Steven, "that was a big bell going off." The Durrance School experience led to a CD on the theme of watershed stewardship called *Running from the Mountains*.[5] The CD "has children from Durrance School and Strawberry Vale School singing songs about watershed stewardship." The couple gained "sponsorship for it right away." Holly and Stephen "started working with Lenny Ross, who is a leading environmental educator at Strawberry Vale School," and Holly began presenting concerts in the University of Victoria auditorium. Parents and community members would attend, "expecting the usual school concert," and were delighted to see their children actively involved and genuinely enthused. "It was just electrifying," remembers Holly.

Kevin "wasn't musically involved" in the early years of the project but rather worked as the "technical guy" after he met the couple in 2003. He was still gigging with local rock bands, but his role in Voices of Nature kept growing, as he added graphic design to his other technical production efforts. He "became more involved with the Artist Response Team" as well, which was developing alongside Voices of Nature, including putting together the team's first website.

Foster was "the foundation of everything," according to Kevin. The dual projects, ART and Voices of Nature, were his "brainchild." Therefore, Holly and Kevin "had to really pick up the slack" when Foster died in 2005. Despite her considerable talent, Holly could not do the school programs by herself. It would not be possible to compose, perform, and take on all of Foster's backstage responsibilities. David Sinclair, their talented guitar player and "an old friend," did not want to take on the difficult role. Eventually, that led to Kevin becoming a partner in operations and management as well as half the musical duo. "I came in not so much as a musical component," noted Kevin, "but more as a helper." Holly remembers Kevin helping her set up the PA system, bringing tea, and being "all hands on deck" to help produce programs involving "hundreds of kids."

"But then we were in the school in Squamish," remembered Holly, "and what happened was, Kevin walks in, and after a day I realized, wow, he really likes the kids, and the kids really like him." Holly realized that Kevin was perfect for an onstage role. "So then," Kevin continued, "we started writing music together."

"I guess at some point," he went on, "I wasn't just the guy behind the scenes." They "started doing the school programs as a duet," as well as "writing songs" for a CD called *I Am the Future*. The new band was called "Holly Arntzen, Kevin Wright and the Dream Band," a name they were using as late as 2010. "Eventually that got to be just too much of a mouthful," laughed Kevin, so in the past couple of years, they have been referring to the entire band, themselves included, as simply "The Wilds."

It was then Holly's turn to tell her story. Her musical training started even earlier than Kevin's. Her "mom and dad were both musicians," as were all five of her siblings. Holly's father, Lloyd Arntzen, is a well-known jazz clarinetist, sax player, guitarist, banjoist, and folk singer. He penned several songs that have come to be considered Canadian classics, including "Where the Coho Flash Silver (All Over the Bay)."[6]

In addition to being a professional performer, Lloyd Arntzen was a music educator, which is "how he paid the bills." "He'd be a teacher during the day," remembers Holly, "and then he'd go play at Shakey's Pizza at night . . . and then he had his jazz band." Whereas many aspiring musicians have no idea what they are getting into, the professional music world was a known quantity to Holly from the very start. She could not imagine doing anything else with her life and career.

Holly helped her father out on occasion, including in his production work for the Canadian Broadcasting Corporation (CBC). "I would go down to the Vancouver Hotel where the CBC studios used to be," she explained, "and I'd record" the show *Sing-Out* "with him," a program that Lloyd produced. Coming full circle, Holly's grade-school teacher would present the show to her class every week. From an early age, Holly was combining musical production and education in a seamless manner, an ideal training process for her adult musical career.

Holly started learning music through the Orff method. Named after German composer Carl Orff, who created the teaching strategy along with his colleague, Gunild Keetman, the Orff method uses a multidisciplinary, play-based approach to learning music. Holly fondly remembers starting out on "xylophones and glockenspiels" at the age of five. She began taking piano lessons at seven and then at twelve fell in love with the French horn. By age seventeen, she was first horn in the Vancouver Youth Orchestra's senior division.

"Along the way, of course," Holly added, "I was always singing folk songs, and I picked up guitar a little bit." After high school, Holly and her boyfriend Simon Kendall formed a "little duo act where we would do Irish rebel songs" in Vancouver's Irish pubs. However, a scholarship from the Koerner Foundation took Holly away from the BC pubs and to Brno, Czechoslovakia, to study French horn under the tutelage of Frantiçek Solz. But she quickly tired of learning among "East European music students" who "had no problem rehearsing" their instruments "for four hours a day." Holly thought to herself, "I don't think I'm gonna cut it here. . . . No, I'm not gonna do this." She spends at least four hours per day on her music, and has done so since childhood, but the intense specialization required for perfecting a single instrument and gaining virtuoso control as a young instrumentalist was not appealing to Holly, whose ambitions ran more toward the creative life of a singer-songwriter.

So Holly came back to the Salish Sea. She first set up camp on Cortes Island in 1974, one of the northern Gulf Islands, situated halfway between Vancouver Island and the BC mainland. On Cortes, Holly became a tree planter. She met Klaus Maiebauer on Cortes, a luthier who built dulcimers. "I heard the dulcimer for the first time, and it was the same as with the French horn," she explained. "It was like a deep internal experience." She compared it to "going into a cathedral." After hearing and then start-ing to play the dulcimer, Holly "had no desire to be a guitar player." She "started writing songs" on Cortes and playing gigs in the local area, in venues like the Whaletown Community Hall. In addition to her own songs, she started performing "Where the Coho Flash Silver (All Over the Bay)," which her father had written just four years earlier. "It's been recorded by lots of artists now," she noted. Holly sang her father's song for me during the afternoon interview, accompanying herself on dulcimer, another beauti-ful musical illustration.

In the late 1970s, Holly recorded "Where the Coho Flash Silver (All Over the Bay)" in her bedroom and sent it out to festivals. She was then hired to perform at the prestigious Winnipeg Folk Festival as well as the Vancouver Folk Festival in 1979 and 1980. That exposure led to Canada Council touring grants that enabled her to showcase her music at venues throughout Canada. During that time, Holly performed solo as well as with a quartet and also did "lots of performing with my dad."

Holly met and married Stephen Foster on Cortes Island. She described Foster as "a builder, and a poet, and an architect." He "had just this fervent love of this place (the Salish Sea), and he had a very highly developed environmental awareness, which I really didn't have at that time." She credits Foster with making her more environmentally aware. He fished his entire life and used fish as "his barometer" for the ecological decline of the Salish Sea. Foster "knew what it was like to go fishing up off Campbell River when the fish were bumping up against the bottom of the boat in the 1950s, and it wasn't that way anymore in the '80s."

Foster saw that Holly's "voice was a way to take out messages about equality" and environmental problems, and that led to Voices of Nature. Unfortunately, there was no way to make a living as an artist on Cortes, so the couple moved down to Vancouver in 1985. They sold the "beautiful handmade property" Foster had built and "invested" most of their money in music and Holly's career. Holly and Stephen sold the place for $90,000 and invested nearly half the proceeds in an LP album titled *Woman in the Mirror*.[7] "We put everything we had into the music," explained Holly, and "tried every possible way to succeed in the music business." "In the late

'80s, I was performing a lot and doing environmental benefits." She compared the way Foster built her career to the way he built homes, starting with an explicit "blueprint to get there," and then described those early days as a performer as like "trying to scale the castle walls of the music industry and just continually getting doused in boiling oil," lamenting that "there was just no way to get over the top." So the couple found another way to make a living through music: the Artist Response Team and Voices of Nature.

ARTIST RESPONSE TEAM

In 1989, Holly and Stephen conceived of the idea for the Artist Response Team. After Holly performed in a number of benefit concerts in the 1980s, the pair decided that something like ART was needed "to support artists and music communicating about the environment." Their first activist performance as ART took place in English Bay. "There was an American nuclear-armed warship in English Bay," explained Holly. "Greenpeace had organized a protest," so Holly, Stephen, and friends took their act onto a sailboat, PA system and all. The "sailors were all up there, and they were just looking at us down there, and they're snapping their fingers." Holly called it "a beautiful, ironic spot." She said that was the birth of the Artist Response Team as "a cultural SWAT team to respond to environmental issues." In other words, ART and the Raging Grannies began in roughly the same place and time, focused on the same anti-nuclear issue.

In 1990, ART produced a tour called "Last Spike" to "draw attention to the shutdown of VIA Rail." Concerts in Victoria, Nanaimo, Duncan, and Courtney brought attention to the need for passenger rail. Meanwhile, Foster "was always raising investment." The tour generated an album, *Last Spike: The Great Canadian Whistlestop Tour*, with high-profile participants like Paul Hyde and Rick Scott.[8] Unfortunately, "not one station would play a song" from the album. "It was a national issue," explained Holly, "because the government was really cutting back on the trains, so we did this tour to say, hey, trains are environmentally sensible." "We don't make decisions about which songs we're gonna add on rotation," explained one local station director. "That decision's made out of Toronto." So Foster went to

Toronto to argue his case. As a result of Foster's efforts, ART "produced a national broadcast campaign," EcoFest, involving "eighty artists recording public service announcements about the environment." ART recruited "six hundred broadcast outlets all over the country" and raised "$375,000 from the government of Canada and corporate sponsors," as well as more than "$1.5 million in in-kind contributions" for the campaign. And that was before Kickstarter and other crowd-funding services existed.

"In the course of doing" the national campaign, Holly also "managed to get a licensing deal with Warner" for an eponymously titled album. Two singles from the CD—"Rushing River" and "Tracktown"—were added to the playlists of "about seventy stations across the country."[9] However, Holly's timing was off. Loreena McKennitt's album came out at the same time, and Warner "had a much bigger financial stake" in McKennitt's album. "Well, there's only so many airplay spots, right?" explained Holly, noting that radio stations were hesitant to "add two female artists such as myself and Loreena in the same week." The situation for women performers is still not great today, but it was even worse in the early 1990s, especially before Sarah McLachlan and other artists succeeded in opening up new spaces for women in North American popular music. However, the chart's loss might have been nature's gain.

VOICES OF NATURE: MUSIC AS ENVIRONMENTAL EDUCATION

The Voices of Nature program is clearly beneficial for everyone involved, from schoolchildren and their parents to sponsors and musicians. Given its success, it is surprising such programs are not more common around the world. The program's advantages for students, instructors, administrators, parents, and musicians are outlined above, but the benefits go beyond the human community to the wider ecosystem and non-human community. Kevin points to a very specific example in the *Salish Sea Handbook for Educators*, noting that the curriculum prepares students for field trips so that kids do not "tromp all over the intertidal zone once they arrive there." Their curriculum takes students through the "seven intertidal zones," including the "eelgrass meadow and the kelp forest," teaching them to appreciate life in the places they visit, and helps them understand how to steward and protect the intertidal ecosystem.

Perhaps funding has been an obstacle to the growth and spread of more such programs. Obtaining funding takes entrepreneurial drive in addition to a good idea and talent. Holly and Kevin keep one eye on project objectives and another on sustaining their effort in the long term. Seemingly small details like presenting every child's name on concert CDs make a difference to the students, their families, the school, and the project's bottom line. The CDs are sold in the community to recoup costs for Voices of Nature, leaving profits for additional school programming. "It was a way of bringing more funding into the arts and schools at a time when" arts programs were experiencing major cuts. In an era of cutbacks, schools desperately needed some way to keep those programs going. "So, ironically," explained Holly, "with the cutbacks to music, this program kinda took off."

In addition to being the audio engineer, videographer, and web designer, Kevin has a rock sensibility that appeals to kids. "He's brought a really strong rock influence into the songs," said Holly, pointing to their popular song "Up Your Watershed" as a tune that motivates kids to become enthusiastic singers and learners. Evidence of that is presented at Ecosong.net, including videos of various school choirs uninhibitedly singing the song onstage along with Holly, Kevin, and The Wilds (formerly the Dream Band) over the past several years.[10] Kevin explained that the song was "inspired by a Sammy Hagar tune called 'Mas Tequila.'"

Kevin referred to his collaboration with Holly as "backgrounds colliding."

They started writing songs together in 2006. Holly had observed Kevin's effect on kids, especially in grades six and seven. His voice and presence "made them cock their heads" and suddenly come alive in the rehearsal room, explained Holly. Kevin brought something new to the project. As ethnographer JoEllen Fisherkeller notes, children are always searching for their "possible selves," adult models representing who and what they might want to emulate some day.[11] Sadly, good models are often missing. Kevin and Voices of Nature are ideally designed to correct the problem chorale scholar Patrick Freer refers to as the "missing male."[12] Young people in school programs, particularly the boys, look at Kevin and see a "possible self" onstage. This makes them more willing to listen to what Holly and Kevin have to teach them.

Kevin and Holly have had the same positive influence in each other's creative lives. As soon as their story hit 2006, the year they started writing together, each took turns bulleting names of songs they had written together since, clearly energized by the music they have created. Holly began piling CDs onto my take-home stack, each one telling a new story about their creative lives and specific collaborations with teachers and kids over the years. Voices of Nature was clearly not plan B for a would-be rock star and folk musician; it is a creatively fulfilling enterprise.

Part of the duo's success has to do with the fact that they do not compose "children's songs." "They're not kids' songs," explained Kevin, "and we don't write them that way at all." They do not worry if some of the song's meaning goes over the heads of younger students. Holly compared kids singing and learning their songs to children singing Christmas carols. "I really didn't understand about frankincense and myrrh," she offers as an example, but "as I got older, I started to understand bits and bits more of what I was singing." "It's really okay to have children sing things that they don't understand totally," she added. "It's actually very good for them." "They learn vocabulary," she explained, and "they get introduced to ideas."

Occasionally The Wilds now see adults who took part in the program as schoolchildren singing along at their concerts. For example, after the band performed in White Rock, British Columbia, recently, a twenty-four-year-old woman came up and said she still knew every word, having taken part in the very first Voices of Nature school program sixteen years ago at Durrance, when she was ten. At the same show, they brought a teenager onto the stage after seeing him mouth all the words to "Up Your Watershed." He, too, had participated in a past program.

The scale of Voices of Nature is somewhat daunting. Two people do most of the background work and pull the production team of scientists, illustrators, and curriculum developers together to produce an integrated set of learning resources. These resources are used in the classroom and combined with two- to three-month music programs, all of which culminate in large community concerts where two hundred to four hundred students perform with Holly, Kevin, and The Wilds. Their community audiences can exceed seven hundred parents, relatives, friends, and community members. These huge concerts feature students, the "decision makers of tomorrow," speaking and singing to adults and "the decision makers of today," as Kevin describes it.

In addition to being very hard work, it is a bit of a balancing act to pull all of that off. Holly explained that "it's very hard to get into schools" and that "it can't be forced." Kevin added that Voices of Nature "can't be political." That balancing act extends to funding as well. Because the program is essentially a free community service for school districts, it requires sponsorship to make it all work.

SPONSORSHIP

Building on Foster's entrepreneurial model, Holly and Kevin continue to tap "untraditional funds for this work." Parks Canada and Fisheries and Oceans Canada were the first agencies to back them, two "federal departments" that "proposed establishing a national marine conservation area in the southern Strait of Georgia." Holly noted that these agencies "realized" that "parents all come to the concerts," making it "a way to reach people with messages about marine conservation that they would really pay attention to." She continued: "They don't read a government brochure, and they don't go to environmental meetings, but they'll pay attention when their kids sing." Holly's point echoes Joe Hill's famous dictum: "A pamphlet, no matter how good, is never read more than once, but a song is learned by heart and repeated over and over."[13] "There's a bunch of working professionals sitting in the audience," explained Holly, "and that's exactly (with whom) they need to communicate. . . . It's not airy-fairy at all; it's demographically justified."

The above vignette is a good window into the negotiation process between artist, audience, and interceding institutions. For example, Holly explains that "field trips can be a scary thing for teachers," and their curriculum makes it a little less so by integrating and facilitating "experiential learning." She noted that *The Salish Sea*, for example, is about "intertidal zones," adding, "Typical pop song material, right?" In other words, Voices of Nature is a complex system connecting sponsors to communities, to schools, to music, to teachers, to local environments, and so on. Nonprofits like the Pacific Salmon Foundation, funded in part by fishing license fees, and the Electronic Products Recycling Association, funded by surcharges on electronic device sales, find in Voices of Nature an ideal forum for getting their messages to the public, as do other public-private consortia like Tire Stewardship BC, which is required by law to use a consumer surcharge on new tire purchases for public education. These and other organizations find Voices of Nature an ideal way to accomplish the sort of hands-on environmental education work that they are in no way equipped to do themselves.

As a result of their hard work and ingenuity, Holly and Kevin have "created a niche" and "gotten to the point where it's like we're not so much the typical starving artist where we're just trying to find the gig." In fact, some sponsors for Voices of Nature have been with the program for thirteen years. "They've really latched on to what we're doing," noted Kevin, "because they have mandates for educational outreach in their fields." Groups like the Habitat Conservation Trust have even funded the duo's preparatory trips through local watersheds. Kevin explained how some conservation organizations had changed in terms of their thinking and budgetary allocations: "These people used to think inside the box where only their money would go into, like I said, hands-on stream restoration projects. Now they're starting to think outside, and their committees are starting to come around, and they're starting to go, 'We really need public support, and we really need public awareness to really help what's going on,' because nobody knows what they're doing. They're doing all this work, spending millions and millions of dollars every year, but the public has no idea."

Nevertheless, the duo are getting somewhat weary of making a living that is so completely tied to sponsorship and the school schedule. As Holly put it, she would like to find a way for their music to earn them a living "in our sleep" as well as onstage. Yet she counts herself fortunate that, "since 1999, we've never had a failure." "We never had a single concert where we've ever come out of it thinking, 'That was a bust. . . . That sucked.'" "I really treasure that, being able to write these songs," she summarized, "and have people like them and be able to perform them." Both recognize how fortunate they are to make music professionally that is also a "social and environmental vehicle for change."

As such, they would like to scale up, and there is something they would like to do with their related Artist Response Team project in particular. "There are a lot of kids out there who are . . . just listening to crap music these days, and it means nothing," said Kevin, noting that the goal was not just expanding the program but extending the message, education, and meaning beyond British Columbia.

Such growth requires clever marketing and promotions. Marketing is "the hardest hurdle for any artist," said Kevin. You can perform in "the wickedest band" with "the greatest songs," he said, but "all of those albums are gonna sit in your closet because you have no marketing and you don't know how to go about doing it." "It gets to the point where you're being like 80 percent admin and 20 percent musician." Yet that is precisely what most starting musicians need to hear. For every musician who achieves escape velocity at an early age, and thus never needs to become "80 percent admin," there are far more artists who have to find some other way to cobble together a living through music. Holly and Kevin provide an innovative and highly successful model for making music that really matters, and making a living doing so.

SETTING AND PLACE IN ENVIRONMENTALIST MUSIC

Kevin explained their songwriting process: "A lot of our songs come from stories, from situations and real-life experiences." In all stories, setting is as important as character and plot. In environmentally themed music, place takes on a particularly important role. That was apparent in each song Holly and Kevin described. For example, "Waiting for Orca" "was born on Malcolm Island," which is located off the "tip of Vancouver Island." Sointula, the main settlement on Malcolm, sits on the southern side of the island. Kevin and Holly were camped on the north side, the Wild Side, when they wrote "Waiting for Orca."[14]

"There's a beach out there, a point kilometers long," said Kevin, that "consists of super-smooth round pebbles that are about that big." He moved his thumb and index finger about three centimeters apart. Holly then walked out of the room and brought in an example, a smooth round pebble from the Wild Side of Malcolm Island. These rocks are important because they make the perfect surface for orcas to rub against each year. Locals call it the "rubbing beach."[15]

Kevin and Holly's friends study orcas on Malcolm Island, setting up tents in order to witness the event as soon as the whales arrive. A few years ago, Kevin and Holly went to the island to help their friends observe the great cetacean massage session. Unfortunately, the whales never arrived, so they wrote the song "Waiting for Orca" instead. In fact, the duo returned in each of the following years, only to be similarly stymied in their attempts to see the storied phenomenon. One hypothesis is that the chinook salmon runs were low in those years, and those are the really big salmon that orcas prefer. The orcas had to expend more energy seeking smaller fish and could not afford the luxury of spending time at the rubbing beach.

"Waiting for Orca" represents an idiosyncratic social activity in a unique place that evokes universal themes, including loss of biodiversity. "That's what you do the whole time" on the rubbing beach, explained Holly. "You're looking out." "You're constantly looking out to see if you can spot them, if they're on their way in," Kevin continued. "Sometimes you see them come in and you see like a whole pod, and you see their dorsal fins going," said Kevin, his voice and excitement rising. "It's like watching soldiers in a line coming toward you." After their first visit, Kevin and Holly donated money for a hydrophone, so the group would not need to rely solely on binoculars to spot the incoming pod. A hydrophone "can pick up orca sounds for about ten kilometers," and when connected to "a little speaker right at the camp," it frees the group from having to constantly scan the horizon.

Kevin and Holly argue that it is important to create art about "iconic species" like the orca, polar bear, gorilla, lion, and grizzly bear so that people have a more visceral sense of what is at stake. Environmental education researchers Erin Barney, Joel Mintzes, and Chiung-Fen Yen agree that "environmental educators" should "consider the plight of individual species" in the classroom, especially "charismatic megafauna." Their research indicates that when done well, the focus on "charismatic megafauna" can arouse the students' interest in environmental science, help teach ecological principles, and encourage better stewardship of ecosystems.[16] However, as they also point out, interest in a species does not always translate into the sort of knowledge that might help preserve species or their habitats: "Although children are interested in diverse animal groups and tend to bond with large conspicuous animals and pets, these attitudes alone do not translate readily into environmentally friendly behavior, nor apparently does instruction that focuses only on knowledge. We suggest that well-financed, carefully crafted, age-appropriate, mass media campaigns targeting specific environmentally friendly behaviors may ultimately contribute more than any other approach."[17] That is positive endorsement of curricula like Voices of Nature, in which connections between environmental science, cultural expression, and "specific environmentally friendly behaviors" are artfully cultivated.

"Waiting for Orca" is an example of using "glocal knowledges" to speak toward global concerns.[18] Just as Robert Livingston argues for turning local-and-global knowledge into "forms of responsibility," Kevin and Holly's song encourages conservation and change, not just spiritual veneration and self-satisfying contemplation. Complexity is retained and polysemy made possible through the song, yet core themes are clearly communicated, including the argument that the sublime wonders of nature should be preserved for future generations of whales and people.

Waiting for Orca

Holly Arntzen and Kevin Wright

Waiting for Orca on a beach so blue
Looking out to Malcolm Point where the fog is rolling through
Can you hear them anywhere?
Can you see them, are they there?
Are they there?

Waiting for Orca on the wild side
Scanning the horizon, eyes open wide
Where do they come from, where do they go?
Why do they come here to rub?
Nobody knows

Chorus:
There are so many things about life that we don't understand
Knowledge and wisdom reside in our hearts and heads and hands

All that lives is holy, everything struggling
To live with man
All we have to do is break through

Waiting for Orca, it's been so long
Remembering how it feels just to hear the song
I can see them . . . so divine
Heading to the beach like soldiers in a line

Chorus

You're the gorillas of the Congo, the white bears of the North
Tigers of the Far East, an iconic hunter of this coast
On the rocks I'm waiting for you, to come back, come back, ohhhhh

Chorus

Related to the question of place, much has been made in the ecocritical humanities of Bruno Latour's "Agency at the Time of the Anthropocene."[19] Latour's article is a somewhat belated recognition in the poststructural humanities that material realities greatly influence how humans think, act, and perceive the world. Our semiotic capacity as a species can fool us into a somewhat solipsistic sense that we are in fact at the center of everything, "constructing" the world in such a way that it can become virtually anything we would make of it. As the world keeps reminding us with various climate-related catastrophes and subtler, slow-burning developments, we are not able to simply create whatever realities we choose. Material conditions and limits often override our abilities to imagine and innovate our way out of problems.

Place exerts agency in a number of ways and in various human discourses. Scientists document threats to species in data and express that information in reports to colleagues. In addition to science, the people of Malcolm Island discuss the matter in terms of memory, folklore, and sense impressions in order to comprehend what is happening to the place they love. We see the agency of place, including its material aspects, in the song "Waiting for Orca." In this case, the composers express the matter with denotative lyrics. Pensive verses float on arpeggiated minors and unresolved sevenths, communicating an anxious wait by the sea. Major chords and a suddenly bright, bouncing melody provide the chorus with a hopeful sense of possibility, signaling the orcas' arrival. The underlying rhythms similarly move from expectation to celebration, ending with a final lesson regarding what is needed to make the ecstatic chorus and return of the orca a reality.

Each of these song elements resulted from a human choice and was based on observations drawn from human perception. The song is communicated using human languages, both verbal and musical. Nevertheless, there is something there, in the originally referenced space of the rubbing beach, that informs the song and communicates to listeners. There is a material context and a narrative setting that matter.

Granted, it is not a simple and linear process. This thing we call "nature" does not dictate what humans do and think. There is no teleological power in the Earth or Gaia waiting for us to obey her quiet commands. Woody Guthrie's dam music serves as evidence that how we conceive of place matters a great deal. We change place. We can make radically different, even oppositional discourses out of the same material context. Guthrie's Columbia is different from that perceived and plowed by a large landholder, mapped by a government agent, or fished by an indigenous resident.

Nor are our nature discourses neutral in regard to how we, in turn, treat the nonhuman world. To go back to Guthrie's Columbia Pacific Northwest case, the choice of whether or not to dam the Columbia River has had radical impacts on salmon, people, and the entire ecosystem. What we do now to solve environmental problems is similarly a matter of debate. For example, Holly and Kevin disagree with me over what to do about climate change and threatened salmon populations. They support what they describe as "an ocean pasture restoration project" undertaken in Haida Gwaii, British Columbia, a project that I find objectionable. Here is their explanation of the project:

> We undertook the 40 Million Salmon Can't Be Wrong project to draw attention to the connection between the decline of our wild salmon runs on the west coast, and the depleted state of plankton pastures in the open ocean. The Haida Salmon Restoration Corporation (HSRC) did an experiment in 2012 to attempt to restore plankton pastures in the ocean west of Haida Gwaii, BC. It became highly controversial, and the project got shut down before the results of the experiment could ever be published. We felt

that the controversy obscured the important issues: (1) we have loaded a vast amount of CO_2 into the atmosphere, which is having a lethal effect on oceans, plankton, and all ocean life; (2) we have damaged and destroyed open ocean ecosystems; (3) we have a sacred responsibility to restore what we have damaged; (4) we need to invest in urgent research to understand what is happening in ocean pastures; (5) people need to become educated about the role of oceans in our land-based lives. Those 40 million sockeye that returned to the Fraser in 2010 are the best scientists of all: when conditions are good, they thrive and return in great numbers; when conditions are bad, they don't come back. That is scientific evidence about which we understand very little; there may be answers there that will help us to develop solutions and bring back the fish.

However, in no way does our disagreement over ocean pasture restoration through iron fertilization keep me from believing that the overwhelming majority of Holly and Kevin's efforts have been place-positive, connecting kids to sound science and information that can help them carefully steward the places where they live.[20]

In that ecological system connecting people to place, place has its say. Sabine Feisst notes that composer John Luther Adams is "guided by a vivid musical imagination and moral strength nourished by the extraordinary landscapes of Alaska."[21] The words "nourished by" artfully capture the ethical relationship between composer and place. Similarly, songs like "Waiting for Orca" are nourished by places like the rubbing beach of Malcolm Island.

In turn, place is re-created, in some small part, through music. Neither I nor other listeners can now visit Malcolm Island or think about it without our conception of that specific place being informed by "Waiting for Orca," and that act of creation has ethical consequences. In the case of "Waiting for Orca," I believe those consequences to be very positive. Much like a Voices of Nature student treading more softly in the intertidal zone, visitors to Malcolm Island who have "Waiting for Orca" as their mental soundtrack are more likely to understand, appreciate, and protect the "wild side" of the island for future generations of people and whales. Holly and Kevin's beautiful song helps make place sacred, giving it new voice in the human community. The value of music like "Waiting for Orca" lies not merely in its ability to draw upon the aesthetic virtues of place, spiritual benefits, or profit-generating potential. Among its other virtues, "Waiting for Orca" reminds us to listen more closely to the sound of whales rubbing rocks; in other words, to hear the music of place.

NOTES

1. Sticking with the policy of referring to my informants by first names, I will do so here. However, I alternate between referring to Stephen Foster as "Stephen" and "Foster," depending on whether the narrative is mainly from Holly's and Kevin's perspective (that of his friends) or my own exposition of information in the abstract. It is inappropriate for me to refer to him by his first name, not having known him, whereas when presented in relation to Holly and Kevin, it is more respectful to represent Mr. Foster as their friend and colleague, Stephen.

2. Nooksack Salmon Enhancement Association, "Education," accessed January 6, 2015, http://www.n-sea.org/educational-programs-1/students-for-salmon.

3. *Salish Sea*, Holly Arntzen and the Saltwater Singers, Artist Response Team, 2000.

4. Joel Bennett, "Turk and the Rat," YouTube video, accessed July 31, 2015, https://www.youtube.com/watch?v=aT5Y1uDu1io.

5. *Running from the Mountains*, Holly Arntzen and the Watershed Choir, Artist Response Team, 1999.

6. "Where the Coho Flash Silver (All Over the Bay)," Lloyd Arntzen, The British Columbia Folklore Society, accessed July 31, 2015, http://folklore.bc.ca/where-the-coho-flash-silver/.

7. *Woman in the Mirror*, Holly Arntzen, Artist Response Team, 1986.

8. *Last Spike: The Great Canadian Whistlestop Tour*, various artists, Artist Response Team, 1990.

9. *Holly Arntzen*, Holly Arntzen, Artist Response Team, 1991.

10. "Up Your Watershed," Holly Arntzen and Kevin Wright with the Dream Band, Artist Response Team, 2010, YouTube video, accessed August 3, 2015, https://www.youtube.com/watch?v=mogHCWnWjxY; "Up Your Watershed," Holly Arntzen and Kevin Wright with the Dream Band, Artist Response Team, 2011, YouTube video, accessed August 3, 2015, https://www.youtube.com/watch?v=g3kVAAkVdLU; and "Up Your Watershed," The Wilds, Artist Response Team, 2012, YouTube video, accessed August 3, 2015, https://www.youtube.com/watch?v=D77cH62OqXI.

11. JoEllen Fisherkeller, "Everyday Learning about Identities among Young Adolescents in Television Culture," *Anthropology & Education Quarterly* 28, no. 4 (1997): 467–492.

12. Patrick K. Freer, "Two Decades of Research on Possible Selves and the 'Missing Males' Problem in Choral Music," *International Journal of Music Education* 28, no. 1 (2010): 17–30.

13. Gibbs M. Smith, *Joe Hill* (Salt Lake City, UT: Peregrine Smith Books, 1984), 19.

14. "Waiting for Orca," The Wilds, Artist Response Team, 2013, YouTube video, accessed August 3, 2015, https://www.youtube.com/watch?v=egFNKcUoXTc.

15. It is not known exactly why Northern Resident Killer Whales rub their bellies on rocky shores. Because that behavior is mostly restricted to these whales, it is widely believed to be a learned social behavior and not one with other physiological functions such as dealing with parasites. See R. Williams et al., "Stimulus-Dependent Response to

Disturbance Affecting the Activity of Killer Whales," *Scientific Committee of the International Whaling Commission, Document: SC/63/WW5* (2011): 3.

16. Erin C. Barney, Joel J. Mintzes, and Chiung-Fen Yen, "Assessing Knowledge, Attitudes, and Behavior toward Charismatic Megafauna: The Case of Dolphins," *Journal of Environmental Education* 36, no. 2 (2005): 54.

17. Ibid., 53.

18. Robert Eric Livingston, "Glocal Knowledges: Agency and Place in Literary Studies," *Publications of the Modern Language Association of America* (2001): 145–157.

19. Bruno Latour, "Agency at the Time of the Anthropocene," *New Literary History* 45, no. 1 (2014): 1–18.

20. The following references provide context on the referenced project, including works that both support and criticize it: Sonia D. Batten and James FR Gower, "Did the Iron Fertilization Near Haida Gwaii in 2012 Affect the Pelagic Lower Trophic Level Ecosystem?" *Journal of Plankton Research* 36, no. 4 (2014): 925–932; D. Biello, "Can Controversial Ocean Iron Fertilization Save Salmon?" *Scientific American*, October, 24, 2012, http://www.scientificamerican.com/article/fertilizing-ocean-with-iron-to-save-salmon-and-earn-money/; H. J. Buck, "Village Science Meets Global Discourse: The Haida Salmon Restoration Corporation's Ocean Iron Fertilization Experiment," 2014, https://geoengineeringourclimate.files.wordpress.com/2014/01/buck-2014-village-science-meets-global-discourse-click-for-download.pdf; CBC News, "Volcanic Eruption Led to BC Salmon Boom: Scientist," October 25, 2010, accessed August 16, 2015, http://www.cbc.ca/news/technology/volcanic-eruption-led-to-b-c-salmon-boom-scientist-1.890331; Henry Fountain, "A Rogue Climate Experiment Outrages Scientists," *New York Times*, October 18, 2012, accessed July 29, 2015, http://www.nytimes.com/2012/10/19/science/earth/iron-dumping-experiment-in-pacific-alarms-marine-experts.html?_r=0.; Russ George blog, http://russgeorge.net/; Haida Salmon Restoration Corporation, http://www.haidasalmonrestoration.com/; Martin Lukacs, "World's Biggest Geoengineering Experiment 'Violates' UN Rules," *Guardian*. October 15, 2012, accessed July 29, 2015, http://www.theguardian.com/environment/2012/oct/15/pacific-iron-fertilisation-geoengineering; Jeff Tollefson, "Ocean-Fertilization Project Off Canada Sparks Furor," *Nature* 490, no. 7421 (2012): 458–459, http://www.nature.com/news/ocean-fertilization-project-off-canada-sparks-furore-1.11631; Charles G. Trick et al., "Iron Enrichment Stimulates Toxic Diatom Production in High-Nitrate, Low-Chlorophyll Areas," *Proceedings of the National Academy of Sciences* 107, no. 13 (2010): 5887–5892; Robert Zubrin, "The Pacific's Salmon Are Back, Thank Human Ingenuity," *National Review*, April 22, 2014, accessed March 26, 2016, http://www.nationalreview.com/article/376258/pacifics-salmon-are-back-thank-human-ingenuity-robert-zubrin.

21. Sabine Feisst, "Music as Place, Place as Music: The Sonic Geography of John Luther Adams," in Bernd Herzogenrath, ed., *The Farthest Place: The Music of John Luther Adams* (Lebanon: University Press of New Hampshire, 2012), 47.

FIGURE 6.1

The Irthlings: Sharon Abreu and Michael Hurwicz. The Irthlings;
used by permission.

6

Orcas Island's Irthlingz

Community Art as Activism

Sharon Abreu's *The Climate Monologues* is a community-based performance combining music, spoken word, and art. Based on the stories of real people, *The Climate Monologues* brings global climate change down to a human scale. Sharon seeks to raise awareness of climate change through her performance of the piece.

On June 6, 2014, I watched Sharon perform *The Climate Monologues* in Anacortes, Washington. It was a remarkable evening, not just for the quality of the performance, but also for the way in which music, spoken word, visual art, and community organizing blended together, without activism overwhelming art or vice versa.

The Anacortes show came about when Sharon answered a call for coal-related art, a serendipitous opportunity. She had been working on *The Climate Monologues* for several years. The Anchor Art Space was planning an exhibit called *Coal* to showcase work by area artists interpreting the Cherry Point coal terminal plan, the same initiative Dana Lyons is fighting with his Great Coal Train Tour (chap. 1). Sharon proposed her show in order to bring live performance into the visual art exhibit.

Anacortes is a small town on the edge of the mainland and the launching point for ferries to the San Juan Islands, Washington, and to Sydney, British Columbia, on Vancouver Island. Like Bellingham, Anacortes is a hub of opposition to the proposed coal terminal at Cherry Point. The city has a troubled environmental history, experiencing both the benefits and disadvantages of having two oil refineries in town. Both are easily visible from downtown Anacortes, about a mile across Fidalgo Bay, disgorging white smoke into the air most of the day.

Recently, a group of residents started protesting rail shipments to the refineries, going so far as to chain themselves to the train tracks in 2014.[1] The Seattle gaggle of the Raging Grannies blockaded the entrance to the Washington Department of Ecology in solidarity with the Anacortes protesters.[2] Opposition to the proposed Cherry Point coal terminal is fueled by new information as well as decades of experience dealing directly with large energy companies like Tesoro and Shell, which currently own Anacortes's refineries.

Local fears of environmental degradation have been reinforced by data provided by environmental scientists, activists, and educators. However, few people are mobilized by science, so community organizers are increasingly drawing on artists like Sharon to communicate ideas and information to people in more direct and visceral ways.[3]

MAKING *THE CLIMATE MONOLOGUES*

Moved by a combination of "external irritation" and "inspiration,"[4] Sharon interviewed people whose lives and families have been adversely affected by climate change and carbon-based pollution (e.g., coal mining). She specifically sought out "stories of people" who are fighting back. Those interviews became the raw material for monologue-and-song pairings, each presented from the perspective of an informant. "Songs jumped out of the stories," explained Sharon. Brief clips are available at Ecosong.net, although the media available do not always do full justice to the live experience of community-based art, both because of the social-media production values and because co-presence is so essential to the musical experience in shows like *The Climate Monologues*.

The following monologue and song are based on the story of Maria Gunnoe from Bobwhite, West Virginia:

The town that I live in is called "Bobwhite." It wasn't named after a man; it was named after a bird. The cliffs on the back side of my property is where the bobwhite quails nested at. When the birds would call through the morning and through the evening, you could hear 'em throughout the valley. It echoed. It sounded like twenty birds was calling instead of one. It's been probably close to fifteen years now since I've even heard a bobwhite quail. This is the most biodiverse region in the United States, second on the globe, you know, and we're blowin' it up.

My grandfather and my family before me worked as underground union coal miners. And it was very hard for me to begin organizing against coal because coal had always been such a source of pride in our family. Coal is the basis of the whole economy here in West Virginia, and they very much control the employment here. There's one area that we're working on right now to preserve that is viable for wind energy. That's jobs forever and it's renewable energy, clean energy. And the coal company wants to blow the mountain up. If they blow the mountain up, it's no longer wind viable. So, you know, I mean, this is permanent. It's permanent if they blow up that mountain, and it's permanent if we put windmills on it.

For more than a hundred years now, there's been a massive taking from the people of central Appalachia. The prosperity is showin' up on Wall Street, but when you look at the places here where this coal was being extracted, prosperity is not what comes to mind.

I've lived on this property myself forty-one years, all my life. As a kid, I spent my life playin' in the stream that runs through this property. In 2000, the West Virginia Department of Environmental Protection permitted this stream to be what they called a national pollution discharge elimination system. Now, they don't openly call it that. They call it an NPDES stream 'cause it sounds so nice. But once I investigated and found out what this meant, it was like, "Oh my goodness!" There's toxic levels of selenium in the stream that runs through my property now. I didn't have a say in that process. You know, we have a functional farm, and throughout my life we've raised our own meat. We've raised our own gardens. And when your groundwater, your aquifer, becomes polluted, you can't do that anymore. You can't raise healthy gardens or healthy cattle. People's water is being polluted, by the coal companies, and it's silent. People know nothing of it until they start having health impacts.

This is the headwaters of the drinkin' water, throughout the southeastern United States. This is not just mine and my kids. It runs by my house but this is where it starts at. It runs from here into the Kanawha and into the Ohio and into the Gulf. Exactly how many people are drinking the water that runs by my house? I often wonder that. I've lost friends that I went to school with from cancer. My fifteen-year-old daughter just last year lost a classmate to cancer. The process that coal starts with is what makes it dirtiest of all.

The coal industry has done everything possible to try an' clean up their public image, and that is very much what they're doing when they say "clean coal." The experts that I have talked to concernin' clean coal and carbon sequestration say it's a mad science experiment gone bad, that we'll invest hundreds of millions of dollars into this idea, and 'not a proven technology. We know that wind is clean, sustainable, renewable, and available. We should put our money towards that.

I see global warming as being a reason for people to start realizing the impacts of our energy usage. As a country, we do not recognize our impact on our children's future. If I knew that my life was sustained by taking my children's last drink o' water, I wouldn't take it. And that's exactly what we're doin'. We are taking our children's future away from them.

Bobwhite
I long to hear the Bobwhite song.
I haven't heard it in so long.
With ev'ry ridge they blast away,
I walk these ancient woods and pray:
Let the waters run clean,
Let our kids grow up fine,
Let us harness the wind
As we close those killin' mines.

I listen for the Bobwhite song,
Calling out to live free.
Heal his wings and lift us up
From this toxic poverty.

Together I know we can right this wrong,
And we will hear again the Bobwhite song.[5]

To picture the performance, imagine an ethnographic performer like Anna Deavere Smith breaking into song after each of her interview-based monologues. When Sharon first told me about *The Climate Monologues*, I wondered if doing that was a good idea, having a hard time imagining how one could meld songs and monologues into the same piece without it all devolving into bad musical theater. I wondered if Smith's subjects in *Twilight: Los Angeles* would come alive through song, or if musical performance would just detract from the serious social realist performance.[6] Can serious subjects be communicated through musical theater? I had to attend the show to find out.

It was not that I doubted Sharon's musical talent, not in the least. I had heard her sing on other occasions and knew her to be an extremely talented vocalist. Sharon is half of the duo Irthlingz. I first heard the Irthlingz perform on Orcas Island. Sharon and her partner Michael Hurwicz sang a combination of original songs and folk tunes, with a few classical pieces thrown in for good measure. Her classically trained voice works well with Michael's stand-up bass and baritone harmonies. She also brings a range of instruments to the duo, most often acoustic guitar. They tour on occasion and have performed with world-renowned figures like Pete Seeger, who described Sharon's voice as "beautiful."[7] So her voice and musical talent are certainly up to the task.

Nevertheless, I had doubts about the basic concept when first hearing about the show. I attended *The Climate Monologues* with skeptical ears, having hit other dead ends during that dry period in the research. I had been looking for promising cases of environmentalist music around the Salish Sea only to find several very earnest local performances that were too amateurish to warrant case studies and inclusion in the book. That is not to denigrate those performances, which will remain unnamed, but rather to say that I found too little in them to justify further exploration and writing. If the goals of the research were to locate performers and ideas that might inform and inspire other musicians, environmental activists, organizers, music scholars, and anyone else interested in environmentalist art, I was not finding much at the time. I feared that my ferry ride to Anacortes might be yet another dead end for the purposes of this project. I was very wrong.

PERFORMING *THE CLIMATE MONOLOGUES*

About a half hour before the show was scheduled to start, Sharon and Michael sat eating ice cream on the porch stoop, chatting to friends and passersby as if they had nothing else to do that afternoon. There was no green room, just the performer sitting on a broad porch as a steady stream of people entered the Anchor Art Space. Some of the guests nodded to Sharon, others exchanged a few words. For Sharon, community audiences are friends and neighbors, not fans, and she treats them accordingly. From arrival to departure, there was no pretense of separation between performer and community.

Inside, art by local painters and sculptors hung on the walls of a large, whitewashed room. The integration of visual and musical art elevated the *Coal/Climate Monologues* experience that evening. By simply looking out the windows, one could see the problems referenced by each work: forested swaths of mountainside next to clear-cuts, oil refinery smokestacks towering above ancient Douglas firs, clear waters roiling underneath oily sheens left by motorized tugs, ships, and pleasure craft. Some of the art in the *Coal* exhibit referred directly to the negative impacts of fossil fuels, while the rest imagined Anacortes as a relatively idyllic ecosystem, as it was before industrial development or as it could be in a low-carbon economy. Sharon later told me that she believes "music is a way to envision and bring about a healed world."[8] That is clearly what the visual artists were trying to achieve with the *Coal* exhibit as well.

After viewing the exhibit and sampling baked goods, the audience occupied several rows of seats set diagonally across the open room. Several in the overflow crowd had to stand and sit along the sides and back. It was a great turnout. In addition to social media, terrestrial radio helped Sharon get word out about the performance. Four days earlier, on June 2, 2014, KBAI, Bellingham's "progressive talk" radio station, presented an interview with Sharon on *The Joe Show* at noon.

Before Sharon began the Anacortes show, two leaders of Power Past Coal introduced their coalition and presented their views on the coal terminal issue. Most of the audience appeared to be sympathetic to the group's aims. Sharon then performed from a brightly lit corner at the front of the room, as if sitting in a living room with friends.

In addition to Gunnoe, Sharon's characters include Lea Bossler of Missoula, Montana; Hunter Lovins of Boulder, Colorado; Robert Athickal from Patna, India; and Ed Wiley of Rock Creek, West Virginia. *The Climate Monologues* is a contemplative, cathartic, and catalytic work of art. For example, Ed Wiley describes how his granddaughter, Kayla, and her classmates began exhibiting strange symptoms as mountaintop removal mining took place near their Marsh Fork Elementary School. So Ed took action. The implicit message to the audience is this: Follow Ed's example. If Ed can do it, so can we.

Contrary to my pre-show skepticism, *The Climate Monologues* is not musical theater in the conventional sense but rather an attempt—and I think a very successful one—to communicate the fuller emotional meaning of people's climate stories through song. *The Climate Monologues* provided Sharon's Anacortes audience with new ways of understanding and dealing with climate change, bringing it down from a global abstraction to human scale, featuring people, woods, waters, and refineries in and around towns not unlike Anacortes. Although the subjects of *The Climate Monologues* live far from Anacortes, the audience could relate well to their familiar struggles.

The piece appeared to have a cathartic effect on the audience, based on their rapt attention and hearty applause. Yet none of Sharon's monologues and songs provide easy answers. Once again, it is catalytic art. *The Climate Monologues* is designed to get people talking, thinking, and working creatively toward community-based solutions.

The Anacortes *Coal* event illustrates the value of community-based art. Although musicians with distribution deals and global circulation can reach far more ears worldwide, they cannot communicate with the familiarity and intimacy of those who live among their audience. *The Climate Monologues* is a model example of thinking globally and performing locally. National and global stars do the reverse. They draw on local symbols to empower global practices, using place-associated genres, styles, and identities to market themselves in a global music industry: West Coast rappers, Detroit hip-hop, London punks, Nashville country singers, and so on. Such artists might be from a given "music scene," but their globalized musical practice turns places of origin into floating signifiers rather than places of deep community engagement. Place is part of the origin story, persona, and mythology for the national or global star, but rarely part of daily life and performance. There is nothing wrong with that, but it is important to draw a distinction between place-associated stars, on one hand, and place-based community artists like Sharon.

An artist needs to be deeply integrated into place to achieve the level of influence Lyons or the Irthlingz experience in their local communities.

Star performers ignite local interest as they pass through, but local artists more consistently help their communities to contemplate shared challenges, gain a voice, and work creatively toward solutions. They are more akin to "cultural workers" in that sense than are the national and international touring acts many of us listen to on our iPhones or pay to see in concert. In the local shows of place-based musicians, one witnesses "communities in their making."[9] Art, activism, and community are mutually enhanced when local art and community work together, as I believe they did during the Anacortes performance. We create better places together, whether that means a place with less pollution, greater access to healthful food, or some other common good. However, that does not just happen spontaneously. Therefore, one of the main goals of this chapter is to dissect the successful *Coal* event so that those of us who live, work, and perform elsewhere might borrow ideas and inspiration from the case.

Sharon drew direct inspiration from Eve Ensler's *The Vagina Monologues*. Years ago, she performed in a production of the pathbreaking show and was inspired to do a similar service for climate change. Specifically, Sharon performed "Reclaiming Cunt," "a poetic, fun, and beautiful monologue about taking back this word that originally was not at all a dirty word." That performance moved her to write *Reclaiming Compassion* following the 9/11 attacks. That then led to *The Climate Monologues*. She has "been doing climate change education since 2000," when it occurred to her that climate change "was like *The Vagina Monologues*" in that environmental crisis "is something that people don't want to talk about."

As for Sharon's music, several musicians have influenced the Irthlingz. Pete Seeger made a lasting impression on Michael and Sharon early on. As a young child, Michael first heard Seeger over the loudspeakers at a record store. He was shopping with his mother in Minneapolis's "Dinkytown" neighborhood when a track from Seeger's *American Industrial Ballads* album began playing.[10] The seven-year-old Minnesotan begged his mother to buy the album and proceeded to learn every song. Michael was "really touched" by the "grief and the anger and the hope that was in those songs." Seeger was one of the reasons Michael became a folk musician. Later, he learned about Seeger's Clearwater project, which further inspired his environmental music and activism.

In addition to *The Vagina Monologues*, Sharon drew on her experience as a trade union delegate in creating *The Climate Monologues*. In 1998, she was "hired to sing for a trade union during the [United Nations] Commission on Sustainable Development." It suddenly struck her that as a member of the North American Traveling Musicians Union, she and her compatriots were experiencing a deep dilemma, one that most musicians had simply ignored: "We have our own issues with fossil fuels, as you might imagine, and that's something I would really like to have a very vibrant discussion about." Sharon tried to get the conversation started "online a few years ago" with the union's "discussion group," but "it just didn't really go anywhere." Not all communities are ready to consider the problem.

That has not stopped the Irthlingz from doing something about climate change. The duo made a conscious choice to limit their touring in order to reduce fossil fuel use. They still conduct occasional short tours, or "tourlettes," as they call them, a term they borrowed from Charlie King. They were able to shrink their most recent tour so that they, their instruments, and their equipment could all be jammed into a Prius.[11]

The main way the Irthlingz minimize waste is by minimizing touring. It might have been easier for the Irthlingz to give up musical travel than it is for most musicians. They do not have a strong desire to travel. Sharon described touring, a financial necessity for many musicians, as "uprooting," noting that "every other day you're in a completely different city and a completely different place." "Uprooting," as she puts it, works against the Irthlingz's place-based ethic. Politically and ecologically, the Irthlingz prefer to focus on the community in which they live rather than lead a mobile, transient existence. The Irthlingz's ecological consciousness is rooted in the San Juan Islands and the Salish Sea region, more generally. Whereas Lyons has found clever ways to tour and still take root locally, the Irthlingz offer another creative response. *The Climate Monologues* was in part an answer to the touring problem. Sharon asked one of the most difficult questions when planning her musical future: "How can we do this so it's not so consumptive?" Her answer was a one-woman show presented mostly around the Salish Sea region.

At the same time, Sharon notes that touring helps circulate new music and new ideas. Therefore, she still experiences a tension between the desire to make music sustainably and the longing for musical exchange. She argues that "face-to-face" contact remains essential to the musical experience. "In 2006, I met this delegation of folks that came from Appalachia," she explains. "They came from Kentucky and West Virginia to talk about the struggle they were going through with mountaintop removal coal mining." Two of her most moving songs and monologues came from that encounter.

The Climate Monologues also allows Sharon to take advantage of her classical voice training. That preparation involved becoming a voice major at New York University, where she graduated magna cum laude. Subsequent work in opera allowed her to perfect her vocal skills. Sharon provides singing lessons and believes that all voices are worth listening to. For community musicians, the real tragedy is that people do not sing together, not that some have less developed vocal skills.[12] Although she is formally trained, Sharon argues that one does not need to be a trained opera singer in order to sing beautifully or sing with others.

Sharon does not think of herself as an outsider performing the words of southeastern coal miners. Instead, *The Climate Monologues* is the result of an intimate conversation among "neighbors." "We are 300 million neighbors in this country," she notes. Rather than worry about representation or misrepresentation, she argues that the "biggest thing we have in common is we're *not* being represented." "Our government is broken," she explains. "There's too much weight, too much money in the process, and we are not being represented." *The Climate Monologues* presents marginalized voices that, in turn, represent entire communities. Sharon does not speak or sing *for* her informants but rather considers herself to be speaking *with* them.

For Sharon, the meaning of the monologues began to change as related issues hit home in Washington. At first, she thought, "Coal is not a big deal for us in Washington State." "We have other issues," she thought, "like transportation." However, an invitation to perform *The Climate Monologues* for the Washington State Department of Ecology led her to realize that the work was not just about concerns 2,500 miles away. After the invitation was issued, two department officials called Sharon in quick succession to "make sure there's nothing political in this show." "Well, let me give you an example," she replied. "I'm doing this monologue for this woman in West Virginia who's fighting coal." The Department of Ecology official responded, "Oh, you can't talk about coal." "Well, then I can't do my show," said Sharon, and she didn't. That vignette is a good example of how the ecopolitical musician gives the term "suffering artist" new meaning. As if it were not hard enough to find gigs, Sharon's ethical strictures limit the possibilities for paid performance considerably. A similar story of sacrifice runs throughout the cases in this book.

A short while after the Department of Ecology rescinded Sharon's invitation, it announced its plan for the Gateway Pacific coal export terminal at Cherry Point. Suddenly it became clear to Sharon why the department was nervous about the coal content in her performance. The plan would bring massive coal ships across the Salish Sea and past the southern and eastern edges of the San Juan Islands, where the Irthlingz live and perform. That issue gave renewed meaning and purpose to *The Climate Monologues*.

For Sharon, the main objective of *The Climate Monologues* "is to communicate on the heart level," because "the mind alone is not enough." "Why haven't we gotten where we need to go?" she asks. In addition to "big money," she argues, part of the blame lies in our failure to put climate science into a language that people can relate to on the human level. She hopes that *The Climate Monologues* will help "inspire understanding, compassion, empathy" for those who are most immediately and directly affected.

COMMUNITY MUSIC AS ENVIRONMENTAL ACTIVISM

The Anchor Art Space *Coal/Climate Monologues* combination made for an electric evening that left the audience energized. In addition to discussions over where to catch dinner, the room buzzed with debates over the best artworks and references to the coal terminal controversy. The looming presence of Peabody Energy and its creditors fueled an evening of synergistic art, music, and community.

Of course, community does not just happen. It takes a great deal of collaboration, time, and hard work. The Irthlingz see their performances in that light, as cultural work. Sharon describes her audience as "normal, average, everyday people," bringing home the point that her neighbors "did not pop out of the womb being activists." Something has to inspire people to take action.

People often say to Sharon, "Oh, you're an activist." Does that mean some people are "inactivists," she wonders? She argues that activists-versus-others is a spurious distinction. Everyone is active, all the time. Furthermore, all actions are political, just to different degrees and toward different goals. Therefore, when an acquaintance told Sharon, "Oh, I'm not into the environment," she replied, "Well, you are, whether you know it or not."

The Irthlingz have been "into the environment" since their respective childhoods but only began working together in the late 1990s after meeting at a "lefty" hangout in New York City, the People's Voice Café. The two then set about producing "a musical environmental show" in 1998. They performed their show throughout the New York public school system, supported by the Brooklyn Arts Council and good friends at the Clearwater project. Their show "had to meet the New York State academic standards for science" in order to be performed in classrooms. Once again, community connections made all the difference. The Irthlingz's partnerships with local arts councils and schools served them well in New York, a lesson they brought to their work in Washington State, although their rural residence provides far fewer opportunities for professional networking than are available to artists based in urban areas.

Fortunately, the Irthlingz do not require music in order to make a living. Not being dependent on music for their entire income allows them to be more selective when choosing gigs. For example, a few weeks before I interviewed Sharon about *The Climate Monologues*, the Irthlingz performed at an alternative energy conference on Orcas Island. Visiting scientists, academics, and entrepreneurs enjoyed having relevant musical entertainment at the conference, telling the pair that they added extra "energy" to the event. A musician who depends on live performances for the entirety of his or her income might not be able to take on small contracts like that and would have to pass up good gigs that pay less than corporate events and weddings.

Sharon feels that music humanizes environmentalist messages, allowing oppositional audiences to hear them without becoming overly defensive. She believes that music, so employed, can promote meaningful dialogue within a community. That ethic was in evidence when Sharon sang her testimony at a local scoping hearing on the Cherry Point coal terminal proposal. She converted the song "Sixteen Tons" into a tune about carbon emissions.[13] Showing the same ingenuity at the Paddle in Seattle protest, she made up the song "Shell No" on the spot as others joined in.

Sharon notes that even protest organizers sometimes say, "Oh, we don't have time for a song." "They think they don't have time for it," notes Sharon, "but what they don't realize is that those three minutes [of music] will make a big difference in the entire energy of the whole event." Yet, as Michael pointed out in the same interview, "I've been at several things lately where I said if it had been half as long, it would have been twice as good." Including art in protest is not always the same thing as "artful protest," but a few minutes of song might be worth as much as an hour of dry speeches.

Like Lyons, Sharon views music done well as a means of reaching out to new audiences, including those who are afraid of losing their jobs: "I've had people come up to me just seething, because they see me as an environmental person as looking to take away their jobs working at the coal plant for a good wage or a union wage." Sharon sees that common challenge as an opening for dialogue and emphasizes listening over preaching when confronted in that manner. Perhaps music is good training for community activism in that regard. The musician learns to listen to other musicians rather than play, sing, or speak at others. Sharon is a particularly skillful listener.

Sharon has trained with Eban Goodstein, author of *The Trade-Off Myth: Fact and Fiction about Jobs and the Environment*.[14] Like Goodstein, she argues that jobs too often become a wedge, forestalling community deliberation around matters of environmental stewardship. In line with Goodstein's thesis, she finds authentic dialogue more effective than blasting information at an ostensible opposition, a Freirean ethic of community education and participation.

Michael explained the matter of musical activism a bit differently, reminding us that people have very different priorities:

> If I wasn't working on these issues through music, I really wouldn't be working on them, because music is what connects me to the world. . . . I mean, I'd be signing petitions online and writing to my congressmen and stuff like that. I'd be a participating citizen, but I wouldn't call that an

activist. So for me, the ability to do it through music [is important]. . . . It connects me to myself and it connects me to other people. And if I hadn't happened to stumble into this particular type of music, I'd be doing some other kind of music. . . . Music is what allows me to do this work. And it allows me to communicate on a larger scale.

Michael provided an important insight and reminder, that the question is not just a matter of how activists "use" music, as if the activist identity were primordial, but rather a matter of how musicians perform politics. Many musicians consider their status, role, and identity as a "musician" to be an inextricable part of who they are and what they do. As such, whatever they do, they will do it as a musician, not someone "using" music for some other, more fundamental purpose.

Michael's point led me to wonder if the practice I have been describing throughout this book as "musical activism" would be more accurately represented as "activist musicianship." It might actually matter which word is qualifier and which is qualified. The term "musical activism" turns music into a method, whereas with "activist musicians," the qualified word, "musicians," is the more fundamental identity. Michael's core identity is that of "musician." He is a musician who uses his art and identity to engage ethically with the world. That is different from a person whose central identity is, instead, "activist," someone for whom music becomes one way of communicating his or her core political principles and identity. It is an important distinction, because it reminds us that most of the people profiled in this book are not activists who strategically pick up an instrument or sing in order to further their environmentalist goals but rather musicians who, as musicians, would bring their art to bear regardless of the topic or context. While it is never a simple either/or proposition, one identity, musician, tends to be more integral to these artists' sense of self. They are musicians who, as it so happens, dedicate their art to environmental activism (among other things).

In other ways, the question of what one does with either music and/or activism matters more than which of the dual identities dominates. Musical activism or activist music can be done well or poorly, depending on the context and goals. For example, Michael argues that we have to beware of becoming "prophets of misery or doom," a matter of environmentalist rhetoric and genre that transcends musical communication. The Irthlingz use music to inspire catharsis, humor, and hope, a theme that runs throughout the cases in this book and therefore an orientation that most successful cases of environmentalist musicianship seem to have in common.

Musical humor is "medicinal," added Sharon, citing *Monty Python's Flying Circus* and *Saturday Night Live* as seminal influences: "So I just have to laugh. I'm an opera singer, and I have laughed through operas that are not funny—no comic relief—not through the whole thing, but at certain point I just start laughing, 'cause it's just too tragic and I can't take it. So for me it has to be fun, and that's the whole thing behind Clearwater. That's celebration. It's about coming together, celebrating what we have done, what we can do, who we are—and why not? It changes our energy. It gives us energy." Therefore, Sharon finds it "tragic" that so many people think they "can't sing." She notes that this often stems from people being told at an early age that they cannot sing. Once again, she believes that there is musicality in everyone and that expressing oneself is essential. Despite her advanced operatic training, Sharon takes the opposite approach of musicians who rely on exclusivity to legitimate their musicianship. She considers herself a success to the extent that her music is accessible and, whenever possible, participatory. For Sharon, an egalitarian musical ethos is essential to community-based art.

Could the average person pull off something like *Coal/Climate Monologues* in his or her own community? No, but neither did Sharon. She relied on a host of neighbors to make it all work: a talk show host, community organizers, a venue owner, artists, a partner, an audience, and many others.[15] Sharon used her considerable talents to mount a one-woman show but depended on others to make it all work. That is how community art and organizing are done, when done well.

In this case, musical performance and visual art worked well together. They were done well. Combining multiple community arts around an environmental theme elevated the event from a typical community arts program to a transformative, community-making moment. Art can help communities recall a collective past, contemplate the present, and deliberate the future. Nothing could be more practical.

NOTES

1. Martha Baskin, "Protestors Stall an Oil Train for Hours at Anacortes," *Resistance: Daily Movement News and Resources*, accessed January 8, 2015, https://www .popularresistance.org/protesters-stall-an-oil-train-for-hours-at-anacortes/.

2. Earth First! "Raging Grannies Blockading Entrances and Exits of WA Department of Ecology," *Earth First! Newswire*, October 30, 2014, accessed March 28, 2016, http:// earthfirstjournal.org/newswire/2014/10/30/breaking-raging-grannies-blockading -entrances-and-exits-of-wa-department-of-ecology/.

3. It should be noted that scientists also use narrative and visual art to communicate their ideas, whether they are reinforcing data presented in TED talks, taking part in films like *An Inconvenient Truth* (dir. Davis Guggenheim, 2006), or explaining their findings to colleagues.

4. All quotes reproduced here and not directly attributed to other sources are derived from the author's interview with the Irthlingz, May 30, 2014.

5. Sharon Abreu, "*The Climate Monologues*: Excerpts," YouTube video, accessed January 8, 2015, https://www.youtube.com/watch?v=okbwBrs6pkM.

6. Anna Deavere Smith, *Twilight: Los Angeles, 1992* (New York: Dramatists Play Service, 2003).

7. Irthlingz, "Sharon Abreu, Executive Director," Irthlingz, accessed January 8, 2015, http://greendept.com/io/sharon-abreu-executive-director/.

8. Sharon Abreu, "A Few Words about Sharon Abreu," Irthlingz, accessed January 8, 2015, http://www.sharmuse.com/sharword.htm.

9. Amy Jo Goddard, "Staging Activism: New York City Performing Artists as Cultural Workers," *Social Justice* (2007): 105.

10. *American Industrial Ballads*, Pete Seeger, Smithsonian Folkways, 1992.

11. Charlie King, Charlie King Music, accessed January 9, 2015, http://www .charliekingmusic.com/.

12. Lee Higgins, *Community Music: In Theory and in Practice* (Oxford: Oxford University Press, 2012).

13. "Sixteen Tons," Merle Travis, *In Boston, 1959*, Rounder Records, 2003.

14. Eban Goodstein, *The Trade-Off Myth: Fact and Fiction about Jobs and the Environment* (Washington, DC: Island Press, 1999).

15. The venue, Anchor Art Space, went out of business in December 2014. However, the show could have just as easily been held at a public site, such as the local library.

FIGURE 7.1

Adrian Chalifour with his band, Towers and Trees.
Towers and Trees; used by permission.

Victoria's Towers and Trees

Together Alone Online

This chapter is about Adrian Chalifour, lead singer of the group Towers and Trees, and his YouTube video "This Land Is Your Land."[1] Adrian performed the song in the woods behind his sister's house on Galiano Island, his brother filmed it, and they then uploaded the video to YouTube. I feature the video here because I believe that what Adrian did is worth seeing, hearing, reading about, and, most importantly, emulating. His example demonstrates how musical activism can go beyond the traditional bounds of face-to-face organizing to include new forms of expression. Throughout this chapter, I encourage readers to follow Adrian's innovative example by making and sharing their own videos at Ecosong.net.

Adrian rewrote the lyrics to Woody Guthrie's folk anthem "This Land Is Your Land" in order to express concerns over clear-cutting, oil shale mining, and other threats to the Salish Sea community. The song references urban blight in "Downtown Eastside" Vancouver, where people live behind "boarded windows" surrounded by "pins and needles." In the lyrics, environmental imagery drawn from Vancouver's urban core illustrates the province's disintegrating safety net and dystopian decay, while the forested setting of the video indicates that much remains to be protected outside the city. Juxtaposed to the forest backdrop, the developments Adrian narrates seem like sacrilege, affronts to people and planet. The soft-spoken bard warns us about these problems as if waking the viewer from a deep sleep.

Throughout its seventy-five-year history, people have often rewritten "This Land Is Your Land." In fact, Guthrie himself borrowed the melody. He did so in order to craft a musical response to Irving Berlin's jingoistic "God Bless America."[2] Therefore, what makes Adrian's YouTube version compelling is not that he changed the words but rather the honest and straightforward way that he performs the song.

In the video, a lone musician sings about preservation of a place while sitting in the middle of that actual place. You might think that would be a rather common phenomenon, a distinct genre of music video "of place, for place, and in place." However, it is not, and that is the main point of this chapter, that such a genre should exist and that such videos should be more common in the era of social media. It would be a powerful thing if place-based musical arguments like Adrian's were shared via social media more often.

Adrian's video represents a fairly old genre updated for very new media. It draws on the power of a time-honored, Thoreauvian dynamic: the lone figure who strikes out into the woods to contemplate place, nature, and society. Similarly in the tradition of Henry David Thoreau, Adrian shares his "solitary" reflections with the world.[3] It is therefore a performative form of contemplation, more public than private despite the ostensible solitude at its center. Adrian, like Thoreau and Rachel Carson before him, chose to present his critical message via artful expression rather than dry prose.[4]

When I first viewed Adrian's "This Land," it had registered barely 900 hits despite having been posted more than a year earlier. As of this writing, it still has received only 1,321 hits on YouTube, although by the time you read this, I hope the count will have risen significantly.[5] Therefore, this is not a study of a popular sociological phenomenon or emerging trend. Some of the most popular cat videos receive that many hits every six minutes. Environmentalist music videos like "This Land" will probably never rival skateboard fails in popularity. However, I do very much believe that Adrian has provided us with an innovative, artful, powerful, and doable way to share musical expressions of place regardless of where one lives. If practiced and shared more widely, the music-in-place video genre could become an effective form of online activism.

After seeing Adrian's remarkable video, I scoured YouTube and Vimeo for more, assuming that many more like it must be posted on social media. All it takes is a camera and a backyard or park. It seems like a natural in the age of social media, a new way to express our age-old connections to place. Unfortunately, I found few such examples. The few I did find are embedded at Ecosong.net, so please do send in more, including your own.

As I watched and listened to Adrian's surprisingly unique music video, I kept wondering why more of us are not doing this. I continue to be fascinated by Adrian's elegant work of art and was moved to contact the performer in order to learn more about the video and his motivations for creating it. Two interviews, a concert, and hours of listening later, I remain convinced that Adrian's backyard video contains considerable potential and will develop the case for it here, drawing on the work of Thoreau, Sherry Turkle, and Woody Guthrie.

It might seem odd that I would delve more deeply into theory here than in previous chapters. After all, this chapter involves the most directly practical example, one that might seem to speak for itself. However, I do so in order to make the case for an idea that, unlike the other examples, has not yet revealed its merit. It is an argument based on speculation and hope rather than manifest evidence of success, making this example different from those in other chapters. Therefore I turn to historical precedent and social media scholarship to help make the case.

WHAT WOULD HENRY DAVID DO?

In addition to writing new lyrics for "This Land Is Your Land," Adrian inserted a minor chord declension at the end of each refrain, adding a more contemplative tone to Guthrie's prose. Adrian's vocal tone indicates that the singer is tired of witnessing each of the ecopolitical insults he documents in the song. Similarly, Guthrie's first drafts of the song presented the famous refrain as a question: "Was this land made for you and me?" Adrian communicates a similar message with voice inflection and probing lyrics. His voice is more resolute than accusatory, if perhaps a bit weary, similar to how Guthrie often sounded in performance. Despite each depredation listed in Adrian's version of the song, a single voice can be heard singing truth to power, as in the original. The forest scene provides resolute support for the singer's environmental testimony, something that is somewhat different than the original. We are made for Galiano's woods as much as it was "made for you and me."

Adrian is the lead singer, songwriter, and central driving force behind the band Towers and Trees. However, he went solo for "This Land," putting aside complex band logistics to produce a simpler, more elegant statement:

This Land is Your Land
This land is your land
This land is my land
From the clear-cut forests
To the northern tar sands

Foreign names and
Stolen islands
This land was made for you and me

I went out walking
Downtown Eastside
Pins and needles
Stealing man's pride

Wandering thin ghosts
Boarded windows
This land was made for you and me

I saw the spirit
Of a nation
Held in bondage
On a reservation

The chains were straining
Pretty soon they'll be breaking
This land was made for you and me

Now the old-growth forests
Once stood so grand

Brought to the ground by
Supply and demand

The smoking gun lies
In your and my hands
This land was made for you and me

Our rugged coastlines
Mines and smelters
Dying mill towns
And homeless shelters

The mighty Skeena (River)
Sold-out arenas
This land was made for you and me

This land is your land
This land is my land
The sacred Earth where
Sea and Sky land

Is it too late now
For to take a stand?
This land was made for you and me

Adrian sings each phrase with a sense of contemplative anxiety. His performance brings to mind Thoreau's *Walden* and is worth examining in that light. In their respective works, Thoreau and Adrian each experience a deep connection to a very specific place and feel moved to share their contemplations with the outside world. Both perform their profound sense of reverence and ecological awareness for distant audiences, turning private contemplations into public lessons.

In fact, that impulse toward advocacy helps us make sense of what might otherwise seem like a basic contradiction at the heart of Thoreau's transcendental philosophy: the individual seeks truth in solitary communion with nature yet then widely broadcasts that experience, transforming contemplative solitude into what could be read uncharitably as narcissistic spectacle. In other words, Thoreau was writing with the intention of being read. There was never anything purely solitary about it. His

Walden was a highly public and collective act from the outset. The intention and consciousness of public mediation make all the difference in the case of *Walden* and Adrian's "This Land" video.

However, as Thoreau made clear at several points in his journal, and Adrian makes evident from the outset, neither performer ever sought hermetic isolation. Instead, both present themselves as ethical interlocutors for distant audiences. They offer their audiences a chance to relate to place rather than to spectate. Performers in the Thoreauvian mode interpellate their audiences as fellow travelers.

Conversely, monks, hermits, and New Age spiritualists retreat to nature for the sake of self-discovery and/or connection to the divine. They escape contemporary urban life by retreating to landscapes and soundscapes more conducive to their individual well-being. Their goal is not preservation of place per se, as it was for Thoreau. In fact, most forms of escape into nature (e.g., travel, adventure, second homes) significantly increase the individual's ecological footprint. Escape comes at great cost, ecologically speaking.

Of course, it is not surprising that people seek spiritual escape from the noisy, alienating realities of modern existence and urban life, a world where one is constantly assaulted with loud noises and artificial images, a world where we are digitally connected to other people, systems, and machines at all moments.[6] It is little wonder that so many people seek rural retreat. However, neither Adrian's nor Thoreau's work represents such a retreat. Both draw links to ideological, political, historical, and economic contexts far beyond the forest and pond, confronting disturbing truths that spiritual isolationists instead work hard to forget.

Despite being separated by the breadth of a large continent and two centuries, a dynamic of contemplative engagement links Thoreau's *Walden* and Chalifour's "This Land." Adrian lays down a challenge to dominant political systems, as did Thoreau. Both use solo performance in nature to advocate for ideological, political, institutional, and ecological change.

In that sense, transcendentalism is a communal act. Thoreau clearly knew, even hoped, that someone would be reading over his shoulder. At some basic level, he obviously hoped to serve as the reader's conduit to nature. He was an advocate. Hitting its mark, Thoreau's *Walden* exerted the greatest influence on environmentalist thought in the United States up to the publication of Rachel Carson's *Silent Spring* more than a century later and remains among the most influential works by any environmentalist author.[7]

Among other virtues, Adrian's music video presents a model that, much like Thoreau's, is easily emulated (not duplicated, but emulated).[8] Modern-day Thoreaus can pick up a camera or smartphone and make their way to a place that is similarly dear to them. Everyone has his or her own song to sing and a place to steward.

PERFORMING PLACE

The first time I interviewed Adrian, he mentioned being particularly moved by the final three verses of Guthrie's "This Land Is Your Land":

As I went walking I saw a sign there
And on the sign it said "No Trespassing."
But on the other side it didn't say nothing,
That side was made for you and me.

In the shadow of the steeple I saw my people,
By the relief office I seen my people;
As they stood there hungry, I stood there asking
Is this land made for you and me?

Nobody living can ever stop me,
As I go walking that freedom highway;
Nobody living can ever make me turn back
This land was made for you and me.

Those stanzas typically are redacted from school versions.[9] The young Canadian composer got the idea to perform "This Land Is Your Land" after hearing Bruce Springsteen sing the three "missing" verses. Adrian realized that the song he had learned in the Canadian classroom, like the versions sung in US schools, "hollowed out the original intentions of the song."[10] Inspired, he "decided to write a version that was real" for him, one "that resonated," a version that would be "written in the context of the Pacific Northwest."

However, Adrian never intended to make a video. The idea of filming on Galiano Island came about spontaneously, several weeks later. Galiano is a Canadian Gulf Island situated between Vancouver Island and the BC mainland. Adrian and his brother were "standing out in the woods." "It was so incredibly quiet and peaceful," explained Adrian. "I could hear ravens; there was a mist. It was just gorgeous." Adrian had just started actively playing music again. He decided to sing "This Land" and have his brother film the performance.

By choosing YouTube, Adrian "was trying to stick with the new DIY ethic of today's musician." "It seems kind of rude to find this picturesque forest scene," said Adrian, "and think 'Ah, I should make a video in it. Shoot it!'" But he decided that it "seemed like a fitting song to do in that setting." The video signals the importance of the forest setting by panning in slowly, showing the enormous trees before revealing Adrian, who is framed by the trees rather than foregrounded. "The nice thing about framing the video in that way," explained Adrian, "is that there is value in preserving that setting."

I asked Adrian to explain what he was thinking about while singing "This Land." "I was thinking, 'This is the first video that I'll share with the world,'" replied the young artist. "I wonder if it will resonate?" He added, "I'm always intent on sharing, so there is always a performance aspect." The talented singer-songwriter was "trying to capture that moment to the best of my abilities so that hopefully it would resonate with other people."

I recently asked the same question of Hannah Lewis, a young musician who performed a sung version of Thoreau's *Walden* at Walden Pond. Peter McMurray filmed and edited her performance into a video titled *Sound and Solitude*.[11] Hannah's answer was revealing and delightfully honest: "I was thinking about getting the next note right."

Both Adrian's and Hannah's responses reminded me that these are first and foremost performances, representations of reflective moments in nature rather than moments of reflection per se. Neither Hannah nor Adrian answered the question in terms of contemplating nature, the answer that I was expecting. At the moment of being filmed, they were paying more attention to medium, performance, and audience than their natural surroundings.

Might that be true of Thoreau's experience as well? Remember that Thoreau wrote reams of journal entries, speeches, and essays. Writing, like singing and filming, takes a great deal of time and influences one's orientation to the subject. A tree is seen not just as a tree in its own right but rather in order to be revealed in writing. A bird is heard not just for the beauty of its voice but in order to be presented in an audio recording. The experience is mediated by specific technologies and genre expectations that performer and audience alike carry into the woods with them. Pencil and paper, the field of natural history, transcendental philosophy, and a conscious recognition of his audience mediated Thoreau's reflective experiences in nature.

Just as Thoreau hoped his writings would be published and actively sought out a publisher, Adrian wondered how his audience would react to his song and video: "I was hoping that it would resonate," he explains, and "not just with people in this region." "The environmental context of each region is distinct," he continued, including "environmental issues and sociocultural issues." However, there are "common themes that reach across regions." He hoped that by "capturing this specific context" in the "Cascadian region . . . someone, whether in Victoria, Nanaimo, Duncan, or Vancouver, or someone in Minnesota," could relate to the performance, "because on some level we can relate to things going on in our own backyards that are similar."

Adrian hoped that filming "specifically in this little patch of forest on a Gulf Island" would allow audiences to identify with it as an actual place. "That sort of pristine natural setting looks very different from region to region, but I still feel like someone in Texas can appreciate the backdrop that I have because they know what their own little idyllic, natural setting looks like." In other words, distant others might be able relate because the Galiano scene is specific and distinct, rather than generic and placeless.

Of course, there are many differences between Adrian's spontaneous project and Thoreau's time in the woods. For example, Thoreau repeatedly writes about the virtues of solitude, making more of a point of being alone in the woods: "I find it wholesome to be alone the greater part of the time. To be in company, even with the best, is soon wearisome and dissipating. I love to be alone. I never found the companion that was so companionable as solitude."[12] Yet here, as elsewhere, Thoreau is clearly engaging in a dialogue with others, even while contemplating and communicating his preference for solitude.[13]

TOGETHER ALONE ONLINE

It is interesting, therefore, that social media critic Sherry Turkle chose Thoreau as her model for contemplative retreat. She uses Thoreau as a romantic foil for the digitally mediated present, arguing that "connected" persons must "retreat" in order to think clearly. She recommends purposeful retreats from media, what she calls "Walden 2.0."[14]

Among the problems with social media, argues Turkle, is that instant communication favors nondeliberative dialogue. Once again, Turkle uses Thoreau as a foil. "Thoreau complained that people are too quick to share an opinion," she explains. "Online, social networks instruct us to share whenever there's 'something on our mind,'" she complains, "no matter how ignorant or ill considered."[15]

I agree with Turkle's assessment of social media, in the main, but examples like Adrian's "This Land" demonstrate that it is possible to share more fully developed ideas, inspire deliberation, and create contemplative dialogue through the use of social media, just as Thoreau did with pencil and paper. Most tweets, text messages, and posts are instantly forgettable. So is most writing. Rarely does print rise to the level of *Walden*. Yet, with all its limitations, we continue to write because it is the medium we know. The same can be said of social media. It might be better to find ways to use it well than to dismiss it altogether.

Turkle describes modern, networked life depressingly well. Obligatory communication technologies enable people to be alone together.[16] Bodies share space, but people fail to connect in meaningful ways. Consciousness is "out there" somewhere, distracted by text messages and data arriving from far beyond our immediate space. People engage in constant out-of-body experiences, neglecting the people, life, and places all around them for the sake of digitized others. Digital deterritorialization turns places into mere spaces, physical locations without meaning, places for cohabitation with others whose consciousness roams elsewhere. As one of Turkle's informants explains, "No one is where they are."[17]

Turkle argues that new communication media have turned living beings into relativized objects wherein life has less meaning, a robotic orientation toward the living world. All things, living and dead, become digital representations and, as such, are assigned instrumental use-values. For the people Turkle describes, "aliveness" has "no greater intrinsic value" than the lifeless objects we use, covet, and collect.[18] The implicit message is that people within reaching distance matter less than digitized distant others. Of course, once the digital native is actually with those distant others, the same alienating behaviors take place, indicating that it is not the actual others that matter but rather their digitized representations. Rendered digitally, these others are narcissistic projections of the social media consumer's self, rather than autonomous and valued human beings in their own right. Digitization provides a feeling of control over one's world, a world where people are reduced to digital objects.

I agree with the main thrust of Turkle's argument. However, there are certainly exceptions, and Adrian's "This Land" is a promising alternative. It is the inverse of Turkle's *Alone Together*, providing the possibility of being "together alone" for a collective purpose for which place and people matter very much. In watching the video, we are neither "tethered" in the oppressive way Turkle describes nor allowed to simply escape, happy in our individuated privilege.[19] Instead of being alienated from the real bodies surrounding us, we draw connections between people and places, even if we are physically alone. Adrian's "This Land" is a call to what Turkle describes as "communion," the antithesis of being alone together.[20]

Granted, face-to-face community building is often preferable to the "weak ties" encountered in digital communities. "Communities are constituted by physical proximity, shared concerns, real consequences, and common responsibilities," explains Turkle, contrasting the Second Life virtual world with the real community to which her grandparents belonged. "What real life responsibilities do we have for those we meet in games?" she asks. "Am I my avatar's keeper?" [21]

These are excellent questions. I find Turkle's argument accurate for social media in the main, but face-to-face communities, like their digital equivalents, can be either liberating or oppressive. Digital media is equally complex from the perspective of environmental ethics and impact. For most of the Anthropocene, we managed to mess things up rather well without the internet. Off-line activities were almost wholly responsible for the sixth great extinction, and, theoretically, replacing unnecessary travel with digital communication could improve global ecosystems.

However, online and off-line existences have become interrelated ecosystems, not separate realities. For example, Adrian's "This Land" is more than a YouTube broadcast. It is also hyperlocal communication with people whom Adrian knows well and interacts with on a daily basis: bandmates, family members, friends, community leaders, and fans, among others. In that sense, social media can become more local than mass-media equivalents from the analog age. Therefore, it is not just a matter of substituting digital representations for face-to-face communication; it is a question of how the two forms of social engagement interrelate. The argument here is that they interrelate very well in "This Land" and social media videos like it.

Another of Adrian's musical works, "Flesh and Bone," as recorded by Towers and Trees, illustrates that same point. There are two videos for the song, both performed with the full band. One presents a very polished performance in a local church for the Chapel Sessions.[22] The production values and cost of that video far exceed those for "This Land." Therefore, it is not something most nonprofessionals could ever emulate. The other video for "Flesh and Bone" is set in a pub.[23] That video also represents a performance beyond the abilities of most nonprofessionals. However, both videos provide interesting contrasts to the much simpler video, "This Land."

"This Land," unlike "Flesh and Bone," is not the sort of song Adrian or Towers and Trees would perform in a pub. Songs like "Flesh and Bone" allow the young Canadian singer-songwriter to bring environmental messages into live contexts and otherwise apolitical music scenes, albeit much less directly than would be the case with his rendition of "This Land." In other words, as opposed to what we might expect from a reading of Turkle, social media rather than live performance allows for deep ecopolitical engagement. Musical interventions like "This Land" defy digital deterritorialization, extending and deepening relationships between people, place, and nonhuman communities despite being communicated digitally.

As Dana Lyons argued during one of our interviews, as social media becomes omnipresent and almost obligatory, why not figure out how to use it for positive purposes? Perhaps exhibit number one is *Sustainable Music*, a blog penned by ethnomusicologist and Thoreau scholar Jeff Todd Titon, a social media site that has profoundly influenced my thinking throughout this work and has similar influenced many contemporary music scholars.[24]

THE POLITICS AND POWER OF SOUND

Thoreau touted the sonic advantages of human solitude: "The bullfrogs trump to usher in the night, and the note of the whip-poor-will is borne on the rippling wind from over the water. Sympathy with the fluttering alder and poplar leaves almost takes away my breath; yet, like the lake, my serenity is rippled but not ruffled. These small waves raised by the evening wind are as remote from storm as the smooth reflecting surface. Though it is now dark, the wind still blows and roars in the wood, the waves still dash, and some creatures lull the rest with their notes. The repose is never complete." Yet at no time was Thoreau simply reveling in the moment. His aims were less spiritual, in the conventional sense, than political. Thoreau sought to communicate ways of being in nature that most of his compatriots lacked. He presaged his readers' most basic question: "For what reason have I this vast range and circuit, some square miles of unfrequented forest, for my privacy, abandoned to me by men?" Sound was central to his answer. "There can be no very black melancholy to him who lives in the midst of Nature and has his senses still," he explained. "There was never yet such a storm but it was Aeolian music to a healthy and innocent ear."[25]

We can see that part of Thoreau's mission was to heal himself, his readers, and what he viewed as a colonial experiment gone wrong. Much like Adrian's "This Land," Thoreau's solitary experience and writings were acts of civil disobedience, matching his more overt protests against the US invasion of Mexico. Regarding these moral commitments, Thoreau paraphrased Confucius: "Virtue does not remain as an abandoned orphan; it must of necessity have neighbors."[26] In context, Thoreau appears to mean that fairly literally. One cannot communicate with oneself alone and expect to lead a virtuous life. His retreat facilitated political engagement: "However intense my experience, I am conscious of the presence and criticism of a part of me, which, as it were, is not a part of me, but spectator, sharing no experience, but taking note of it, and that is no more I than it is you."[27]

Communication with self and other seems to be at the heart of Adrian's YouTube video, just as that dynamic runs throughout Thoreau's writings at Walden Pond. Thoreau's anticolonial commitments and abolitionist activism demonstrate a deep dedication to action and show that he sought much more than spiritual redemption in the woods. Similarly, the implicit message of Adrian's video, and his explicit explanation in the interviews, is that sustainability, biodiversity, and environmental justice can be effectively communicated via social media in intimate, individual, place-based performances.

Adrian's music and video performance is not just about global abstractions like climate change or colonialism but is fundamentally about knowing oneself in relation to place, about being grounded enough to make a difference. Thoreau argued: "One hastens to southern Africa to chase the giraffe; but surely that is not the game he would be after. How long, pray, would a man hunt giraffes if he could? Snipes and woodcocks also may afford rare sport; but I trust it would be nobler game to shoot one's self."[28] He argued for the critical contemplation of place and against more mindless forms of mobility:

> Direct your eye right inward, and you'll find
> A thousand regions in your mind
> Yet undiscovered. Travel them, and be
> Expert in home-cosmography.[29]

As Jeff Titon writes, it was "sound" that "led" Thoreau "to ecstasy and the sublime" in nature.[30] A similar sense of sound underlies Adrian's "This Land" video. The sublime reveals itself through expressions of wonder in nature, the ineffable sense that nature cannot be fully understood, captured, or collected. Adrian's voice never rises to the level of a natural disturbance but instead retains hushed tones of reverence, allowing his criticisms to come across all the more powerfully. He is modeling deep listening, as did Thoreau in his writings. In the musical expressions of both Thoreau and Adrian, the sublime is more than a feeling of wonder at nature's spectacle; it is a genre of environmental communication with the power to stir others into action.

WHAT WOULD WOODY DO?

Having made an analytical link to the writings of Thoreau and Turkle, it is important to explore the connection between Adrian's "This Land" and Guthrie's song, remembering that Guthrie borrowed much of the melody from the Carter Family Singers and their rendition of the Baptist hymn, "Oh, My Loving Brother."[31] It is important to note that Guthrie was not concerned with sustainability. His interest in advancing the cause of labor excluded environmental concerns. As noted in chapter 1, Guthrie championed the Bonneville Power Administration's (BPA) dam projects, salmon-destroying edifices that the contemporary left now seeks to remove. Guthrie's Columbia River Cycle was composed for the BPA, written under commission, the only such commission the folk icon ever accepted (and later appeared to regret having done so).[32] As with most of the Old Left, Guthrie looked at the landscape in terms of labor use-value, not as something to be carefully stewarded. To most eyes in Guthrie's day, nature's bounty appeared endless, although the Dust Bowl awoke some of Guthrie's contemporaries to the need for conservation.

Guthrie and others envisioned the BPA as a progressive bulwark against powerful interests. Damming the mighty river would literally bring power to the people, or so he and the BPA hoped. The dam project had ironic results, however, further enriching bankers, large landowners, and conservative interests rather than bettering the plight of small farmers and migrant labor. Given Guthrie's lack of attention to environmental politics, it is interesting how Adrian's "This Land" borrows and repurposes the folk hero's song for environmental advocacy.

Although they do not share environmentalist ideologies, Guthrie and Adrian share an intense interest in place. Guthrie most often presented place in the form of travelogue and montage. Being on the move much of the time, he helped make "the road" a central motif in twentieth-century American popular music, yet he was no less fascinated by place. He created a sonic geography in his songs and traced paths between places by telling stories of workers' oppression, resistance, and triumph. In that sense, Adrian's version pays homage to Guthrie's original song in connecting people's plights to place. Conversely, the heavily redacted school versions of "This Land Is Your Land" that we were taught as children turned the song into a patriotic anthem. Today, commercial uses of the song, such as the North Face's glitzy "This Land" campaign, turn Guthrie's rebel song toward promoting consumption as opposed to citizenship. In this and other ways, Adrian's version is truer to Guthrie's.

In reference to Guthrie's use of place, Adrian noted, "You sing about the things that aren't right because you love the place and care about it," drawing connections between Guthrie's place-based patriotism and his own. "When I think about capturing the West Coast in our music," said the young artist, "what I really celebrate about the West Coast is its ruggedness, this wildness, the natural." He went on to explain that he did not want the music to sound as if it had been recorded in a studio but rather hoped it would retain the feel of an actual place and natural accents from the region.

Adrian noted that his music "embraces the geography as metaphor or even more than that," an "homage to the many faces of the West Coast, good and bad." He explained that "in BC we've had a lot of issues on the radar of late with pipeline construction, oil and gas development, natural gas development, and First Nations land claims," all of which are "part of the political and social landscape here." That sense of natural belonging burst off the stage at Towers and Trees' Butchart Gardens show on August 2, 2013 (see back cover photo). The band's "new folk" sound fit that scene, surrounded by towering Douglas firs and native cedars, as if part of the natural habitat. That might ultimately be one of the important differences between Guthrie and Adrian. Guthrie was a fairly rootless Dust Bowl refugee who made the entire United States, and even much of the world, his itinerant home. Adrian's "This Land" is more deeply rooted in place, as is Towers and Trees' music in general. The band engages in their share of musical travel in songs like "Devil on the Highway" and "Montreal,"[33] but as Adrian noted in our interview, "place was a very prominent theme" in Towers and Trees' first EP, *Broken Record*, and will be "more so in the next album." Giving a preview, Adrian explains that the working title of the next "full-length album" could be "The West Coast."

WHAT THEN MUST WE DO?

This project came full circle when, linking the first and last chapters, I asked Dana Lyons to provide advice to aspiring artists. His main suggestion was to emphasize social media. "YouTube is a miracle for small artists or publishers," he explained. "Basically, anyone in the world can have their own TV station." He mentioned two viral versions of "Cows with Guns," both animated videos created by people he did not know, one garnering more than 1.5 million hits[34] and the other achieving 3 million views.[35] However, he was quick to point out that it does not take 3 million hits for a video to matter. "Tell your friends who care about the issue, and they can spread it around," he suggested. "Maybe one hundred to three hundred people watch it, maybe a few thousand." He noted that the margin of difference in many elections is smaller than that:

> So many elections come down to a handful of votes. If you push an election by 1 percent or if you frame a debate [you can make a difference]. Maybe a few thousand people will watch it. If it touches a number of those people, and they go, "That's right," and they say it to their relatives, you can have a ripple effect, and maybe you influence ten thousand people. Maybe that election comes down to 1,500 votes, as many of them do. That's a powerful thing.

Not realizing that I had been studying a video (Adrian's "This Land") with many of the very same components he was suggesting, Dana continued:

> I'd advise, in particular to musicians, if there's something you care about, I recommend writing a song about it. You can do the age-old Woody Guthrie and Pete Seeger. Some call it plagiarism, and some call it the folk tradition. "We Shall Overcome," "If I Had a Hammer," "This Land Is Your Land'—these are all previously existing tunes. I just mentioned that I'm doing a song based on the Village People's "YMCA." It can be as silly as taking a pop song and changing the words, or maybe you write your own original piece of music. Any songwriter knows that some of your songs are pretty good, and some of your songs are not pretty good. It's just the way it is. It can make a difference. It's worth trying. If you write a mediocre song, then fine. You don't put it out. If you write a song about an issue you care about, maybe it's going to be an election or maybe you're fighting to create a new park or a new school or whatever. If your friends seem to like it or your supporters seem to like it, make a simple YouTube video of it.

Dana went on to offer further advice for the aspiring YouTube artist-activist:

> I would recommend making the budget as close to $0.00 as possible. That's the great thing about YouTube. I don't think people want slick on YouTube. It's kind of cool that it's a little funky. Even if it's just you playing the guitar or the piano and singing your song, just make a YouTube video.

Tell the people who are interested in that subject about it. If they think it's helpful, then they'll tell their friends, and it gets spread around. It can help frame a debate. It can help draw a community together.

Rather than differentiating what he does, as a professional, and what YouTube performers and activists are doing on an amateur basis, Dana closely equates the two forms of musicianship. In line with the Raging Grannies, Dana considers the activist aspect more important than professionalization:

It's funny. I've been doing this for a really long time, but it's only recently that I realized this is really important. I need to spend more time on doing songs about issues and doing videos. That's my primary work now. Now, it's unclear how I'm going to get paid to do that, but that's my passion. . . . I gig to make money. Most artists don't get paid anything. You don't need to get paid. Obviously, we all do what we need to do to pay our bills, but if you've got a friend with a video camera, you can do something cool and simple on YouTube that's powerful.

As Billy Bragg suggested: "Start your own revolution and cut out the middle man."[36]

If Adrian, Dana, Henry David, and Woody have not persuaded you to make a music video in and about a place that matters deeply to you, perhaps a little additional prompting will do the trick. Pick any hymn, folk song, or other tune in the public domain. Rewrite the words to express your own message. "This Land Is Your Land" is an excellent example and serves as the template on Ecosong.net, where you will find a few additional resources that might be of use as well. However, as Joe Hill discovered more than a century ago, the hymnals and folk archives are full of songs waiting to be repurposed for the present, as has been the folk tradition for millennia.[37] It is what keeps musical traditions alive.

Perhaps you would be willing to film yourself or a friend singing your song in a place that matters to you, whether it is your backyard, back forty, or backwoods? If you do, please consider sharing your video with us at Ecosong.net. We will work to get your musical message a bit farther out into the world.

Hopefully the artists chronicled here have in some way inspired you or provided a few ideas. As my bandmates and I have worked on music videos for local watersheds, the lessons contained in these pages have been invaluable. Adrian's example is one of the most inspiring in that all one needs is a smartphone and guitar to make a difference.

NOTES

1. "This Land Is Your Land," lyrics by Adrian Chalifour, melody by Woody Guthrie, performed by Adrian Chalifour, Towers and Trees, accessed January 7, 2015, http://www.towersandtreesmusic.com/2012/02/29/this-land-was-made-for-you-and-me/.

2. "God Bless America," *The Best of Kate Smith*, words and music by Irving Berlin, performed by Kate Smith, BMG, 1967.

3. Henry David Thoreau, *Walden*. Project Gutenberg. Accessed January 7, 2015. http://www.gutenberg.org/files/205/205-h/205-h.htm.

4. Rachel Carson, *Silent Spring* (Boston: Houghton Mifflin Harcourt, 2002).

5. "This Land Is Your Land," lyrics by Adrian Chalifour, melody by Woody Guthrie, performed by Adrian Chalifour, YouTube video, accessed January 7, 2015, http://www.youtube.com/watch?v=oJwZFV6J-eA.

6. The term "nature" is used here in the colloquial sense, to represent material realities that exist independently of human construction in the simplest and broadest terms (i.e., we did not invent the universe of objects nor does the universe require us to keep thinking about it in order to exist). No matter how problematic, I argue that words like "nature" remain a meaningful part of social discourse that must be engaged and applied, not simply deconstructed. For a very different position, see Timothy Morton, *Ecology without Nature: Rethinking Environmental Aesthetics* (Cambridge, MA: Harvard University Press, 2007).

7. Jeff Todd Titon, "Conservation, Environmentalism, Ecology," Sustainable Music, accessed January 7, 2015, http://sustainablemusic.blogspot.com/2012/11/conservation-environmentalism-and.html.

8. I am speaking in terms of media here, not quality of writing. Few writers can match Thoreau in that regard.

9. "This Land Is Your Land," lyrics by Woody Guthrie, WoodyGuthrie.org, accessed January 7, 2015, http://www.woodyguthrie.org/Lyrics/This_Land.htm.

10. All of Chalifour's quotes were derived from two interviews with the author, one live in Victoria on August 2, 2013, and the other via phone on November 15, 2013.

11. Hannah Lewis and Peter McMurray, "Sounds and Solitude (Walden)," Vimeo Video, accessed April 1, 2016. https://vimeo.com/78756447.

12. By using Project Gutenberg's full-text edition of *Walden* online, the reader will be able to search out these passages and read them in context. Henry David Thoreau, *Walden*, Project Gutenberg, accessed January 7, 2015, http://www.gutenberg.org/files/205/205-h/205-h.htm13. .

14. Sherry Turkle, *Alone Together: Why We Expect More from Technology and Less from Each Other* (New York: Basic Books, 2012), 275–277.

15. Ibid., 276.

16. Sherry Turkle, *Alone Together: Why We Expect More from Technology and Less from Each Other* (New York: Basic Books, 2012).

17. Ibid., 277.

18. Ibid., 4, 28.
19. Ibid., 171–186.
20. Ibid., 127–147.
21. Ibid., 239.
22. "Flesh and Bone," Chapel Sessions, YouTube video, accessed January 7, 2015, https://www.youtube.com/watch?v=B-yqt-Fltbo.
23. "Flesh and Bone," Live at the Canoe Brew Pub, words and music by Adrian Chalifour, performed by Towers and Trees, YouTube video, accessed January 7, 2015, https://www.youtube.com/watch?v=9ZtlwW39qq4.
24. Jeff Todd Titon, Sustainable Music, accessed January 7, 2015, http://sustainablemusic.blogspot.com/.
25. Henry David Thoreau, *Walden*, Project Gutenberg, accessed January 7, 2015, http://www.gutenberg.org/files/205/205-h/205-h.htm.
26. Ibid.
27. Ibid.
28. Ibid.
29. Ibid.
30. Jeff Todd Titon, "Emerson's Eye and Thoreau's Ear," Sustainable Music, accessed January 7, 2015, http://sustainablemusic.blogspot.com/2012/02/emersons-eye-and-thoreaus-ear.html.
31. The melody of Guthrie's "This Land" closely resembles that of the anonymous Baptist hymn, "Oh, My Loving Brother," which was popularized by the Carter Family Singers as, "When the World's on Fire." Carter Family Singers, *When the Roses Bloom in Dixieland: Their Complete Victor Recordings (1929–1930)*, Rounder Records. 1995.
32. Mark Pedelty, "Woody Guthrie and the Columbia River: Propaganda, Art, and Irony," *Popular Music and Society* 31, no. 3 (2008): 329–355.
33. "Devil on the Highway," *Broken Record*, words and music by Adrian Chalifour, performed by Towers and Trees, 2012; "Montreal," *Broken Record*, words and music by Adrian Chalifour, performed by Towers and Trees, 2012.
34. "Cows with Guns," words, music, and performance by Dana Lyons, video animation by Cameron Edser and Michael Richards of GooRoo Animation, YouTube video, accessed January 7, 2015, https://www.youtube.com/watch?v=a5s5qGgo1nE.
35. "Cows with Guns," words, music, and performance by Dana Lyons, video animation by Bjorn-Mange Stuestol, YouTube video, accessed January 7, 2015, https://www.youtube.com/watch?v=FQMbXvn2RNI.
36. Billy Bragg, "Waiting for the Great Leap Forward," on *Workers' Playtime*, Cooking Vinyl, 2006, CD.
37. Benjamin Robert Tubb, Public Domain Music, accessed January 7, 2015, http://www.pdmusic.org/.

Conclusion

Common Themes and Connections

FERDINAND: Where should this music be? i' the air or the earth?
It sounds no more: and sure, it waits upon
Some god o' the island. Sitting on a bank,
Weeping again the king my father's wreck,
This music crept by me upon the waters,
Allaying both their fury and my passion
With its sweet air: thence I have follow'd it,
Or it hath drawn me rather. But 'tis gone.
No, it begins again.

    —William Shakespeare, *The Tempest*, act 1, scene 2

Like Shakespeare's Ferdinand, I have tried to make sense of a unique and fascinating soundscape. I do so by talking to musicians and observing them in performance. This book raises many of the same questions Ferdinand asks in act 1 of *The Tempest*: What sort of music is made in this place? What does it mean? Who makes it? Why? What does this captivating music do?

I have been visiting the Salish Sea for three decades and have lived here each of the past fifteen summers, yet I feel as if I am just beginning to answer these difficult questions. Culture and place are always stories in the making, not static things to be captured. By using terms like "ecosystem," "community," and "place" we attempt to gain psychological control over extremely complex realities that ultimately defy reductionism. Place is always plural. Ferdinand's place is not Prospero's. My Salish Sea is not the same as Sharon Abreu's or Shell Oil's.

In fact, each of these musicians lives in a different world, despite sharing overlapping geographies. As I sat chatting with Dana Lyons at cafés in Bellingham, toured an aquarium with Bobs & Lolo in Vancouver, watched Towers and Trees in Butchart Gardens, and so on, each musician revealed a slightly different conception of the Salish Sea.[1] They each represent very different identities, communities, and genres.

Yet consciousness of a shared ecosystem is growing. There is an emerging recognition that all living in and around the Salish Sea are connected by a larger web of life, rock, and rain. In material terms, there is a bounded ecosystem that could fairly be described as "the Salish Sea." Nevertheless, the incredible complexity of material ecosystems makes modeling an ecosystem in its entirety nearly impossible. That is why environmental scientists study and model specific subsystems rather than entire ecosystems. Nevertheless, just knowing that one is materially connected to others—human and nonhuman—can change one's behavior. Ecosystems are useful ideas.

Add the reality of culture to material ecosystems and you have a real mess, something so complex that no single model could ever suffice. Unlike a material ecosystem, "the Salish Sea" as a culturally conceived place is in no way bounded by natural laws or material limits. The Salish Sea is a shifting and nearly infinitely variable set of cultural realities that could never be captured in their entirety. Our subjects' symbolic productions—culture, music, nature, communication, and place, to name just a few examples—make a mockery of positivistic methods and epistemologies.

Instead, cultural research is intertextual. We tell stories about stories, relating the lives, cultures, and rich symbolic meanings encountered in the field. That makes our work intersubjective as well. Cultural research represents an engagement between subjects rather than a mapping of static cultural realities that exist "out there" in the field. Culture changes, we change, and vantage point matters. Despite very much believing in the power of positivistic science to uncover natural processes, such as hydrologic cycling, I am certain that no such method is possible when it comes to studying cultural realities like music and place. The best we can do is to provide salient interpretations. I hope I have given an adequate interpretation of the musical work these artists have been doing around the Salish Sea. Perhaps some of what I have related will prove useful to readers.

Throughout the Salish Sea, musicians are working with community organizations to educate and advocate for environmental justice, health, and biodiversity. Common themes rose out of the combined cases. I conclude by dealing with six of them: voice, place, scale, identity, humor, and communication. However, I think of this chapter as a segue rather than an end point. A book is too brief to touch on the hundreds of artists creating environmentalist music in some form or fashion worldwide, so the sharing of ideas, songs, and videos continues at Ecosong.net. The book is ending, but ecomusical activism seems to be just getting started. However, having presented seven detailed case studies, it is useful to examine common themes that arise out of the study as a whole, starting with the subject of voice. This chapter and book concludes with a discussion of applied ecomusicology, considering some of the ways that the information in these pages might be put to use.

VOICE

Voice is invoked in each of the case studies, as a metaphor for both empowerment (voice as agency) and visceral phenomenon (vocalization). These cases remind us that voice is much more than a metaphoric stand-in for agency.[2] Throughout these cases, we see how important it is for people to gain an actual voice in the public arena. Voice is the most essential and profound medium for human communication.

That point is made most compellingly in the case of Cecilia Point, an MC for the Musqueam Nation. The self-proclaimed "suburban hockey mom" who was terrified of public speaking now speaks to thousands of people each year and orchestrates music-filled protests.

All the musicians featured here found their voices at key turning points in their lives, and they have repeatedly rediscovered the power of voice in the public sphere and policy-making arenas.[3] Each story is about the power of voice to create positive change.

The human voice produces not only words but also powerful sound waves, making voice a physical, visceral, and intersubjective phenomenon. The complex communicative qualities of vocal sound move listeners every bit as much as the alphabetic messages carried by vocal sound waves. Voice communicates nonverbal messages through subtle changes in timbre, tone, volume, and pitch. Those qualities matter as much as the rhetorical content of speech.[4] That is one of the reasons why Ecosong.net is repeatedly referenced throughout the book, because it allows the reader to access artists' actual voices: Lyons's folksy baritone, Bobs & Lolo's pitch-perfect blend, the Raging Grannies' destabilizing dissonance, Chalifour's resolute concern, Abreu's operatic soprano, and the calm command in Point's voice at a protest. Listening is as important as reading.

Musical voice is a collective phenomenon, a question of creating community. As Lee Higgins argues, "Community music is an expression of cultural democracy."[5] Communities are realized and performed, in part, through giving voice to collective concerns and interests.

It is not just a matter of collective expression but also one of collective listening. "The transformative act of listening," explains Jan Curtis, is key to the "inner life of community."[6] Movements and organizations that listen well also tend to communicate their message effectively to the outside world. The Raging Grannies model this every week during community center rehearsals. Similarly, Idle No More is creating listening strategies that have led to effective collaboration across disparate cultural groups.

Julie Rickwood provides a similar example of collective expression and listening. She studied Ecopella, "a network of six community choirs" in Australia.[7] Ecopella is tackling some of Australia's most pressing environmental challenges, using music to organize, inform, and inspire. Rickwood explains how Ecopella uses voice to represent themselves and the interests of other living creatures. Ecopella's "choralecology" serves as a potent symbol of how communities gain agency through voice. In Australia, as around the Salish Sea, music is helping movements find their voice in soundscapes dominated by industrial interests.[8]

Of course, listening can become insular. Rickwood raises the problem of Ecopella "preaching to the converted," or, as we say in the United States, "preaching to the choir."[9] Environmentalist organizations can sometimes fall into a pattern of speaking mostly to themselves rather than reaching

out to, and listening to, the wider community. As a result, environmentalists may fail to inform, move, or persuade others. Here is where music and
the principles of community music, in particular, help by emphasizing
inclusion rather than impenetrable walls of specialized rhetoric.[10]

However, Ecopella and the Cascadian cases in this book also show that
preaching to the choir has its place, if it is not taken to extremes. Music is
important for group morale and solidarity. Song coheres communities and
inspires creativity, as it did during the early civil rights movement and all
successful movements. For example, "We Shall Overcome" reinforced
group resolve during trying times. When sung loudly by marchers, the
song expressed group solidarity and let both passive observers and violent
opponents know that the movement was there to stay. "We Shall Not Be
Moved" did similar cultural work. For activist communities, making
music together helps people create a collective voice.

PLACE

Throughout recorded history, human beings have used music to express a sense of connection to the natural world. Given archaeological
evidence of musicality going back at least thirty-five thousand years,
people have probably been using music to communicate and express ecological ideas for as long as the species *Homo sapiens* has existed, if not
longer (other species in the genus *Homo* probably communicated through
music as well).[11] Therefore, connections to place have been formed through
music for many millennia. As ethnomusicologist Travis Stimeling explains, "topophilia," or "the human being's affective ties with the material
environment," is expressed and fostered through music.[12] From ritual
expressions of reverence for animals to colonial anthems of conquest, music
mirrors, expresses, and influences how humans interact with the rest of
the living world.

Every performer and all the songs featured in this book express conceptions of place. Environmentalist musicians communicate what it means
to live in places like Anacortes, Orcas Island, and the Fraser River Watershed. Theresa May studied similar, performative connections in Northern
California. Through stories, indigenous Californians "create a matrix of

belonging, a living tissue between past and present, and between human and nonhuman communities."[13] As Bruno Latour has argued, the nonhuman world exerts agency and influences how human beings feel, think, live, die, and sing.[14] It is one reason that music made around the Salish Sea differs from music made in northern Minnesota or southern Florida. Place has its say in music.

Place is at the heart of Coast Salish music. For the Salish as for the indigenous cultures in California, "nothing of the earth or made by human hands is inanimate."[15] "The land is filled with ancestral stories," explains May. The same is true for music. For First Nations, the voice of a place includes land, wind, water, plants, animals, and ancestors. Increasingly, indigenous worldviews have been informing nonnative environmentalists' perspectives. From Gordon Hempton's *One Square Inch of Silence* to Dana Lyons's songs about the Salish Sea, the influence of Coast Salish culture is evident, and neither represents cultural appropriation. That is part of what makes Idle No More's broad coalition possible, the fact that many nonnatives have over the years learned from First Nations' perspectives. New Age appropriation of indigenous culture still takes place to an alarming degree, but an undercurrent of more positive influence is also evident.

That intercultural dynamic is part of what makes place. Over time, communities develop spatial identities and express them through music: Coast Salish log drums, the "Seattle sound," or a raven's gurgling chortle. All are sonic signifiers of place. Musical sound is particularly important to place making. Lawrence Grossberg calls music "a territorializing machine."[16] Songs like "Where the Fraser River Flows" and "Roll On Columbia"[17] color our territorial imaginations.[18]

Musical place making has a strong ethical dimension, as illustrated by the following excerpt from Bobs & Lolo's "I'm a Beat":

I'm a sound
Traveling through the ground
Or up in the air
You hear me everywhere

My favourite sounds
Come from the natural things

Wind, water, and wood
They all sound so good

You're a sound
With the voice that you've found
Sing in harmony
Come and sing with me[19]

Bobs & Lolo use sound to draw an ethical connection between kids and the Vancouver landscape.

Abreu offers another contemplation of place in *The Climate Monologues.* The piece is ostensibly about West Virginia, Colorado, and India—places thousands of miles from the Salish Sea—but once performed in Anacortes, it became very much about the Salish Sea. As the Anacortes community debated coal terminals and oil trains, Abreu's performance took on new, localized meanings. As Adams and Gynnild argue, most "interpretations are localized" in environmental communication.[20]

That is part of what differentiates environmentalist music from environmentally themed music as a broader category. The musicians profiled here are not just singing about local people and communities for the sake of crafting musical messages, such as when someone far from Mississippi borrows a guitar riff from the Delta Blues to communicate a sense of loss and lament in a song. For these musicians, place is more than a floating signifier. Environmentalist expressions of place are deeply embodied, material exigencies that make place intrinsically important to a song's meaning. It is not just place for music's sake but also music for place's sake. That might be one of the main distinctions between environmentalist music and music in general. We might never know if the hundreds of artists who use Pacific Northwest place-names in their music actually care about these places beyond their utility as musical signifiers, but we can be certain that Dana Lyons, The Wilds, and musicians like them care very deeply about the places they reference in song. As those musicians have made very clear in this book, their songs are very explicitly intended to help sustain those places.

The above argument goes for other environmentalist arts and artists. Take the case of Lummi artist Jewell James. Washington's master carver has promoted the development of a coalition to purchase land at Cherry

Point, the site proposed for a controversial coal-export terminal. He advocates for turning the threatened coastline into a marine sanctuary. Paralleling his political action, James's famous carvings present artful conceptions of place that take dirt, rock, people, water, and whales seriously, rather than appropriating them to simply serve his art as abstract metaphors. It is an ecologically connected ethic and aesthetic shared by the musicians profiled here. Of course, environmentalist artists use metaphor as well (a whale is never just a whale), but they also draw deep connections to actual whales, forests, birds, and ecosystems, expressing an ethical stake in their stewardship.[21]

SCALE

As Adams and Gynnild argue: "When communicating about the environment it is essential to speak of, about, and to place."[22] No matter how global the problem, most people relate to environmental issues on a local level. Abreu's songs about coal and climate change gain greater meaning when sung in a place like Anacortes, where people are struggling with similar energy production problems. Likewise, when sung in the ranch towns of eastern Montana, Lyons's "Sometimes" becomes a local entry into the global problem of climate change, not by presenting it as an abstract, global problem, but by putting the complex matter into a vernacular story form to which people in that region can readily relate: a community's struggle with coal companies.

Environmental inquiry requires ecological imagination, which begins with concern for place. Musical performance, when done well, inspires what is increasingly referred to as "glocal" thinking.[23] Having become a cliché, "think globally, act locally" has been replaced by an awkward portmanteau, "glocal." Whatever we call it, however, environmental science and environmentalist performance alike require an understanding of systemic relationships between different scales of abstraction, including the local in the global. And so, Chalifour's "This Land" draws connections between a pristine forest on Galiano Island and what people suffer in "Downtown Eastside." In the world of the song, seemingly disparate realities are connected to disastrous environmental policies and priorities that overwhelm local interests. Many if not most of the songs featured here seek to connect local consciousness to global contexts. Art encourages people to see and hear the world in a new way. Environmentalist musicians seek to inspire ecological imagination among their listeners, starting with the places they know and love and scaling up.

There is an entirely different question of scale running throughout this book as well: ensemble size. The cases presented here offer a serendipitous opportunity to explore differences between solo, duo, and group musicianship as related to performance and suggest that certain ensemble sizes favor specific ecomusical approaches while disadvantaging other strategies. For example, as soloists, Lyons and Chalifour are able to do things that duos and ensembles find difficult (e.g., it is probably no coincidence that Chalifour produced "This Land" alone and not with his full band, Towers and Trees). The soloist experiences logistic advantages and artistic freedoms that ensembles tend to constrain.

However, larger ensembles more directly represent community objectives and embody those values in concert. Large groups of musicians model group communication by listening to one another and responding rhythmically in model displays of entrainment. They produce sounds and sensations that add up to something much greater than the sum of their individual parts.

Nevertheless, group musicianship works against topicality, environmentalist or otherwise, for all the reasons laid out in chapter 1. It is far easier to hear and focus on words in solo concerts, far easier to fund and stage solo concerts, and far easier for the soloist to forge a coherent musical message than it is for an entire group of musicians to do so. When it comes to topical art, what is lost in collective musicianship is gained in communicative focus when the solo or duo take the stage. In sum, solo and group music represent and accomplish different things.

Increases in ensemble scale appear to have implications for professionalism as well. It is probably no coincidence that I could not find an actively gigging band in the region that dedicates the majority of their time to environmental issues. In all my discussions with musicians and environmentalists around the Salish Sea, I have yet to encounter an ensemble of three or more musicians who consistently work with environmental movements or place environmentally themed music at the center of their public personae. When it comes to bands and other large ensembles, there is simply no parallel to Dana Lyons, Bobs & Lolo, and the Irthlingz. In this book, the leap from duos to groups is also one from professionals to amateurs.

Free association works great for groups like the Raging Grannies, but it is an ineffective organizing principle for professional music groups. Of course, established folk, rock, jazz, and classical ensembles occasionally lend their weight to environmental efforts around the region, even if their lyrics and music have little to do with environmentalism. That is an extremely important phenomenon, one worthy of its own book. However, such bands are not "environmentalist musicians" in the way I am using the term here. Whereas Dana Lyons, Bobs & Lolo, The Wilds, the Irthlingz, and the Raging Grannies dedicate much of their time and effort to making music about environmental issues, professional bands do not.

In truth, very few musicians place ecological principles, environmental education, or environmental organizations at the core of their public personae. Nor should musicians be expected to do so. There is simply not enough audience to go around. Because of that, musicians who successfully synthesize musical performance, environmental activism, and professional performance have tended to operate on a very small scale. They are mainly soloists and duos, at least in the Cascadian context. We could hope that one day a full environmentalist band could match the touring success of Dana Lyons and Bobs & Lolo, but for now that sort of success appears to be out of reach. It would require a much more environmentally engaged audience and culture. Holly and Kevin, through facilitating full band concerts with The Wilds at the end of each school term, offer a promising model for larger-scale musical efforts.

Perhaps as more people become aware of and care about environmental challenges, the audience for environmentalist music will grow. However, there is at present no economy of scale for environmentalist or environmentally relevant music. If the underlying premise of this book holds true—that environmentalist music matters—then the hope is that in the near future there will be nothing terribly odd about a critic or fan referring to an entire band as "environmentalist." If bands can be viewed as anarchist (various punk bands), feminist (riot grrrl groups), and so on, why not environmentalist?

IDENTITY

Dominant cultural identities—race, ethnicity, nationality, gender, and class—are evoked and performed throughout environmentalist music. For example, it means something very different for a Musqueam drummer to perform a song-prayer on unceded territory than it does for a white musician to perform that same song.

In fact, the most effective performers are aware of how they are perceived by audiences, especially in terms of identity. A musician's persona is always negotiated with the audience. No matter what persona the performer projects, it is meaningless and useless if the audience does not recognize it as both interesting and legitimate. That is why performers often try out several personae before hitting on one that works. For example, Bob Dylan (Robert Zimmerman) and Joe Strummer (John Graham Mellor) both experimented with "Woody" before settling on their now-famous names and stage personae.

It is not a trivial matter. How an audience perceives a performer, in terms of identity, will radically affect how they will hear that performer, or whether or not he or she will be heard at all. Identity is central to perception, including articulations of race and genre. For example, the audience cedes Lyons a certain level of credibility when he inhabits the singer-songwriter "cowboy" archetype because that image has been so closely associated with whiteness and masculinity in the United States. A black woman might have a harder time inhabiting that role. We need look no further than Nina Simone for evidence. "If I had to be called anything it should be a folk singer," complained the American musical icon in response to critics and scholars who labeled her a "jazz singer." Simone argued that the misperception came about because she "didn't fit into white ideas of what a black performer should be."[24] The reverse is equally true, evidenced in the way many white rappers are labeled "wannabes." Environmentalist identities and stage personae are similarly influenced by popular and relatively narrow conceptions of race as it relates to genre.

The same can be said of gender and genre. Bobs & Lolo perform mostly within their audience's gendered expectations. If two men danced about in bright rain slickers and boots, they might have a harder time convincing parents to bring their children to concerts. Identity would become an obstacle to communicating environmental messages rather than an effective instrument. In other words, Bobs & Lolo do not take on the task of challenging gender expectations, it is more than enough to push the needle regarding environmental attitudes. Nor is Dana Lyons's main goal to change people's perceptions of whiteness or masculinity. Instead, many environmentalist musicians perform within recognizable archetypes and develop rich stage personae so that they can communicate effectively about environmental justice, biodiversity, and sustainability to audiences who might otherwise not be receptive to their message. And so ethnicity, gender, and age prefigure what is possible for many artists, including genre and style choices. Performers may adopt any persona or musical style they choose, but it does not mean that the audience will buy into their act or listen to them. A great deal of cultural work goes into the complex negotiation between artist and audience, and a number of interceding gatekeepers, from record labels to venue managers, mediate that relationship as well.

Nowhere does the connection between music and identity become more evident than in the case of the Raging Grannies. The Grannies are "growing old disgracefully," to borrow the subtitle from Andy Bennett's fascinating study of age and music.[25] In a time-honored tradition of political resistance, the Grannies have turned stigmatic identities of "old women" into potent weapons against politicians, military leaders, and CEOs who still have no idea what to do with older women dressed in outlandish granny costumes, singing clever lyrics, and performing provocative street theater. The Grannies turn identity from a social deficit into an effective weapon.

Intersectionality extends beyond race, class, and gender to place-based identities and stage personae. Musicians like Jimi Hendrix, Bikini Kill, Kurt Cobain, and Macklemore lend a sense of regional identity to local acts, circumscribing what is and is not cool for young rock and rap musicians around the Salish Sea to perform. Environmentalist identities are similarly connected to place. Ernest Callenbach's *Ecotopia*, first published in 1975, helped popularize a utopian conception of Cascadia.[26] Ever since, there has been a widespread perception that the Pacific Northwest is a place for iconoclasts, "eco-freaks" who identify with old-growth forests, and New Age philosophies.

However, the area's ecotopian reputation can be misleading. The widespread desire to be somewhere "natural" has, rather ironically, led the Pacific Northwest to differ wildly from its progressive reputation as a haven of sustainability. The region boasts some of the worst urban sprawl in the United States, with traffic and development patterns more akin to Southern California than Ecotopia. The situation is no better offshore. Salish Sea waterways are crowded with motor craft. The Salish Sea's archipelagos have become extensions of the mainland, just as dependent on Costco for subsistence as is the rest of suburban Seattle or Vancouver, with residents required to travel farther to shop there. The environmental costs of living in a supposedly remote, natural setting are extremely high, resulting in decreased biodiversity, ecosystemic integrity, and environmental injustice (i.e., the wealthy get paradise and others pay the costs).

Cascadia is one of those odd places where political liberalism (left-of-center politics) and economic liberalism (laissez-faire policies) overlap. Although populated by more liberals than conservatives, the Pacific Northwest retains strong remnants of a frontier mentality, a belief that nature's bounty is limitless. "Better to ask forgiveness than permission" is said with a nod and a wink, a way of sidestepping environmental protections. For example, in the San Juan Islands, organic farmers (many of whom are more accurately described as gardeners) on occasion join with libertarian Republicans in fighting proposals for stricter wetland setbacks, the distance between a sensitive wetland habitat and land that can be tilled or developed for residential occupation. The belief that all lands should be turned to agricultural or residential use, no matter how inefficient or ecologically unsustainable, drives many to support policies that work against biodiversity and sustainability.

That is true both north and south of the border, in Washington as well as in British Columbia. Both territories share the ecotopian reputation, yet neither is, in the main, substantially different in terms of policy and practice from the rest of the continent. Strategic uses of landscape for tourism and well-publicized acts of environmentalism give the rest of the world a sense that environmental stewardship is more successful in Cascadia than elsewhere. Unfortunately, public relations and reputation often substitute for reality. Although the number of musicians who sing about environmental issues might be slightly higher in Cascadia than elsewhere,

because of a very robust environmentalist subculture, these artists perform on cultural terrain that is perhaps only slightly more welcoming than
what musicians encounter elsewhere in the world.

An international border further frustrates attempts by environmentalists to promote regional identification with the Salish Sea ecosystem.
Looking across the Salish Sea from the hills above Bellingham, one can
easily see Vancouver Island to the west and metropolitan Vancouver to
the north. The city of Vancouver is a short drive away. However, crossing
the border can take hours. The border remains a very real obstacle to
cultural and political exchange. It is far easier for sea life to swim back and
forth across the border, or for goods to flow both ways, than it is for people
to walk, drive, sail, or bike across it. Cross-border consciousness and cooperation remain relatively weak as a result.

For these and other reasons, environmental movements tend to be
local, national, or global in scope, rather than regional. Each local organization operates on its own side of the border. Although Greenpeace started
in Vancouver, it now takes on challenges all over the planet, one of the few
nongovernmental organizations that crosses borders as effectively as
transnational corporations and markets do. Yet few organizations are
dedicated to the entirety of the Salish Sea and its special needs; they almost always stop at the international border.

Canadian First Nations and Native American tribes in the United
States are the other notable exception. Indigenous peoples were moving
throughout the region long before the border was drawn and continue to
work across national boundaries today. Indigenous cross-border cooperation is symbolized by annual canoe journeys and gatherings.[27] Each First
Nations community prepares its canoes and canoeists over the year and
then joins with other bands and nations in broad circuits, passages, and
central gatherings.

Coast Salish communities also instruct nonnatives on the cultural heritage of the Salish Sea, in part using music as the instructional medium.
For example, on June 7, 2014, I watched as members of the Swinomish
Indian Tribal Community and Samish Indian Nation taught visitors from
surrounding communities about the canoe tradition. The event, which
emphasized principles of environmental stewardship, began with drumming and singing, led by seven Swinomish and Samish musicians holding

frame drums, rattles, and striking sticks. After a song-prayer was offered, veteran canoeists helped local kids and their parents into a giant dugout canoe, instructed them on basic paddling techniques and safety protocols, and headed off across Bowman Bay. Coast Salish communities use the time-honored canoe journey tradition to promote conservation as well. Working with the United States Geological Survey, canoeists collected water samples, studied water quality, and educated the wider public during their journey.[28]

However, there is the danger of falling into the "ecological Indian" discourse when discussing Coast Salish conservation efforts and music. Shepard Krech criticizes that tendency in *The Ecological Indian: Myth and History*.[29] Yet, as Casey Schmitt argues in contrast to Krech, many Native American and First Nations activists are "explicitly linking environmental concerns to social issues that Westerners have not historically considered as 'environmental' matters, including housing, healthcare, social welfare, and economics."[30] To say that indigenous groups are leading environmental efforts around the Salish Sea is not to say that there is some intrinsic connection between indigeneity and stewardship. Few Idle No More activists, for example, claim essentialist connections to conservation. Depending on band, tribal, or national affiliation, native activists sometimes struggle as much against their own tribal councils and corporate boards as with outside forces like Enbridge.[31] To assume that a person or group will automatically work to steward resources because of indigenous identity is quite simply wrong.

However, Idle No More activists have tended to avoid the dehumanizing rhetoric Krech critiques. Instead of playing on "European perceptions of noble savagery," Idle No More's argument is based on advocacy for specific policy goals, alliances with the international environmental justice movement, and complex intersectional identification. As Schmitt argues, First Nations activists are adopting very different "ecological Indian" identities than the racist and essentialized "environmental identities" Krech decries.[32]

In fact, one of the strengths of Idle No More is that while activists draw very heavily on environmental identities and First Nations traditions, the movement avoids simplistic notions like (bad) "Western" versus "non-Western" (good) others, the simplistic binary many scholars seem reluctant to jettison. West-versus-the-rest rhetoric is ostensibly aimed at critiquing racism and colonialism, but that simplistic inversion is barely any better than the scientific racism underlying Western hegemony. Flipping the moral binary is evidence of hegemony rather than an effective form of resistance against it. With a more nuanced and critical view of power, Idle No More names specific institutions, bills, proposals, and policies rather than abstract conceptions like "Western society." Neither "West" nor "Western" is employed anywhere on the Idle No More website, The movement avoids dichotomous identity rhetoric in favor of more grounded and nuanced references and coalition-building rhetoric.[33] To circle back to the initial point, First Nations are playing an important role in restoring and advancing cross-border collaboration among environmentalists. In fact, that more nuanced and complicated sense of social dynamics holds true for most of the musicians featured here. Community organizers cannot afford to draw fixed lines of opposition or treat people as if they are simply either allies or enemies.

Unfortunately, unsustainable institutions have been creating cross-border coalitions with even greater success than First Nations. Companies like Canada's Enbridge and Kinder Morgan have effectively coordinated activities and allied interests across the border for years, and the Canadian and United States' governments have facilitated those exchanges at the expense of local biomes. Meanwhile, most Cascadian organizations, activists, and artists operate either north or south of the border but rarely across it.

Fostering a regional identity is essential to collaborative stewardship of the shared marine ecosystem. Music has an important role to play in that regard, but as each case in this book demonstrates, that potential has not yet been realized. Other than the accidental spread of Raging Grannies gaggles, there is little evidence of musical networking across the border at this point. My hope is that this project can in some small way contribute, and there are elements of Ecosong.net dedicated to that as well. For example, several of the musicians profiled here expressed interest in performing a transnational tour around the Salish Sea to coincide with the release of the book. If that happens, maybe it will provide some small indication of how more transnational collaborations could be executed in the future.

HUMOR

Believe it or not, toxic pollution and climate change have their humorous sides. Rather than deadly serious doom-and-gloom rhetoric, most of these artists use humor to bring home their environmental messages. With songs like "Cows with Guns," Lyons grabs his audience's attention and performs with a disarming charm that allows serious ideas to be communicated. Similarly, the Raging Grannies make audiences laugh and think. So, too, Bobs & Lolo get kids laughing, singing, and dancing instead of boring them with didactic detail. Humor has been integral to the performers' success.

Martin Branagan discovered the same connection between music and humor in his study "Environmentalist Education, Activism, and the Arts."[34] He argues that laughter is more productive than tears. Similarly, Alison Bodkin argues that comedic performances are extremely good at exposing "illogical claims that sound ecologically savvy," such as "clean coal."[35] Both scholars show how comedic performance builds community, propels movements, and welcomes the wider public into the conversation.

Conversely, some common environmental communication techniques repel audiences.[36] For example, doom-and-gloom environmentalism may scare away audiences. Born during the Cold War, environmentalism took on many of the same apocalyptic tendencies as Cold War rhetoric, with environmental apocalypse simply substituted for nuclear annihilation.[37] While environmental problems do rise to the level of crisis, millenarian rhetoric does little to inform, persuade, or mobilize.

The perception of environmental doom and gloom might be reinforced by popular culture. Environmentalists and environmental scientists tend to deal with either global abstractions (e.g., climate change) or matters on the microscopic scale (e.g., toxins). Both are beyond human vision and, as Jennifer Peeples explains in her work on the "Toxic Sublime," invisible environmental issues take a great deal of creativity to meaningfully represent in science, art, and the press.[38] Given the gap between human perception, on one hand, and the micro- and macroscopic scales of environmental problems, on the other, fictional texts might unfortunately become intertextual stand-ins for public audiences. Films and novels serve as a lens through which environmental information is understood and metaphors for engaging frightening unknowns. In film, television, and fiction, environmental crises often result in apocalypse. That might lead some audiences to convert serious environmental data and predictions into dystopian visions of the future, even when scientists or environmentalists communicate information in a more nuanced frame of reference. For example, as Naomi Klein points out in *This Changes Everything*, venture capitalists and geo-engineers have employed hyperbolic narratives in order to profit from environmental problems while potentially worsening the situation through technological quick fixes.[39]

Humor takes the conversation in a very different direction. In a climate dominated by doom and gloom, humor opens the door to more sober consideration of environmental problems and probabilities than is possible with apocryphal tales and apocalyptic rhetoric. Therefore, environmentalist musicians have found humor to be a useful form of communication. Scientists, environmental campaign organizers, and policy makers could learn a lesson from these successful musicians, in terms of not only adopting their rhetorical strategies but also relying a bit more on music and the arts to get their messages across. As an emotive medium, music is particularly good at helping audiences consider matters that might otherwise seem overwhelming and immutable.

COMMUNICATION

Which brings us to the final common theme: communication. Surprisingly, despite a robust subdiscipline called "environmental communication," few communication scholars have studied environmentally themed music. A photo of the Raging Grannies made the cover of *Environmental Communication* in June 2012, but there has been very little in the journal beyond passing mentions of music.

Yet when it comes to communication, the arts and music play roles every bit as important as science and policy. Take the case of coal and oil transportation policy across the Pacific Northwest and western Canada. Musicians like Lyons, the Raging Grannies, Chalifour, and the Irthlingz, as well as Idle No More activists, have been every bit as essential to impeding the plans of Enbridge, Kinder Morgan, Peabody Energy, and other giant energy companies as have scientists and others speaking out against them. The arts and activism, in addition to science, play important roles in environmental regulation. Although art, science, and policy seem to be distinctly different rhetorical modes, media, and professions, they blend together in practice more often than is imagined or modeled in the academic world. Systematic, relational, and holistic models of environmental communication—in other words, *ecological* models of communication—should include the arts and popular culture as well as science, policy making, and social movements when attempting to figure out how environmental ideas, rhetorics, and information circulate. As argued at the outset of this chapter, ecosystems are made up of much more than their material components and processes. Culture plays a strong, if not overdeterminant role.

Fortunately, communication researchers have begun examining how the performing arts express environmental messages. For example, Richard Besel and Jnan Blau's *Performance on Behalf of the Environment* provides several good examples of how creative performance mediates environmental matters.[40] Perhaps that book is a harbinger of more good work to come. Music is, among many other things, an essential medium for human communication. It is useful to know how individuals, communities, and institutions craft musical messages, exchange information, frame debates, and create new visions of the future through music. Studying music as communication can help us better understand how music coheres communities, assists coordination, expresses identity, fosters creativity, and delivers messages.

Even musicians tend to underplay the power of their art. For example, only after decades of success did Lyons fairly recently come around to the belief that music "can help frame a debate" in addition to promulgating messages. Based on this research, I very much agree. Lyons chose his words well. Music *helps* frame debates, working intertextually with scientific information, rhetorics of social justice, allied arts, and, most importantly, social movements.

Similarly, Patricia Cué illustrates the "layered" nature of environmental framing in her study of Mexican wall paintings and music advertisements.[41] She demonstrates how muralists visually frame public soundscapes. Her work reminds us that musical soundscapes are deeply articulated with visual references, including the landscape.[42] As another example, wildlife artist Robert Bateman uses a line from Joni Mitchell's "Big Yellow Taxi" to describe his painting *Cardinal and Wild Apples*: "give me spots on my apples but leave me the birds and the bees." Like the Mexican muralists Cué studies, British Columbia's Bateman makes music without emitting a sound.[43]

In addition to intertextual expressions of meaning, environmental music communicates informational messages. Kids learn about animal and plant life through Bobs & Lolo's recordings and performances as well as The Wilds' Voices of Nature songs and school curricula. Lyons's songs and between-song banter present important information to the audience. For example, he made the following joke at one concert I attended: "They're just saying how great it is to put frog genes in fruit trees and mouse genes in pigs and human genes in rice. Enjoy your rice!" That might seem like a good joke, a hyperbolic take on a serious problem (artistic license), but all three of those seemingly preposterous gene transfers have been accomplished or proposed for regulatory approval.[44] Granted, a concert is not the place for sober deliberation of environmental policy, but it might be where some people learn that there is a debate to be had in the first place, much as many rock fans in the 1980s learned about apartheid at human rights benefits or how labor union tenets have been communicated musically for more than a century. A concert or a song is not the best medium for conveying detailed information, perhaps—Lyons does not claim to be an expert on GMOs—but music is an essential form of expression and, as such, a very effective headline service.

Environmentalist musicians ask audiences to feel and care more deeply about environmental issues. Typically, scientific information does not move people to love nature and cherish habitats. People are often unaware of how a local ecosystem functions in scientific terms, even though they greatly value and protect it. Instead of an intellectual engagement with place, people experience place with their full range of senses, creating emotional connections through smelling an ocean breeze or listening to the comforting sound of seagulls or watching the drizzle drift through cedar branches. Music tends to work that way as well, via sense impression more than denotative communication. From time immemorial, humans have expressed their sense of belonging to a given place by referencing its natural attributes, through music, art, and other forms of expression. Therefore, it is little wonder that environmentalists turn to music to express their concerns and communicate with audiences.

Environmental communication scholars have much to add to the study of how people relate to place through music, joining musicologists, ethnomusicologists, cultural studies scholars, anthropologists, and others who have taken up the subject. The most robust academic arena for that interdisciplinary discussion thus far has been a growing field called "ecomusicology."[45]

TOWARD AN APPLIED ECOMUSICOLOGY

Ecomusicology is certainly not the first field of scholarly research to consider music and environment. That started at least as far back as 1838, with the publication of William Gardiner's *The Music of Nature*.[46] Music-and-nature has been an important theme in musicology and a central concern of ethnomusicologists as well. So why start a new conversation called "ecomusicology"? As renowned ethnomusicologist Tony Seeger joked at the 2012 Shasha Seminar for Human Concerns, at Wesleyan University, Connecticut: "I am glad to see that they are giving a new name to what we have always been doing."

While it is true that music-and-nature has been an important theme in music research for years, music studies scholars have tended to neglect environment in the ecological sense and have not consistently engaged with scientists and other researchers in environmental studies. The meta-discipline of environmental studies has engaged everyone from biologists to poets in meaningful conversations around environmental health, biodiversity, sustainability, environmental justice, and other concerns related to the keyword "ecology." If musical research concerning nature does not fit into that very big tent—and thus far it rarely has—matters like biodiversity, environmental health, and environmental justice are probably getting short shrift in music studies as well. Therefore, in 2002, Alexander Rehding suggested the term "ecomusicology" for a more robust and interdisciplinary conversation around music and the environment.[47] Since then, publications like Aaron Allen and Kevin Dawe's *Current Directions in Ecomusicology* have advanced our understanding of how music relates to ecological questions, and upcoming publications promise to greatly advance the field, including the *Oxford Handbook of Ecomusicology* edited by Sabine Feisst.[48]

As for the role of environmentalist advocacy and activism in music, Tyler Kinnear put the matter into perspective in the "Sound, Environment, and Action" special issue of *Music and Politics*: "While humanities research on humans and the physical world is not new, the emerging field of ecomusicology seeks to develop discursive tools for the study of music during a time of rapid environmental change. Only recently has 'politics' received critical attention in ecomusicological scholarship."[49] Over the years, there has been a great deal of study on the ways in which organology and composition reflect the natural world, but surprisingly little attention has been paid to how music relates to environmental crises, biodiversity, environmental health, or environmental justice. Ecomusicology responded to that gap in disciplinary knowledge.[50] Aaron Allen, Kevin Dawe, and Jennifer Post are among the leaders of that effort, taking the study of instrument manufacture toward a more complete understanding of how materials and meanings circulate, with specific reference to sustainability and biodiversity.[51] Their work shows how music and musicians relate to issues like deforestation and climate change. That is just one example of how ecomusicological research has taken the musicological conversation into ecological terrain.

Nevertheless, few scholars have studied ecopolitical advocacy through music, although several have called for such study to take place. For example, in *The Book of Music and Nature*, David Rothenberg suggests that we study music as "protest."[52] Similarly, David Ingram observes: "Further research is needed in reception studies to investigate how particular pieces of music have actually affected listeners, and whether they have played a part in organizations or subcultures involved in environmental activism."[53] This book takes on Rothenberg's and Ingram's calls to study music as "environmental activism" and "protest" as illustrated by the lifelong work of Lyons, the Raging Grannies, Idle No More, the Artist Response Team, and Abreu and by Chalifour's "This Land" video. This research has been guided by the following questions: How does music contribute to environmental movements? What does environmentalist music mean to those who create it? How might we, as environmentalists, more effectively perform music in the service of biodiversity, sustainability, and environmental justice? I believe that the musicians interviewed, observed, and profiled here provide intriguing answers based on their many years of experience, experimentation, and success. That is what brought me to each one's doorstep, song catalogs, and concerts.

So what are we to do with the knowledge these case studies provide? As an applied scholar, I hope this is actionable intelligence. One of the main reasons I undertook this work was to find new ways of composing, recording, distributing, and performing community-based music from an ecological standpoint. I was interested in learning from successful artists, and, having mined the Salish Sea region for best cases, I have discovered many worth emulating. Scholars of community music have long encouraged us to take our work beyond the academy, borrowing good ideas from one another.[54] "The new advocacy ethnomusicology," explains Jennifer Post, "is used to seek solutions for contemporary social problems."[55] That is the objective of this work, to use real-world examples in order to provide musicians, organizers, students, music researchers, and other citizens with new ideas regarding how we might advocate for more effective environmental policies, institutions, and actions.[56]

So what is the reader to do with all this? How does it help anyone to know how Dana Lyons puts together campaign-tours, The Wilds teach children about intertidal zones, the Raging Grannies agitate for ecological sanity, Adrian Chalifour sings for trees, the Irthlingz bring together a community, or Idle No More builds broad coalitions throughout Canada? I cannot say for certain, but I do know that there is much more to be done in the applied study of environmentalist music. And so this work continues on Ecosong.net, a digital exchange designed to continue and expand the conversation.

Ecosong.net is based on the principles of community music. Lee Higgins explains community music as a commitment "to the idea that everybody has the right and ability to make, create, and enjoy their own music."[57] Ecosong.net provides a platform for sharing music related to environmental issues and ecosystems.[58] Specifically, it is a social networking site for the exchange of songs, music videos, and ideas. Please consider taking part in that exchange.

Reading about these inspiring artists will, I hope, be a catalyst for cultural action. Performance is "particularly important for environmental movements," explain David Terry and Anne Marie Todd, "because effective environmental activism must be able to not only critique existing relationships" but also model "alternative modes of belonging."[59] Alternative "modes of belonging" must be imagined and performed before they are realized. Most people appreciate the beauty and meaning in music, but we sometimes forget how important music is to our collective lives. As these talented artists have demonstrated time and again, when it comes to preserving a planet, community, or sea, nothing is more essential than music.

AFTERWORD

On May 9, 2016, the Army Corps of Engineers denied a permit for construction of the Gateway Pacific Coal Terminal at Cherry Point, near Ferndale, Washington. It was a landmark victory for the Lummi Nation and their environmentalist allies including Dana Lyons, the Raging Grannies, the Irthlingz, and Idle No More activists throughout the Salish Sea region.

NOTES

1. I return to using the performers' last names in this chapter in order to more clearly identify them in context and distinguish them from one another. Whereas the case studies lent themselves to more personal treatment, bringing them all together in the introduction and conclusion requires the use of stage names and last names.

2. Mikko Keskinen, "Her Mistress's Voice: Gynophonocentrism in Feminist Discourses," *Journal of International Women's Studies* 2, no. 1 (2013): 2. Also see Mark Pedelty and Morgan Kuecker, "Seen to Be Heard? Gender, Voice, and Body in Television Advertisements," *Communication and Critical/Cultural Studies* 11, no. 3 (2014): 250–269.

3. Sabine Feisst, "Animal Ecologies: Laurie Spiegel's Musical Explorations of Urban Wildlife," *Social Alternatives* 33, no. 1 (2014): 16.

4. That might be why works invoking "voice" so often neglect nonverbal qualities of voice. That is both the promise and limitation of books like the edited volume *Voice and Environmental Communication* (see Jennifer Peeples and Stephen Depoe, eds., *Voice and Environmental Communication* [Basingstoke, Hampshire, England: Palgrave Macmillan, 2014]). Such work does great service in bringing voice to environmental inquiry. However, by considering voice as rhetorical metaphor for agency while ignoring actual

sound, such work shows how much further we have to go toward understanding the relationship between voice and environment.

5. Lee Higgins, *Community Music: In Theory and in Practice* (Oxford: Oxford University Press, 2012), 7, 32–37.

6. Jan Curtis, "Ecology and the Arts," *International Journal of the Arts in Society* 5, no. 6 (2011): 277, 284.

7. Julie Rickwood, "Choralecology?: Community Choirs and Environmental Activism," *Social Alternatives* 33, no. 1 (2014): 30–38.

8. For interesting comparisons and analogies between human and animal musics and voices, see Vivek Nityananda and Mark A. Bee, "Finding Your Mate at a Cocktail Party: Frequency Separation Promotes Auditory Stream Segregation of Concurrent Voices in Multi-species Frog Choruses," *PLOS One* 6, no. 6 (2011): e21191; and also see Archie Powell and Sara Ramsden, *Why Birds Sing*, BBC Productions, accessed January 11, 2015, http://watchdocumentary.org/watch/why-birds-sing-video_7f9015c5d.html.

9. Page 36 in Julie Rickwood, "Choralecology?: Community Choirs and Environmental Activism," *Social Alternatives* 33, no. 1 (2014): 30–38.

10. Lee Higgins, *Community Music: In Theory and in Practice* (Oxford: Oxford University Press, 2012), 7, 32–37.

11. Nicholas J. Conard, Maria Malina, and Susanne C. Münzel, "New Flutes Document the Earliest Musical Tradition in Southwestern Germany," *Nature* 460, no. 7256 (2009): 737–740.

12. Travis D. Stimeling, "Music, Place, and Identity in the Central Appalachian Mountaintop Removal Mining Debate," *American Music* 30, no. 1 (2012): 3.

13. Theresa J. May, "Indigenous Theater in Global Times: Situated Knowledge and Ecological Communities in *Salmon Is Everything* and *Burning Vision*," in Richard D. Besel and Jnan A. Blau, eds., *Performance on Behalf of the Environment* (Lanham, MD: Lexington Books, 2013), 193.

14. Bruno Latour, "Agency at the Time of the Anthropocene," *New Literary History* 45, no. 1 (2014): 1–18.

15. Theresa J. May, "Indigenous Theater in Global Times: Situated Knowledge and Ecological Communities in *Salmon Is Everything* and *Burning Vision*," in Richard D. Besel and Jnan A. Blau, eds., *Performance on Behalf of the Environment* (Lanham, MD: Lexington Books, 2013), 206.

16. Lawrence Grossberg, *We Gotta Get Out of This Place: Popular Conservatism and Postmodern Culture* (New York: Routledge, 2014), 104.

17. "Where the Fraser River Flows," Joe Hill, performed by Utah Phillips, YouTube video, accessed January 2, 2015, https://www.youtube.com/watch?v=7Rww4Fx5NeY; "Roll On Columbia," Woody Guthrie, *Columbia River Collection*, Rounder Records, 1988.

18. "This Land Is Your Land," lyrics by Adrian Chalifour, melody by Woody Guthrie (borrowed from the Carter Family Singers), performed by Adrian Chalifour, YouTube, accessed January 7, 2015, http://www.towersandtreesmusic.com/2012/02/29/this-land-was-made-for-you-and-me/.

19. "I'm a Beat," Bobs & Lolo, *Connecting the Dots*, Bobolo Productions, 2011.

20. Paul C. Adams and Astrid Gynnild, "Environmental Messages in Online Media: The Role of Place," *Environmental Communication: A Journal of Nature and Culture* 7, no. 1 (2013): 114.

21. Once again, I am not saying that all or even most music should maintain such a relationship to place-based references—that would be worse than restrictive; rather, I am trying to explain the more specific relationship to place in most environmentalist music.

22. Page 114 in Paul Adams and Astrid Gynnild, "Environmental Messages in Online Media: The Role of Place," *Environmental Communication: A Journal of Nature and Culture* 7, no. 1 (2013): 113–130.

23. William H. Thornton, "Mapping the 'Glocal' Village: The Political Limits of 'Glocalization,'" *Continuum: Journal of Media & Cultural Studies* 14, no. 1 (2000): 79–89.

24. Nina Simone, *I Put a Spell on You: The Autobiography of Nina Simone* (Boston: Da Capo Press, 2003), 69.

25. Andy Bennett, *Music, Style, and Aging: Growing Old Disgracefully?* (Philadelphia: Temple University Press, 2013).

26. Ernest Callenbach, *Ecotopia* (New York: Random House, 2009).

27. "Tribal Journeys to Bella Bella," First Nations in British Columbia, accessed January 11, 2015, http://fnbc.info/event/tribal-journeys-bella-bella-2014.

28. Krista J. Kapralos, "Science Hitches a Ride on Tribal Canoe Journey," *Herald of Everett, Washington,* last modified March 3, 2008, http://www.heraldnet.com/article /20080303/NEWS01/855603740.

29. Shepard Krech, *The Ecological Indian: Myth and History* (New York: W. W. Norton, 2000).

30. Casey R. Schmitt, "Invoking the Ecological Indian: Rhetoric, Culture, and the Environment," in Jennifer Peeples and Stephen Depoe, eds., *Voice and Environmental Communication* (Hampshire, Basingstoke, England: Palgrave Macmillan, 2014), 67–68.

31. Although the documentary *Musicwood* is about an Alaskan conflict, it provides an interesting glimpse into intratribal conflicts over conservation, with official leadership promoting clear-cutting of old-growth forests of Sitka spruce while many members oppose the profit-driven efforts to accumulate personal wealth at the expense of future generations of indigenous and nonindigenous residents alike. Maxine Trump, dir., *Musicwood,* DVD (Brooklyn, NY: Helpman Productions, 2013).

32. Casey R. Schmitt, "Invoking the Ecological Indian: Rhetoric, Culture, and the Environment," in Jennifer Peeples and Stephen Depoe, eds., *Voice and Environmental Communication* (Hampshire, Basingstoke, England: Palgrave Macmillan, 2014), 67–68.

33. Idle No More, accessed January 9, 2015, http://www.idlenomore.ca.

34. Martin Branagan, "Education, Activism, and the Arts," *Convergence* 38, no. 4 (2005): 33–50.

35. Alison Bodkin, "Eco-comedy Performance: An Alchemy of Environmentalism and Humor," in Richard D. Besel and Jnan A. Blau, eds., *Performance on Behalf of the Environment* (Lanham, MD: Lexington Books, 2013), 53.

36. Ibid., 68.

37. M. Jimmie Killingsworth, "From Environmental Rhetoric to Ecocomposition and Ecopoetics: Finding a Place for Professional Communication," *Technical Communication Quarterly* 14, no. 4 (2005): 359–373.

38. Jennifer Peeples, "Toxic Sublime: Imaging Contaminated Landscapes," *Environmental Communication: A Journal of Nature and Culture* 5, no. 4 (2011): 373–392.

39. Naomi Klein, *This Changes Everything* (New York: Simon and Schuster, 2014), 31–62.

40. Richard D. Besel and Jnan A. Blau, eds., *Performance on Behalf of the Environment* (Lanham, MD: Lexington Books, 2013).

41. Patricia Cué, "On the Wall: Designers as Agents for Change in Environmental Communication," *Visible Language* 48, no. 2 (2014): 70–83.

42. Also see Daniel Grimley, "Hearing Landscape Critically," University of Oxford Faculty Research, accessed January 15, 2015, http://www.music.ox.ac.uk/research /projects/hearing-landscape-critically/. The University of Oxford project is dealing with sound and the role of aural analysis in "interpreting the role that landscape, space and place have played in ideas of occupation, reservation, institution, restitution, academy, capital, knowledge, authenticity and legitimation."

43. Robert Bateman, *Cardinal and Wild Apples*, accessed January 15, 2015, http:// robertbateman.ca/paintings/CardinalWildApples.htm.

44. See Rick Weiss, "USDA Backs Production of Rice with Human Genes," *Washington Post*, last modified March 2, 2007, http://www.washingtonpost.com/wp-dyn/content /article/2007/03/01/AR2007030101495.html; Andrew Pollack, "Move to Market Gene-Altered Pigs in Canada Is Halted," *New York Times*, accessed April 3, 2012, http://www .nytimes.com/2012/04/04/science/gene-altered-pig-project-in-canada-is-halted.html?_r =1&.http://www.utsandiego.com/news/2014/oct/31/breeding-better-stone-fruit/; and Nan Sterman, "Breeding Better Fruit," *San Diego Union Tribune*, accessed October 31, 2014, http://www.utsandiego.com/news/2014/oct/31/breeding-better-stone-fruit/.

45. Aaron Allen and Kevin Dawe, *Current Directions in Ecomusicology* (New York: Routledge, 2015).

46. William Gardiner, *The Music of Nature* (Boston: J. H. Wilkins & R. B. Carter, 1838).

47. Alexander Rehding, "Review Article: Eco-Musicology," *Journal of the Royal Musical Association* 127, no. 2 (2002): 305–320.

48. Aaron Allen and Kevin Dawe, *Current Directions in Ecomusicology* (New York: Routledge, 2015).

49. Tyler Kinnear, "Introduction to Special Issue: 'Sound, Environment, and Action,'" *Music and Politics* 8, no. 2 (2014), accessed January 13, 2015, http://quod.lib.umich.edu/m /mp/9460447.0008.201/--introduction-to-special-issue-sound-environment-and-action ?rgn=main;view=fulltext.

50. Ecocriticism Study Group (ESG), *Ecomusicology Bibliography*, American Musicological Society (AMS), accessed January 13, 2015, http://www.ecomusicology.info /resources/bibliography/.

51. Their book, tentatively titled *The Tree That Became a Lute: Musical Instruments, Sustainability and the Politics of Natural Resource Use*, is contracted to University of Illinois Press and planned for release in 2016.

52. David Rothenberg and Marta Ulvaeus, eds., *The Book of Music and Nature: An Anthology of Sounds, Words, Thoughts* (Middletown, CT: Wesleyan University Press, 2013), 7.

53. David Ingram, *The Jukebox in the Garden: Ecocriticism and American Popular Music since 1960* (Amsterdam: Rodopi, 2010), 236.

54. Applied research can be difficult, not only because of the considerable time required for community action, but also because of biases against applied research in the academy. In anthropology, for example, applied work has long been marginalized, partly out of legitimate fears of institutional cooptation, fears generated out of a history of unethical applications of anthropological knowledge for military agencies and corporations. The paid governmental or corporate researcher must first and foremost pay the piper. Unfortunately, that fear has resulted in wider bias against applied research in general. Regarding applied ethnomusicology as it relates to community music, see also Lee Higgins,

Community Music: In Theory and in Practice (Oxford: Oxford University Press, 2012), 124–128.

55. Jennifer C. Post, ed., *Ethnomusicology: A Contemporary Reader* (New York: Routledge, 2013), 10. See also Charles R. Hale, "What Is Activist Research?" *Items and Issues: Social Science Research Council* 2, no. 1–2 (2001): 13–15.

56. This sort of applied work might seem tendentious to some. In response to the first concern, I agree. In fact, there are tendentious assumptions underlying this entire work, but they are the basic ethical principles underlying environmental studies as a whole. Scholars in environmental studies stake out the tendentious position that species retention is preferable to extinction, believe that sustainable uses of resources are better than robbing from future generations, and feel that environmental health and well-being should be shared and that no community should be forced to live in toxic "sacrifice zones." These are moral stances rather than manifest material facts. We like to think those views are informed by logic and evidence, but there is clearly an ethical belief underlying them. After all, from a purely scientific or critical point of view, a dead planet is no worse than a living one. We choose our ethics as musicians, scholars, activists, and people. So, yes, applied ecomusicology is tendentious, just as tendentious as environmental studies, economics, or any other pursuit of knowledge. According to several Gallup polls, environmentalist positions are widely shared by the American public. See Gallup, "Environment," accessed January 15, 2015, http://www.gallup.com/poll/1615/environment.aspx). In relation to environmentalist movements, 18 percent of Americans consider themselves to be "active" and an additional 42 percent "sympathetic," 26 percent see themselves as "neutral," and only 10 percent are "unsympathetic." Holding the above views does not blind ecomusicological researchers any more than sharing them keeps environmental biologists, bookkeepers, and musicians from doing their work well.

57. See Lee Higgins, *Community Music: In Theory and in Practice* (Oxford: Oxford University Press, 2012), 5.

58. My academic interest in the phenomenon was driven partly by a personal desire to learn from successful musical activists. Ongoing collaboration with local groups in Minnesota, like Metro Blooms (metroblooms.org), and Blue Thumb (bluethumb.org), convinces me that part-time musicians and music scholars can also help community organizers and activists achieve their goals. See Mark Pedelty, *Ecomusicology: Rock, Folk, and the Environment* (Philadelphia: Temple University Press, 2012), 129–198.

59. David P. Terry and Anne Marie Todd, "It's a Party, Not a Protest: Environmental Community, Co-incident Performance, and the San Jose Bike Party," in Richard D. Besel and Jnan A. Blau, eds., *Performance on Behalf of the Environment* (Lanham, MD: Lexington Books, 2013), 11. See also Sarah Schweizer et al., "Strategies for Communicating about Climate Change Impacts on Public Lands," *Science Communication* 31, no. 2 (2009): 272.

DISCOGRAPHY

American Industrial Ballads. Pete Seeger. Smithsonian Folkways, 1992.

"Bella Ciao." Solidarity Notes Labour Choir. Accessed January 9, 2015. http://www
.solidaritynotes.ca/mp3s/bellaciaosoprano.mp3.

"Beluga Song." Bobs & Lolo. *Sea Notes.* Bobolo Productions, 2004.

"Beneath the Forest Floor." Hildegard Westerkamp. Compositions. Accessed January 10,
2015. http://www.sfu.ca/~westerka/program_notes/forestfloor.html.

"Buffy Sainte-Marie Demonstrates the Mouth Bow." YouTube video. Accessed January 9,
2015. https://www.youtube.com/watch?v=DkWMC2zS1fU.

"Chief Dan George Prayer Song." YouTube video. Accessed January 9, 2015. https://www
.youtube.com/watch?v=lbXal6XhfAY.

"Coast Salish Anthem." YouTube video. Accessed January 9, 2015. https://www.youtube
.com/watch?v=Nj55oGcNkBs.

"Coast Salish Anthem." YouTube video. Accessed January 9, 2015. https://www.youtube
.com/watch?v=S3KwoaR6VW8.

"Connecting the Dots." Bobs & Lolo. *Connecting the Dots.* Bobolo Productions, 2011.

"Cows with Guns." Dana Lyons. Reigning Records, 1996.

"Cows with Guns." Words, music, and performance by Dana Lyons. Video animation
by Cameron Edser and Michael Richards of GooRoo Animation. YouTube video.
Accessed January 7, 2015. https://www.youtube.com/watch?v=a5s5qGgo1nE.

"Cows with Guns." Words, music, and performance by Dana Lyons. Video animation by
Bjorn-Mange Stuestol. YouTube video. Accessed January 7, 2015. https://www.youtube
.com/watch?v=FQMbXvn2RNI.

"Devil on the Highway." *Broken Record.* Words and music by Adrian Chalifour. Performed
by Towers and Trees, 2012.

"Drop of Water." Dana Lyons. Reigning Records, 1998.

"Flesh and Bone." *Chapel Sessions.* Words and music by Adrian Chalifour. Performed by
Towers and Trees. YouTube video. Accessed January 7, 2015. https://www.youtube.com
/watch?v=B-yqt-Fltbo.

"Flesh and Bone." *Live at the Canoe Brew Pub*. Words and music by Adrian Chalifour. Performed by Towers and Trees. YouTube video. Accessed January 7, 2015. https://www.youtube.com/watch?v=9ZtlwW39qq4.

"Forty Million Salmon (Can't Be Wrong)." The Wilds. Artist Response Team. Accessed July 31, 2015. https://www.youtube.com/watch?v=_fRB8EgnbGk.

"Give the Peace a Chance." Keep the Peace Allstars. Artist Response Team, 2015. YouTube video. Accessed August 3, 2016. https://www.youtube.com/watch?v=jEdGdFJ7XUY.

"God Bless America." *The Best of Kate Smith*. Words and music by Irving Berlin. Performed by Kate Smith. BMG, 1967.

The Great Salish Sea. Dana Lyons. Reigning Records, 2014.

Holly Arntzen. Holly Arntzen. Artist Response Team, 1991.

Hudson Valley Suite. Composed by Robert Starer. MCA Music, 1983.

"I'm a Beat." Bobs & Lolo. *Connecting the Dots*. Bobolo Productions, 2011.

"Label GMO Disco." Dana Lyons. YouTube video. Accessed January 12, 2015. https://www.youtube.com/watch?v=ho2H7b1tUgQ.

Last Spike: The Great Canadian Whistlestop Tour. Various artists. Artist Response Team, 1991.

"Legendary." Words, music, and performance by Mahogany Jones and Nique Love-Rhodes. Video by Piper Carter. *5E Gallery*. Accessed January 11, 2015. Ecosong.org.

"Little Boxes." Composed by Malvina Reynolds. Performed by Pete Seeger. Smithsonian Folkways Recordings, 1999.

"Log Song." Bobs & Lolo. *Connecting the Dots*. Bobolo Productions, 2011.

"Mi Novia." Agustin Lara. Black Round Records, 2011.

"Montreal." *Broken Record*. Words and music by Adrian Chalifour. Performed by Towers and Trees, 2012.

"Muscles." Bobs & Lolo. *Action Packed*. Bobolo Productions, 2008.

"New World Water." Lyrics by Mos Def. Composed by Dante Smith. Performed by Mos Def. Rawkus/Priority, 1999.

"No Frackin' No Way!" Lyrics by Vicki Ryder. Accessed January 7, 2015. http://raginggrannies.net/no-frackin-no-way.

"Now That the Buffalo's Gone." Buffy Sainte-Marie. *It's My Way!* Vanguard, 2006.

"Ocean Blue." Bobs & Lolo. YouTube video. Accessed January 6, 2015. https://www.youtube.com/watch?v=ABFdw7D-jxw.

"Our State Is a Dumpsite." Dana Lyons. Reigning Records, 1985.

"The Preacher and the Slave," Lyrics by Joe Hill. First published in the July 6, 1911, edition of the Industrial Workers of the World's *Little Red Songbook*.

"Raindrop Pop." Bobs & Lolo. YouTube video. Accessed January 6, 2015. https://www.youtube.com/watch?v=ok2fEPJ4060.

"The Rapture." Seattle Raging Grannies. Accessed January 7, 2015. http://raginggrannies.org/seattle/the-rapture/.

"Really Don't Care." Demi Lovato. *Demi*. Hollywood Records, 2013.

"Recycle Wrap." Dana Lyons. Reigning Records, 2006.

"Ride the Lawn." Dana Lyons. Lyons Brothers Music, 2004.

"Roll On Columbia." Woody Guthrie. *Columbia River Collection*. Rounder Records, 1988.

Running from the Mountains. Holly Arntzen and the Watershed Choir. Artist Response Team, 1999.

Salish Sea. Holly Arntzen and the Saltwater Singers. Artist Response Team, 2000.

Sea Notes. Bobs & Lolo. *Sea Notes*. Bobolo Productions, 2004.

"Sea Turtles Are Special to Me." Bobs & Lolo. *Sea Notes*. Bobolo Productions, 2004.

"Sixteen Tons." Merle Travis. *In Boston, 1959*. Rounder Records, 2003.

"Sometimes (The Coal Train Song)." Dana Lyons. Lyons Brothers Music, 2012.

"The Tree." Dana Lyons. Lyons Brothers Music, 1994.

"This Land Is Your Land." Lyrics by Woody Guthrie. Melody by Woody Guthrie (borrowed from the Carter Family Singers). Performed by Woody Guthrie. Washington, DC: Smithsonian Folkways Recordings, 1999.

"This Land Is Your Land." Lyrics by Woody Guthrie. Accessed January 7, 2015. http://www.woodyguthrie.org/Lyrics/This_Land.htm.

"This Land Is Your Land." Lyrics by Adrian Chalifour. Melody by Woody Guthrie. Performed by Adrian Chalifour. Accessed January 7, 2015. http://www.towersandtreesmusic.com/2012/02/29/this-land-was-made-for-you-and-me/.

"This Land Is Your Land." Lyrics by Adrian Chalifour. Melody by Woody Guthrie (borrowed from the Carter Family Singers). Performed by Adrian Chalifour. YouTube video. Accessed January 7, 2015. http://www.youtube.com/watch?v=oJwZFV6J-eA.

"Turn of the Wrench." Dana Lyons. Reigning Records, 2004.

"Up Your Watershed." Holly Arntzen and Kevin Wright with the Dream Band. Artist Response Team, 2010. YouTube video. Accessed August 3, 2015. https://www.youtube.com/watch?v=m0gHCWnWjxY.

"Up Your Watershed." Holly Arntzen and Kevin Wright with the Dream Band. Artist Response Team, 2011. YouTube video. Accessed August 3, 2015. https://www.youtube.com/watch?v=g3kVAAkVdLU.

"Up Your Watershed." The Wilds. Artist Response Team, 2012. YouTube video. Accessed August 3, 2015. https://www.youtube.com/watch?v=D77cH62OqXI.

"Waiting for Orca." The Wilds. Artist Response Team, 2013. YouTube video. Accessed August 3, 2015. https://www.youtube.com/watch?v=egFNKcUoXTc.

"Waiting for the Great Leap Forward." Billy Bragg. *Workers' Playtime*. Cooking Vinyl, 2006.

"When the World's on Fire." Carter Family Singers. *When the Roses Bloom in Dixieland: Their Complete Victor Recordings (1929–1930)*. Rounder Records, 1995.

"Where the Coho Flash Silver (All Over the Bay)." Lloyd Arntzen. The British Columbia Folklore Society. Accessed July 31, 2015. http://folklore.bc.ca/where-the-coho-flash-silver/.

"Where the Fraser River Flows." Joe Hill. Performed by Utah Phillips. YouTube video. Accessed January 2, 2015. https://www.youtube.com/watch?v=7Rww4Fx5NeY.

"Who's Gonna Stand Up?" Neil Young. *Storytone*. Reprise Records, 2014.

"Willy Says." Dana Lyons. Reigning Records, 1996.

"Wish for a Fish: The Sturgeon Song." Bobs & Lolo. *Musica Adventures*. Nettwerk Music Group, 2006.

Woman in the Mirror. Holly Arntzen. Artist Response Team, 1986.

"Your Next Bold Move." Ani DiFranco. Righteous Babe Music, 2001.

BIBLIOGRAPHY

Abrams, Lindsay. "Disney Partners with Oil Firms to Make Pipelines Fun." *Salon*. Accessed January 4, 2015. http://www.salon.com/2013/12/23/disney_partners_with_oil_industry_to_make_pipelines_fun/.

Abreu, Sharon. "*The Climate Monologues*: Excerpts." YouTube video. Accessed January 8, 2015. https://www.youtube.com/watch?v=okbwBrs6pkM.

———. "A Few Words about Sharon Abreu." Sharon Abreu. Accessed April 1, 2016. http://www.sharmuse.com/sharmuse/sharword.htm.

Acker, Alison, and Betty Brightwell. *The Raging Grannies: Off Our Rockers and into Trouble*. Victoria, BC: TouchWood Editions, 2004.

Adams, Paul C., and Astrid Gynnild. "Environmental Messages in Online Media: The Role of Place." *Environmental Communication: A Journal of Nature and Culture* 7, no. 1 (2013): 113–130.

Aigen, Kenneth. "The Voice of the Forest: A Conception of Music for Music Therapy." *Music Therapy* 10, no. 1 (1991): 77–98.

Allen, Aaron, and Kevin Dawe. *Current Directions in Ecomusicology*. New York: Routledge, 2015.

Associated Press. "Washington's Inland Waters Now the Salish Sea." *Oregon Live*. Accessed January 6, 2015. http://www.oregonlive.com/news/index.ssf/2009/11/washingtons_inland_waters_now.html.

Barney, Erin C., Joel J. Mintzes, and Chiung-Fen Yen. "Assessing Knowledge, Attitudes, and Behavior toward Charismatic Megafauna: The Case of Dolphins." *Journal of Environmental Education* 36, no. 2 (2005): 41–55.

Barz, Gregory F., and Timothy J. Cooley. *Shadows in the Field: New Perspectives for Fieldwork in Ethnomusicology*. New York: Oxford University Press, 2008.

Baskin, Martha. "Protestors Stall an Oil Train for Hours at Anacortes." *Resistance: Daily Movement News and Resources*. Accessed January 8, 2015. https://www.popularresistance.org/protesters-stall-an-oil-train-for-hours-at-anacortes/.

Bateman, Robert. *Cardinal and Wild Apples*. Robert Bateman Accessed January 15, 2015. http://robertbateman.ca/paintings/CardinalWildApples.htm.

Batten, Sonia D., and James FR Gower. "Did the iron fertilization near Haida Gwaii in 2012 affect the pelagic lower trophic level ecosystem?" *Journal of Plankton Research* 36, no. 4 (2014): 925–932.

BC Stats. "Ethnicity and Visible Minority Characteristics of BC's Population." Accessed January 11, 2015. file:///Users/markpedelty/Downloads/Ethnicity%20and%20Visible%20Minority%20Characteristics%20of%20BC's%20Population.pdf.

Beierle, Thomas C., and Jerry Cayford. *Democracy in Practice: Public Participation in Environmental Decisions*. Washington, DC: Resources for the Future, 2002.

Bennett, Andy. *Music, Style, and Aging: Growing Old Disgracefully?* Philadelphia: Temple University Press, 2013.

Besel, Richard D., and Jnan A. Blau, eds. *Performance on Behalf of the Environment*. Lanham, MD: Lexington Books, 2013.

Biello, D. "Can controversial ocean iron fertilization save salmon." *Scientific American* (2012). Accessed October, 24, 2012. http://www.scientificamerican.com/article/fertilizing-ocean-with-iron-to-save-salmon-and-earn-money/

Boas, Franz. "The Indians of British Columbia." *Popular Science Monthly* 32 (March 1988). Republished in *Works of Franz Boaz*. Seattle: The Perfect Library, Amazon Digital Services, 2015.

Bobs & Lolo. "Bobs & Lolo 'I Love Bugs' Live in Ottawa." YouTube video. Last modified March 19, 2011. http://www.youtube.com/watch?v=rX8wIunIwaw.

Bodkin, Alison. "Eco-comedy Performance: An Alchemy of Environmentalism and Humor." In Richard D. Besel and Jnan A. Blau, eds., *Performance on Behalf of the Environment*. Lanham, MD: Lexington Books, 2013.

Boucher, David. *Dylan & Cohen: Poets of Rock and Roll*. New York: Continuum, 2004.

Branagan, Martin. "Education, Activism, and the Arts." *Convergence* 38, no. 4 (2005): 33–50.

Buck, H. J. "Village Science Meets Global Discourse: The Haida Salmon Restoration Corporation's Ocean Iron Fertilization Experiment." 2014. https://geoengineeringourclimate.files.wordpress.com/2014/01/buck-2014-village-science-meets-global-discourse-click-for-download.pdf.

Burgess, Jacquelin, Carolyn M. Harrison, and Petra Filius. "Environmental Communication and the Cultural Politics of Environmental Citizenship." *Environment and Planning* 30, no. 8 (1998): 1445–1460.

Callenbach, Ernest. *Ecotopia*. New York: Random House, 2009.

Carson, Rachel. *Silent Spring*. Boston: Houghton Mifflin Harcourt, 2002.

CBC News. "9 Questions about Idle No More." Accessed January 9, 2015. http://www.cbc.ca/news/canada/9-questions-about-idle-no-more-1.1301843.

———. "Volcanic Eruption Led to BC Salmon Boom: Scientist." October 25, 2010, accessed August 16, 2015. http://www.cbc.ca/news/technology/volcanic-eruption-led-to-b-c-salmon-boom-scientist-1.890331.

Cedarsong Nature School. Accessed November 23, 2014. http://cedarsongnatureschool.org/.

Cermak, Michael J. "Hip-Hop, Social Justice, and Environmental Education: Toward a Critical Ecological Literacy." *Journal of Environmental Education* 43, no. 3 (2012): 192–203.

Chess, Caron, and Kristen Purcell. "Public Participation and the Environment: Do We Know What Works?" *Environmental Science & Technology* 33, no. 16 (1999): 2685–2692.

Chor Leoni. "Chor Leoni." Accessed January 9, 2015. https://chorleoni.org/.

Coast Salish Art. "Coast Salish Art." Accessed January 5, 2015. http://coastsalishart.com /videos-coast-salish-anthem-[S3KwoaR6VW8].cfm.

Conard, Nicholas J., Maria Malina, and Susanne C. Münzel. "New Flutes Document the Earliest Musical Tradition in Southwestern Germany." *Nature* 460, no. 7256 (2009): 737–740.

Cooney, Rosie. *The Precautionary Principle in Biodiversity Conservation and Natural Resource Management: An Issues Paper for Policy-Makers, Researchers and Practitioners.* IUCN Policy and Global Change Series no. 2, 2004.

Coss, Roger. "Multicultural Perspectives through Music & Sustainability Education." *Multicultural Education* (Fall 2013): 20–25.

Costanza, Robert. "Ecosystem Services: Multiple Classification Systems Are Needed." *Biological Conservation* 141, no. 2 (2008): 350–352.

The Council of Canadians/Le Conseil des Canadiens. Accessed January 7, 2015. http:// www.canadians.org/.

Cramer, Janet M., and Karen A. Foss. "Baudrillard and Our Destiny with the Natural World: Fatal Strategies for Environmental Communication." *Environmental Communication* 3, no. 3 (2009): 298–316.

Cué, Patricia. "On the Wall: Designers as Agents for Change in Environmental Communication." *Visible Language* 48, no. 2 (2014): 70–83.

Curtis, Jan. "Ecology and the Arts." *International Journal of the Arts in Society* 5, no. 6 (2011) 277–286.

"Dana Lyons Live in Concert to Benefit the Whale Museum." *Journal of the San Juan Islands,* April 21, 2010. Accessed January 4, 2015. http://www.sanjuanjournal.com /entertainment/91760804.html.

"Dana Lyons Performs at Elwha Dam Removal Ceremony." YouTube video. Accessed January 6, 2015. https://www.youtube.com/watch?v=bi7Sc4U_YUg.

Delaney, R. "Musically Challenging." *Horizons* 18, no. 2 (2004): 26–28.

Deleuze, Gilles, and Felix Guittari. *Anti-Oedipus: Capitalism and Schizophrenia.* New York: Viking Press, 1977.

Durkheim, Émile. *The Division of Labor in Society.* New York: Simon and Schuster, 2014.

Earth First! "Raging Grannies Blockading Entrances and Exits of WA Department of Ecology." *Earth First! Newswire.* October 30, 2014. Accessed January 8, 2015. http:// earthfirstjournal.org/newswire/2014/10/30/breaking-raging-grannies-blockading -entrances-and-exits-of-wa-department-of-ecology/.

Ecocriticism Study Group (ESG). *Ecomusicology Bibliography.* American Musicological Society. Accessed January 13, 2015. http://www.ecomusicology.info/resources /bibliography/.

Entman, Robert M. "Framing: Toward Clarification of a Fractured Paradigm." *Journal of Communication* 43, no. 4 (1993): 51–58.

Fairey, Shepard. "Native America." *Rebel Music.* Accessed January 9, 2015. http://www .rebelmusic.com/#!music/rebel-music/episode/native-america.

Falconer, Bruce. "Can Anyone Stop the Man Who Will Try Just about Anything to Put an End to Climate Change? Most Scientists Oppose Russ George's Efforts to Fix the World's Climate. But Who's Going to Do Something about It?" *Pacific Standard,* May 5, 2014. Accessed August 7, 2015. http://www.psmag.com/books-and-culture/battlefield -earth-can-anyone-stop-man-will-try-just-anything-fix-climate-78957.

Fallon, Robert. "Birds, Beasts, and Bombs in Messaien's Cold War Mass." *Journal of Musicology* 26, no. 2 (Spring 2009): 175–204.

Feisst, Sabine. "Animal Ecologies: Laurie Spiegel's Musical Explorations of Urban Wildlife." *Social Alternatives* 33, no. 1 (2014): 16.

———. "Music as Place, Place as Music: The Sonic Geography of John Luther Adams." In Bernd Herzogenrath, ed., *The Farthest Place: The Music of John Luther Adams*, 23–47. Lebanon: University Press of New Hampshire, 2012.

Fisherkeller, JoEllen. "Everyday Learning about Identities among Young Adolescents in Television Culture." *Anthropology & Education Quarterly* 28, no. 4 (1997): 467–492.

Fountain, Henry. "A Rogue Climate Experiment Outrages Scientists." *New York Times*, October 18, 2012. Accessed July 29, 2015. http://www.nytimes.com/2012/10/19/science /earth/iron-dumping-experiment-in-pacific-alarms-marine-experts.html?_r=0.

Fraser River Sturgeon Conservation Society. "Wish for a Fish: The Sturgeon Song by Bobs and Lolo." Accessed January 6, 2015. http://www.frasersturgeon.com/multi_media /wish_for_a_fish__the_sturgeon_song_by_bobs_and_lolo.

Freer, Patrick K. "Two Decades of Research on Possible Selves and the 'Missing Males' Problem in Choral Music." *International Journal of Music Education* 28, no. 1 (2010): 17–30.

Gallup. "Environment." Accessed January 15, 2015. http://www.gallup.com/poll/1615 /environment.aspx.

Gardiner, William. *The Music of Nature*. Boston: J. H. Wilkins & R. B. Carter, 1838.

Garofalo, Reebee. *Rockin' the Boat: Mass Music and Mass Movements*. Brooklyn, NY: South End Press, 1992.

Gaunt, Simon. *Troubadours and Irony*. Cambridge: Cambridge University Press, 1989.

George, Ross. blog, http://russgeorge.net/; Haida Salmon Restoration Corporation, http://www.haidasalmonrestoration.com/Gianturco, Paola. *Grandmother Power: A Global Phenomenon*. Brooklyn, NY: Powerhouse Books, 2012.

Gitlin, Todd. *The Whole World Is Watching: Mass Media in the Making and Unmaking of the New Left*. Berkeley: University of California Press, 1980.

Goddard, Amy Jo. "Staging Activism: New York City Performing Artists as Cultural Workers." *Social Justice* (2007): 97–116.

Goffman, Erving. *Frame Analysis: An Essay on the Organization of Experience*. Cambridge, MA: Harvard University Press, 1974.

Gold, John. "Roll On Columbia: Woody Guthrie, Migrants' Tales, and Regional Transformation in the Pacific Northwest." *Journal of Cultural Geography* 18, no. 1 (1998): 83–97.

Goodall, H. Lloyd. *Living in the Rock n Roll Mystery: Reading Context, Self, and Others as Clues*. Carbondale: Southern Illinois University Press, 1991.

Goodstein, Eban. *The Trade-Off Myth: Fact and Fiction about Jobs and the Environment*. Washington, DC: Island Press, 1999.

Gouzouasis, Peter, Anne Marie Lamonde, and Martin Guhn. "The Fine Arts and Media in Education Project: The Integration of Creative Arts-Based Activities, Wireless Technologies, and Constructivist Teaching Practices in Practicum Classrooms." *From Sea to Sea: Perspectives on Music Education in Canada*. An Open Access, Peer-Reviewed Electronic Book 2007: 1–28. Accessed April 1, 2016. file:///Users/pedeltmh/Downloads/ Chapter%2022%20The%20Fine%20Arts%20and%20Media%20in%20Education%20 %20Project%20(1).pdf

Grimley, Daniel. "Hearing Landscape Critically." University of Oxford Faculty Research. Accessed January 15, 2015. http://www.music.ox.ac.uk/research/projects/hearing -landscape-critically/.

Grossberg, Lawrence. *We Gotta Get Out of This Place: Popular Conservatism and Postmodern Culture.* New York: Routledge, 2014.

Guggenheim, Davis. *An Inconvenient Truth.* Beverly Hills, CA: Lawrence Bender Productions, 2006.

Hale, Charles R. "What Is Activist Research?" *Items and Issues: Social Science Research Council* 2, no. 1–2 (2001): 13–15.

Heise, Ursula K. *Sense of Place and Sense of Planet: The Environmental Imagination of the Globe.* Oxford: Oxford University Press, 2008.

Hempton, Gordon, and John Grossmann. *One Square Inch of Silence: One Man's Search for Natural Silence in a Noisy World.* New York: Simon and Schuster, 2009.

Henry, Jules. *Culture against Man.* New York: Random House, 1963.

"Herstory." Raging Grannies International. Accessed January 6, 2015. http://raging grannies.org/herstory/.

Higgins, Lee. *Community Music: In Theory and in Practice.* Oxford: Oxford University Press, 2012.

Idle No More. "Living History." Accessed January 9, 2015. http://www.idlenomore.ca /living_history.

———. "The Story." Accessed January 9, 2015. http://www.idlenomore.ca/story.

Ingram, David. *The Jukebox in the Garden: Ecocriticism and American Popular Music since 1960.* Amsterdam: Rodopi, 2010.

———. " 'My Dirty Stream': Pete Seeger, American Folk Music, and Environmental Protest." *Popular Music and Society* 31, no. 1 (2008): 21–36.

Irthlingz. "Sharon Abreu, Executive Director." Accessed January 8, 2015. http://greendept .com/io/sharon-abreu-executive-director/.

———. "Sharon Abreu and Michael Hurwicz." Accessed January 8, 2015. YouTube video. https://www.youtube.com/watch?v=kK83uz7nsNY.

Ivakhiv, Adrian. "From Frames to Resonance Machines: The Neuropolitics of Environmental Communication." *Environmental Communication* 4, no. 1 (2010): 109–121.

Jenn, Richard. "Profiles of Pacific Northwest Activists: Dana Lyons." *Whatcom Watch Online,* February, 2014. Accessed January 5, 2015. http://www.whatcomwatch.org/php /WW_open.php?id=1666.

Johnson, Kirk. "Vote on Labeling Modified Foods Spurs Costly Battle in Washington State." Last modified October 30, 2013. http://www.nytimes.com/2013/10/31/us/vote -on-labeling-modified-food-spurs-costly-battle-in-washington-state.html?_r=0.

Kapralos, Krista J. "Science Hitches a Ride on Tribal Canoe Journey." *Herald of Everett, Washington.* Last modified March 3, 2008. http://www.heraldnet.com/article /20080303/NEWS01/855603740.

Keller, Helen. *Helen Keller: Selected Writings.* New York: NYU Press, 2005.

Keskinen, Mikko. "Her Mistress's Voice: Gynophonocentrism in Feminist Discourses." *Journal of International Women's Studies* 2, no. 1 (2013): 1–15.

Killingsworth, M. Jimmie. "From Environmental Rhetoric to Ecocomposition and Ecopoetics: Finding a Place for Professional Communication." *Technical Communication Quarterly* 14, no. 4 (2005): 359–373.

Kinder Morgan. "About Us." Accessed January 9, 2015. http://www.kindermorgan.com /about_us.

King, Charlie. Charlie King Music. Accessed January 9, 2015. http://www.charlieking music.com/.

Kinnear, Tyler. "Introduction to Special Issue: 'Sound, Environment, and Action.'" *Music and Politics* 8, no. 2 (2014). Accessed January 13, 2015, http://quod.lib.umich.edu/m/mp /9460447.0008.201/--introduction-to-special-issue-sound-environment-and-action ?rgn=main;view=fulltext.

Klein, Naomi. *No Logo: Taking Aim at the Brand Bullies*. New York: Picador, 2002.

———. *The Shock Doctrine: The Rise of Disaster Capitalism*. Toronto: Knopf Canada, 2009.

———. *This Changes Everything*. New York: Simon and Schuster, 2014.

Krech, Shepard. *The Ecological Indian: Myth and History*. New York: W. W. Norton & Company, 2000.

Kroeber, Alfred Louis. "The Superorganic." *American Anthropologist* 19, no. 2 (1917): 163–213.

Latour, Bruno. "Agency at the Time of the Anthropocene." *New Literary History* 45, no. 1 (2014): 1–18.

Lewis, Hannah, and Peter McMurray. "Sounds and Solitude (Walden)." Vimeo Video. Last accessed April 1, 2016. https://vimeo.com/78756447.

Livingston, Robert Eric. "Glocal Knowledges: Agency and Place in Literary Studies." *Publications of the Modern Language Association of America* (2001): 145–157.

Lukacs, Martin. "Noam Chomsky Slams Canada's Oil Shale Gas Plans." *Guardian*. Last modified November 1, 2013. http://www.theguardian.com/environment/2013/nov/01 /noam-chomsky-canadas-shale-gas-energy-tar-sands.

———. "World's Biggest Geoengineering Experiment 'Violates' UN Rules." *Guardian*, October 15, 2012. Accessed July 29, 2015. http://www.theguardian.com/environment /2012/oct/15/pacific-iron-fertilisation-geoengineering.

Mattern, Mark. *Acting in Concert: Music, Community, and Political Action*. New Brunswick, NJ: Rutgers University Press, 1998.

May, Theresa J. "Indigenous Theater in Global Times: Situated Knowledge and Ecological Communities in *Salmon Is Everything* and *Burning Vision*." In Richard D. Besel and Jnan A. Blau, eds., *Performance on Behalf of the Environment*. Lanham, MD: Lexington Books, 2013.

McCrea, Edward J. "The Roots of Environmental Education: How the Past Supports the Future." *Environmental Education and Training Partnership*. 2005. Institute of Education Sciences. Accessed September 24, 2014. http://files.eric.ed.gov/fulltext/ED491084.pdf.

Morton, Alexandra B., and Helena K. Symonds. "Displacement of Orcinus orca (L.) by High Amplitude Sound in British Columbia, Canada." *ICES Journal of Marine Science: Journal du Conseil* 59, no. 1 (2002): 71–80.

Morton, Timothy. *Ecology without Nature: Rethinking Environmental Aesthetics*. Cambridge, MA: Harvard University Press, 2007.

Native Drums. "Drum Culture." Accessed January 9, 2015. http://www.native-drums.ca /index.php/Drumming/Culture?tp=a.

Nemeth, Erwin, Nadia Pieretti, Sue Anne Zollinger, Nicole Geberzahn, Jesko Partecke, Ana Catarina Miranda, and Henrik Brumm. "Bird Song and Anthropogenic Noise: Vocal Constraints May Explain Why Birds Sing Higher-Frequency Songs in Cities." *Proceedings of the Royal Society B: Biological Sciences* 280, no. 1754 (2013). Accessed January 4, 2015. http://rspb.royalsocietypublishing.org/content/280/1754/20122798.short.

Nityananda, Vivek, and Mark A. Bee. "Finding Your Mate at a Cocktail Party: Frequency Separation Promotes Auditory Stream Segregation of Concurrent Voices in Multispecies Frog Choruses." *PLOS One* 6, no. 6 (2011): e21191.

Nooksack Salmon Enhancement Association. "Education." Accessed January 6, 2015. http://www.n-sea.org/educational-programs-1/students-for-salmon.

Norton, Todd. "The Structuration of Public Participation: Organizing Environmental Control." *Environmental Communication* 1, no. 2 (2007): 146–170.

Oliveros, Pauline. *Deep Listening: A Composer's Sound Practice.* Bloomington, IN: iUniverse, 2005.

Orca Sing 2013 (14th Annual). YouTube video. Accessed January 4, 2015. https://www.youtube.com/watch?v=JlE0QcIxdUM.

Payerhin, Marek. "Singing Out of Pain: Protest Songs and Social Mobilization." *Polish Review* 57, no. 1 (2012): 5–31.

Pedelty, Mark. *Ecomusicology: Rock, Folk, and the Environment.* Philadelphia: Temple University Press, 2012.

———. "Woody Guthrie and the Columbia River: Propaganda, Art, and Irony." *Popular Music and Society* 31, no. 3 (2008): 329–355.

Pedelty, Mark, and Morgan Kuecker. "Seen to Be Heard? Gender, Voice, and Body in Television Advertisements." *Communication and Critical/Cultural Studies* 11, no. 3 (2014): 250–269.

Peeples, Jennifer. "Toxic Sublime: Imaging Contaminated Landscapes." *Environmental Communication: A Journal of Nature and Culture* 5, no. 4 (2011): 373–392.

Peeples, Jennifer, and Stephen Depoe, eds. *Voice and Environmental Communication.* Basingstoke, Hampshire, England: Palgrave Macmillan, 2014.

Pezzullo, Phaedra C. *Toxic Tourism: Rhetorics of Pollution, Travel, and Environmental Justice.* Tuscaloosa: University of Alabama Press, 2009.

Plec, Emily, and Mary Pettenger. *Greenwashing Consumption: The Didactic Framing of ExxonMobil's Energy Solutions.* New York: Routledge, 2012.

Pollack, Andrew. "Move to Market Gene-Altered Pigs in Canada Is Halted." *New York Times*, April 4, 2012. http://www.nytimes.com/2012/04/04/science/gene-altered-pig-project-in-canada-is-halted.html?_r=1&.

Post, Jennifer C., ed. *Ethnomusicology: A Contemporary Reader.* New York: Routledge, 2013.

Powell, Archie, and Sara Ramsden. *Why Birds Sing.* BBC Productions. Accessed January 11, 2015. http://watchdocumentary.org/watch/why-birds-sing-video_7f9015c5d.html.

Pratt, Ray. *Rhythm and Resistance: The Political Uses of American Popular Music.* New York: Praeger, 1990.

"Public Hearing on the Cherry Point Coal Terminal." YouTube video. Accessed January 5, 2015. https://www.youtube.com/watch?v=I34C4MNTWLQ.

Pulkkinen, Lea. "Ten Pillars of a Good Childhood: A Finnish Perspective." *Childhood Education* 88, no. 5 (2012): 326–330.

Putnam, Robert D. *Bowling Alone: The Collapse and Revival of American Community.* New York: Simon and Schuster, 2000.

Rabin, Lawrence A., and Correigh M. Greene. "Changes to Acoustic Communication Systems in Human-Altered Environments." *Journal of Comparative Psychology* 116, no. 2 (2002): 137.

Raging Grannies. *Raging Grannies Songbook*. Gabriola Island, BC: New Society Publishers, 1993.

———. *Raging Grannies Songs*. Accessed January 7, 2015. http://raginggrannies.net/.

Rehding, Alexander. "Review Article: Eco-Musicology." *Journal of the Royal Musical Association* 127, no. 2 (2002): 305–320.

Rice, Mabel L., Aletha C. Huston, Rosemarie Truglio, and John C. Wright. "Words from 'Sesame Street': Learning Vocabulary While Viewing." *Developmental Psychology* 26, no. 3 (1990): 421.

Rickwood, Julie. "Choralecology?: Community Choirs and Environmental Activism." *Social Alternatives* 33, no. 1 (2014): 30–38.

Rodnitsky, Jerry. *The Decline and Rebirth of Folk Protest Music*. London: Ashgate, 2006.

Rosenbaum, Ron. "Playboy Interview: Bob Dylan." *Playboy* (January, 1978), 12–17.

Rosenthal, Debra J. "'Hoods and the Woods: Rap Music as Environmental Literature." *Journal of Popular Culture* 39, no. 4 (2006): 661–676.

Rothenberg, David. *Thousand Mile Song: Whale Music in a Sea of Sound*. New York: Basic Books, 2010.

Rothenberg, David, and Marta Ulvaeus, eds. *The Book of Music and Nature: An Anthology of Sounds, Words, Thoughts*. Middletown, CT: Wesleyan University Press, 2013.

Roy, Carole. "The Original Raging Grannies: Using Creative and Humorous Protests for Political Education." *Herstory*. Accessed January 6, 2015. http://raginggrannies.org/herstory/.

———. *The Raging Grannies: Wild Hats, Cheeky Songs, and Witty Actions for a Better World*. Montreal: Black Rose Books, 2004.

———. "Raging Grannies and Environmental Issues: Humour and Creativity in Educative Protests." *Convergence* 33, no. 4 (2000): 6–18. Retrieved October 3, 2015. http://web.b.ebscohost.com.ezp2.lib.umn.edu/ehost/detail/detail?vid=3&sid=32601a8a-5086-4cc3-9ceb-cec065aa1d94%40sessionmgr115&hid=115&bdata=JnNpdGU9ZWhvc3QtbGl2ZQ%3d%3d#db=aph&AN=4931134.

Roy, William G. "How Social Movements Do Culture." *International Journal of Politics, Culture, and Society* 23, no. 2–3 (2010): 85–98.

Ryan, Robin. "Toward a New, Musical Paradigm of Place: The Port River Symphonic of Chester Schultz," *Environmental Humanities* 4 (2014): 50.

Sartre, Jean-Paul. *Existentialism Is a Humanism*. London: Methuen, 1960.

Sawchuk, Dana. "Peace Profile: The Raging Grannies." *Peace Review* 25, no. 1 (2013): 129–135.

Schafer, R. Murray. *The Soundscape: Our Sonic Environment and the Tuning of the World*. Rochester, VT: Inner Traditions/Bear & Co., 1993.

Schmitt, Casey R. *If a Text Falls in the Woods . . . : Intertextuality, Environmental Perception, and the Non-authored Text*. Oakland, CA: University of California Press, 2012.

———. "Invoking the Ecological Indian: Rhetoric, Culture, and the Environment." In Jennifer Peeples and Stephen Depoe, eds., *Voice and Environmental Communication*. Basingstoke, Hampshire, England: Palgrave Macmillan, 2014.

SeaDoc Society. "Salish Sea Facts." Accessed January 4, 2015. http://www.seadocsociety.org/salish-sea-facts/.

Sercombe, Laurel. "Researching the Music of the First People of the Pacific Northwest: From the Academy to the Brain Room." *Fontes Artis Musicae* 50, no. 2–4 (2003): 81–88.

Shakespeare, William. *Measure for Measure. The Complete Works of William Shakespeare.* Accessed January 4, 2015. http://shakespeare.mit.edu/measure/full.html.

Shea, Courtne. "Habits of Highly Successful People: Buffy Sainte-Marie." *Globe and Mail,* June 8, 2014. http://www.theglobeandmail.com/arts/music/habits-of-highly -successful-people-buffy-sainte-marie/article19049892/.

Silver-Sweeney, Marlisse. "Anti-pipeline Protest on World Oceans Day." *Global News,* June 8, 2014. http://globalnews.ca/news/1381277/anti-pipeline-protest-on-world -oceans-day/.

Simone, Nina. *I Put a Spell on You: The Autobiography of Nina Simone.* Boston: Da Capo Press, 2003.

Small, Christopher. *Musicking: The Meanings of Performing and Listening.* Middletown, CT: Wesleyan University Press, 2011.

Smith, Anna Deavere. *Twilight: Los Angeles, 1992.* New York: Dramatists Play Service, 2003.

Smith, Gibbs M. *Joe Hill.* Salt Lake City, UT: Peregrine Smith Books, 1984.

Smith-White, Graham. *The Sunrise Review.* Accessed January 15, 2015. http://solarpowered music.com/press.

Stahl, Matthew. "To Hell with Heteronomy: Liberalism, Rule-Making, and the Pursuit of 'Community' in an Urban Rock Scene." *Journal of Popular Music Studies* 15, no. 2 (2003): 140–165.

Sterman, Nan. "Breeding Better Fruit." *San Diego Union Tribune.* Accessed October 31, 2014, http://www.utsandiego.com/news/2014/oct/31/breeding-better-stone-fruit/.

Sterne, Jonathan. "Sounds Like the Mall of America: Programmed Music and the Archi- tectonics of Commercial Space." *Ethnomusicology* (1997): 22–50.

Stimeling, Travis D. "Music, Place, and Identity in the Central Appalachian Mountaintop Removal Mining Debate." *American Music* 30, no. 1 (2012): 1–29.

Strauss, Susan. *The Passionate Fact: Storytelling in Natural History and Cultural Interpreta- tion.* Golden, CO: Fulcrum Publishing, 1996.

Tagg, Phillip. *Subjectivity and Soundscape, Motorbikes and Music.* New York: Routledge, 2006.

Terry, David P., and Anne Marie Todd. "It's a Party, Not a Protest: Environmental Com- munity, Co-incident Performance, and the San Jose Bike Party." In Richard D. Besel and Jnan A. Blau, eds., *Performance on Behalf of the Environment.* Lanham, MD: Lexing- ton Books, 2013.

Thoreau, Henry David. *Walden.* Project Gutenberg. Accessed January 7, 2015. http://www .gutenberg.org/files/205/205-h/205-h.htm.

Thornton, William H. "Mapping the 'Glocal' Village: The Political Limits of 'Glocaliza- tion.'" *Continuum: Journal of Media & Cultural Studies* 14, no. 1 (2000): 79–89.

Tippett, Krista. "The Last Quiet Places: Silence and the Presence of Everything." *On Be- ing.* Podcast. Accessed January 4, 2015. http://www.onbeing.org/program/last-quiet -places/4557.

Titon, Jeff Todd. *Sustainable Music.* Accessed January 7, 2015. http://sustainablemusic .blogspot.com/.

Toliver, Brooks. "Eco-Ing in the Canyon: Ferde Grofé's *Grand Canyon Suite* and the Transformation of Wilderness." *Journal of the American Musicological Society* 57, no. 2 (Summer 2004): 325–367.

Tollefson, Jeff. "Ocean-Fertilization Project Off Canada Sparks Furor." *Nature* 490, no. 7421 (2012): 458–459. http://www.nature.com/news/ocean-fertilization-project-off -canada-sparks-furore-1.11631.

"Tribal Journeys to Bella Bella." *First Nations in British Columbia*. Accessed January 11, 2015. http://fnbc.info/event/tribal-journeys-bella-bella-2014.

Trick, Charles G., Brian D. Bill, William P. Cochlan, Mark L. Wells, Vera L. Trainer, and Lisa D. Pickell. "Iron enrichment stimulates toxic diatom production in high-nitrate, low-chlorophyll areas." *Proceedings of the National Academy of Sciences* 107, no. 13 (2010): 5887–5892.

Trump, Maxine, dir. *Musicwood*. DVD. Brooklyn, NY: Helpman Productions, 2013.

Tubb, Benjamin Robert. Public Domain Music. Accessed January 7, 2015. http://www.pdmusic.org/.

Turkle, Sherry. *Alone Together: Why We Expect More from Technology and Less from Each Other*. New York: Basic Books, 2012.

United States Census Bureau. "Washington." Accessed January 11, 2015. http://quickfacts.census.gov/qfd/states/53000.html.

Vancouver Aquarium. "Sea Star Wasting Syndrome." Accessed January 5, 2015. http://www.vanaqua.org/act/research/sea-stars.

Vancouver Sun. "VPD Officer Injured at Anti-pipeline Protest after Being Hit by a Car." Last modified June 9, 2014. http://www.vancouversun.com/touch/news/officer+anti+pipeline+protest+needs+surgery+after+being/9919925/story.html?rel=831135.

Von Glahn, Denise. *Music and the Skillful Listener: American Women Compose the Natural World*. Bloomington and Indianapolis: Indiana University Press, 2013.

———. *The Sounds of Place: Music and the American Cultural Landscape*. Lebanon, NH: University Press of New England, 2003.

Walker, Gregg B. "Public Participation as Participatory Communication in Environmental Policy Decision-Making: From Concepts to Structured Conversations." *Environmental Communication* 1, no. 1 (2007): 99–110.

Washington State Department of Ecology. "Nuclear Waste Program History." Accessed January 5, 2015. http://www.ecy.wa.gov/programs/nwp/aboutnwp.htm.

Watkins, Holly. "Musical Ecologies of Place and Placelessness." *Journal of the American Musicological Society* 64, no. 2 (2011): 404–408.

Weiss, Rick. "USDA Backs Production of Rice with Human Genes." *Washington Post*. Last modified March 2, 2007. http://www.washingtonpost.com/wp-dyn/content/article/2007/03/01/AR2007030101495.html.

Williams, R., Erin Ashe, Doug Sandilands, and David Lusseau. "Stimulus-Dependent Response to Disturbance Affecting the Activity of Killer Whales." *Scientific Committee of the International Whaling Commission, Document: SC/63/WW5* (2011): 1–27.

Wong, Penelope. "Greening the Elementary Education Curriculum One Course at a Time." *Green Teacher* 85 (2009): 24–27.

Zinn, Howard. *A People's History of the United States*. New York: Harper and Row, 2005.

Zubrin, Robert. "The Pacific's Salmon Are Back, Thank Human Ingenuity." *National Review*, April 22, 2014. Accessed March 26, 2016. http://www.nationalreview.com/article/376258/pacifics-salmon-are-back-thank-human-ingenuity-robert-zubrin.

INDEX

MARK PEDELTY

is Professor of Communication Studies and Anthropology and a Resident Fellow of the Institute on the Environment at the University of Minnesota. His books include *Ecomusicology: Rock, Folk and the Environment* and *Musical Ritual in Mexico City: From the Aztec to NAFTA*. Pedelty teaches courses in environmental communication, musical communication, and ethnographic methods. He also sings, composes, and plays guitar and harmonica for the band Hypoxic Punks.